Backpacking in Mexico

Backpacking in
Mexico

Tim Burford

Bradt Publications, UK
The Globe Pequot Press Inc, USA

First published in 1997 by Bradt Publications,
41 Nortoft Road, Chalfont St Peter, Bucks SL9 0LA, England.
Published in the USA by The Globe Pequot Press Inc, 6 Business Park Road,
PO Box 833, Old Saybrook, Connecticut 06475-0833.

British Library Cataloguing in Publication Data
A catalogue record for this book is available from the British Library
ISBN 1 898323 56 9

Library of Congress Cataloging-in-Publication Data
Burford, Tim.
    Backpacking in Mexico/ Tim Burford.
        p. cm. — (Bradt guides)
    Includes bibliographical references (p.) and index.
    ISBN 1-898323-56-9 (Globe Pequot Press)
    1. Backpacking–Mexico–Guidebooks. 2. Hiking–Mexico–
    Guidebooks. 3. Mexico–Guidebooks. I. Title. II. Series.
GV199.44.M6B87   1996
796.51'0972—dc21   96-47776
                                                                 CIP

Cover photographs
Front: Overlooking Ensenada Grande Bay, Baja California (William Wheeler)
Back: Fiesta figure (representation of a tourist!), San Cristóbal de las Casas,
Chiapas (Tim Burford)
Drawings Wendy Dison
Maps *Inside covers*: Steve Munns   *Others*: Hans van Well

Typeset from the author's disc by Patti Taylor, London NW10 1JR
Printed and bound in Great Britain by The Guernsey Press Co Ltd

CONTENTS

INTRODUCTION

To Europeans, if not North Americans, Mexico seems huge, and it certainly has a wide variety of climates, landscapes and biological habitats. Whatever kind of scenery appeals to you, from tropical beaches through vast deserts and great canyons to high, ice-capped volcanoes, you are almost sure to find something like it here. This guide describes hiking in many of these areas, both day walks and a few tougher overnight hikes; moreover it also reflects the move in the travel sphere towards 'ecotourism', with a wealth of information on geology, biology, and most National Parks and Biosphere Reserves. Scientific names for fauna and flora are given in many places, so that you can refer to more detailed guides, but these can of course be ignored in most cases.

Mexico is one of the easiest 'third world' countries in which to travel, with a sophisticated infrastructure of buses, hotels and supermarkets. However, its people remain its greatest wealth, friendly and generous and welcoming to outsiders while remaining true to their own traditions. At the moment, thanks to a crash in the value of the peso, Mexico is also very affordable, but as its economy comes into line with its NAFTA partners costs are sure to rise. So visit now!

ACKNOWLEDGEMENTS

I am grateful to Eduardo Villalaz, Angeles Morales, Carlos León de la Peña, Renato Calo Mascarello, José Ma. Aguayo Estrada, Juan Naves Zaballa, Alejandro Hernandes, Moises Carréon, Gerardo Rannou, Richard Vogt, Rupert Witherow, Chris Daniel and Tim Means for their help and information; also to Jim Conrad, Steven Vale, Graham Mackintosh, Rob Rachowiecki and Dr Bob Vinton, and as ever to Hilary Bradt, Hans van Well, Patti Taylor, Wendy Dison and the rest of the trusty team.

Part One

GENERAL INFORMATION

2

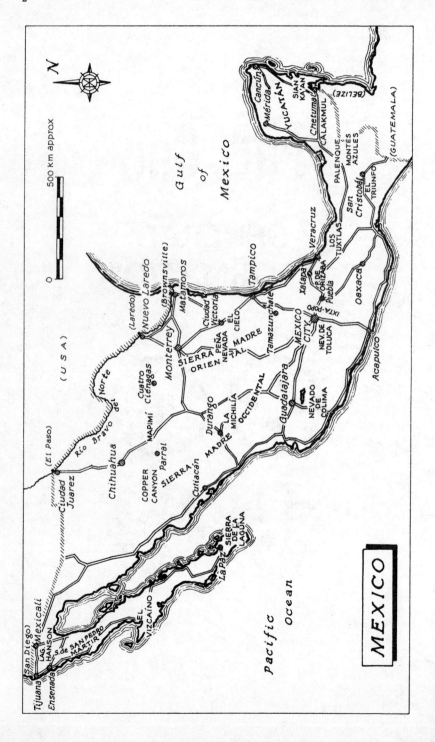

MEXICO

Chapter One

The Land

GEOGRAPHY

Mexico north of the isthmus of Tehuantepec – all of the country except the Yucatán peninsula and Chiapas – is shaped like a horn-of-plenty, curving to the southeast, with Baja California seen as a dribble of wine overflowing from the northwestern brim. In the middle of this horn there's a high tableland, the arid and dusty Northern Plateau or altiplano, the eastern rim of which is formed by the sedimentary Sierra Madre Oriental range (a southerly extension of the Rockies); the largely volcanic Sierra Madre Occidental (a southerly extension of the Sierra Nevada) forms its western rim. Both of these pine-clad ranges provide fine hiking almost anywhere you can gain access to them, and quite a few highways do cross them. The sedimentary lowlands along both the Gulf of Mexico and the Pacific coasts are hot and humid.

In general, the further south you travel on the altiplano, the higher in elevation you'll rise, until you reach Mexico City at 2,240m. The plateau ends just south of here, where the country's highest peaks are found in an east–west band of volcanoes – some of them still active – known by various names such as the Transversal Volcanic Axis or Trans-Mexico Volcanic Belt. South of this, the Valley of the Río Balsas cuts a deep gash across to the Pacific coast; together, the volcanoes and the valley form one of the main dividing points between southern and northern species. To the south of the Balsas the Sierra Madre del Sur occupies much of the states of Guerrero and Oaxaca, ending in the Isthmus of Tehuantepec, which marks the start of Central America, at least in geological terms.

Beyond here the Yucatán Peninsula, with arid thorn forests in the north evolving into rainforests in the south, is a huge flat to gently rolling, low-elevation slab of limestone. Some very interesting hikes can be made visiting ancient, out-of-the-way Maya ruins. Chiapas, Mexico's southernmost state, borders Guatemala; its flora and fauna show more affinities with Central America than they do with the rest of Mexico, and the diversity of species here is greater than anywhere else in Mexico. Chiapas is also home to the most traditional of Mexico's indigenous peoples, thus requiring special sensitivity and watchfulness on the hiker's part. Its Lacandón Jungle and isolated peaks provide some of the most exotic sensations available in Mexico.

This leaves Baja California, jutting south below the US state of California (properly Alta, or Upper, California), but really a world unto itself. It also has Pacific lowlands and Gulf lowlands, though here it's the Gulf of California, not the Gulf of Mexico. It has a mountainous spine, and the uplands are served by a network of trails – often the remnants of historic routes linking colonial missions. As described by Graham Mackintosh, it's also possible to walk along the coast, circumambulating the entire peninsula. Add the fact that Baja's plants and animals are uncommonly interesting and unique, and you have to say that Baja is as much a hiker's dreamland as is mainland Mexico.

Two-thirds of the country is over 800m in altitude, and about 50% is too steep to farm; 50% of the country is arid and at least 20% semi-arid, so that only 15% of the country's area is farmed.

Volcanic activity

In Mexico there are sixteen active volcanoes, some of which emit highly noxious gases, while others seem inactive but can belch forth lava and rocks without warning – something to consider before hiking to the summit. In particular, the country's best-known mountain, Popocatépetl, has been erupting since 1994, and is closed to visitors, although the *Club Alpin Mexicano* does organise the occasional trip.

So how does a volcano form? The active ingredient is magma, molten gas-charged rock which rises after being liquified by subterranean heat and pressure. The various types of magma define the various types of volcano, with soup-like magma spurting over the edge of the volcano in frequent and minor releases of energy, or thick and viscous magma which coagulates and is then blasted violently high into the air. This is the vulcanian type, the norm in Central America. If a large quantity of magma emerges it may leave a void into which the top of the volcano topples, turning the summit into a *caldera*. Years later lakes can form in the calderas of extinct volcanoes.

These beautiful lakes can be your reward if you've struggled up a volcano, although chances are slim that you'll be able to drink from them because they're usually at the bottom of a very steep pit, and almost always excessively alkaline. But they catch the light spendidly and the colours can be stunning.

You'll often find your path covered with pumice stone and obsidian. Usually they're found together because they're created together: pumice is the solidified foam on top of molten obsidian. Once cooled, obsidian can relatively easily be knapped into broad flat areas with sharp edges: just right for arrow and spear heads.

These are inactive indicators of past volcanic activity, but what about current events? In addition to the huge clouds currently belching from Popo', you'll see steam rising from fumaroles on other mountains such as Volcán de Colima; Paricutín is the volcano which appeared from nowhere between 1943 and 1952. In the Los Azufres National Park, in Michoacán state, you can see fumaroles and mudpots, formed by superheated water vapour forcing its way to the surface.

There are also regular earthquakes throughout much of Mexico; it's remarkable that a quake in Acapulco registering 4.1 on the Richter scale produced not a single emergency call.

CLIMATE AND WHEN TO GO

To the backpacker accustomed to temperate-zone seasons, the Mexican climate is confusing. The country is far enough north of the Equator for May-September to be warmer than October-April, but altitude plays a greater role in temperature changes, and in any case these affect the walker (and the farmer) far less than do the rainy and dry seasons.

In general, the rainy season occurs between June and September, and the dry season between January and April. During the rainy season, mornings usually begin clear and dewy-crisp and become progressively hotter and more humid, with clouds forming from mid-morning; by early afternoon the humidity is often oppressive but it usually isn't long before a storm dumps huge amounts of rain on you and drastically cools things off. On an August afternoon after a big rain in Mexico City, you may be glad you brought a warm jacket.

In winter, the Yucatán peninsula and parts of northern Mexico can be affected by winds known as *nortes* from, yes, the north; at this time the nights can be cold enough for you to wish not to be stuck in a beachside hammock without a good sleeping bag. Northern Mexico may have to endure a week or two of drizzly, windy, bone-chilling weather; in January there may be snow flurries along the border, and there are deep drifts in the mountains. The highlands are usually cool or even downright cold, even in summer, when all of low-elevation Mexico is, of course, scorching. The only areas that are wholly frost-free are the coasts and the Yucatán.

El Niño is the name of a sporadic weather system, usually occurring in the northern winter, when a transient body of warm water invades the usually chilly waters off Mexico's Pacific coast. When you hear that this has happened (every five years or so), you'd do well to reconsider any plans for backpacking in northern Mexico – including Baja and the Copper Canyon area. El Niño causes one wave of cold, rainy weather after the other to march across northern Mexico, turning vast saguaro and yucca deserts into veritable lakes. Southern Mexico and the Yucatán remain fairly unaffected by this, but the Gulf coast and the Yucatán can suffer from hurricanes between August and October. Actually, in recent years weather all over the world has been acting crazy, so don't depend too much on any of the above generalisations. In particular, the north of Mexico and southern Texas have been afflicted by a severe drought for several years.

NATURAL HISTORY

Mexico is the third most biologically diverse country in the world, bettered only by Brazil and Colombia; this is because of its great size (1,960,000km²), and more particularly its north–south spread and altitudinal range and the variety of climates and habitats these produce.

It's hard to give precise figures because it's hard to reach consensus on what is a distinct species and what is a subspecies (race or form) of an already established species, and because it's equally hard to know whether what you've found is the same as a specimen recorded in the 18th century in a totally different (and far less detailed) style than is used nowadays. It's rightly said that it's easy to find a new species, but it's very hard to convince the establishment that you have done so. Nevertheless, we can say that between 21,600 and 33,000 of the 250,000-odd known species of higher plants can be found in Mexico (the fourth highest total in the world), including 150 conifers (and half of the world's pines), and around a thousand each of ferns, orchids and cacti. As for animals, Mexico boasts 436–455 mammals (second only to Indonesia – Brazil has just 394), over 1,000 birds (1,018 including accidentals, casuals, introduced species and recent extinctions), 693–717 reptiles (more than any other country), 283–289 amphibians (fourth in the world), 2,000 fish, and hundreds of thousands of insect species (including 25,000 Lepidoptera – more than one per flowering plant species).

It's the high degree of endemicity (species being found nowhere else) that makes Mexico's wildlife especially valuable, and places a heavy responsibility on the country and its rulers: if they fail to preserve these species there's nowhere else (as a rule) that they might be found, nothing that anyone else can do – the species is irredeemably lost. In the 20th century at least five Mexican vertebrates have become extinct: the imperial woodpecker (*Campephilus imperialis*, the world's largest woodpecker, which simply ran out of trees big enough to nest in); the Guadalupe caracara (*Polybotus plancus lutosus*, killed mostly by visiting sailors, although the last nine were actually killed by collectors for the Smithsonian and similar institutes!); the Guadalupe storm petrel (*Oceanodroma macrodactyla*) and the Socorro dove (*Zenaida graysoni*), both wiped out by introduced rats on isolated Pacific islands; and the slender-billed grackle (*Quiscalis palustris*), in the marshy headwaters of the Río Lerma. In addition, about 35 species, such as the 'Californian condor (*Gymnogyps californianus*), grizzly bear (*Ursus arctos*), wolf (*Canis lupus*), wapiti (*Cervus elaphus*, identical to the European red deer), sea otter (*Enhydra lutris*), and river otter (*Lutra canadensis*), are now only found in other countries, and 1,066 of around 2,370 vertebrates are listed as threatened. On the other hand, species thought extinct are occasionally rediscovered, such as the Socorro mockingbird (*Mimodes graysoni*) and the horned guan (see below).

About half of Mexico's higher plant species, reptiles and amphibians, a third of its mammals and 12% of birds are endemic; in mammals endemism is at its highest in the Transversal Volcanic Axis and the Sierra Madre del Sur, in reptiles in the pine-oak forests and arid zones of the north, and in vegetation in the northern deserts. Other centres of endemism include Cuatro Ciénagas (Coahuila), the Barranca de Tolentenango (Hidalgo), and El Cielo (Tamaulipas). These are the areas of most dynamic interaction between the Nearctic (North American) and Neotropical (South/Central American) kingdoms, and thus the areas that scientists are keenest to preserve.

Endemism (the proportion of endemic species) should be distinguished from diversity (the total quantity of species). For instance, landbird diversity is highest in the southeastern lowlands and the Yucatán, where over 230 species can be found in some places, and lowest in the Pacific islands and the southern tip of Baja California; while endemism is highest in the Sierras Madre Occidental and Oriental, the Transversal Volcanic Axis and the Pacific Islands. In mammals, diversity is highest in the Balsas Valley (between Guerrero and Michoacán states) and the nearby stretch of the Pacific coast, and from the mouth of the Río Pánuco (between Tamaulipas and Veracruz) to Oaxaca. Plant diversity is highest in the tropical south, where the state of Chiapas alone boasts 8,250 species, more than any Central American country; in contrast the Sonoran desert has only 2,634 species, but a high proportion of endemics.

Vegetation zones

In very general terms, and all things being equal, as you travel south in Mexico rainfall increases and vegetation becomes more lush: deserts in the north, rainforest in the south. However there are many other factors: on one side of a mountain rainfall may be extremely heavy and the vegetation very lush, while on the other side, in the "rain shadow", there will be nothing but cacti and a few clumps of grass. Altitude is crucial, too, with mountain vegetation usually in fairly predictable zones.

In its original state, southern Mexico was almost entirely covered with forest, but this has now been reduced to a fraction of its original area. The north is dominated by the two great mountain ranges, largely conifer-covered, of the Sierras Madre Oriental and Occidental. Much of the surviving rainforest is (in theory) protected, as are many of the more interesting habitats in the north. This book deals largely with these parks and reserves, in most cases giving specific details of habitats and vegetational communities; here I just give a general overview of the northern forests, which are broadly familiar already to many Europeans and North Americans. The tropical forests and deserts are described in more detail, due both to their ecological importance and to their fascinating complexity.

Tropical rainforest, tropical evergreen forest and **tropical deciduous forest** are what most people rather loosely call jungle (or *selva* in Spanish). In Mexico, tropical rainforest is found only in a few valleys near the Guatemalan border of Chiapas; tropical evergreen (*perennifolia*) forest covers the central and southern Yucatán peninsula and stretches up the coast into Tabasco and Veracruz, and tropical deciduous (*caducifolia*) forest covers the lower parts of Chiapas, Oaxaca and Guerrero, and much of the Pacific slope of the Sierra Madre Occidental. There is effectively no winter, but some trees will shed their leaves for a brief period in the dry season, to conserve water. In Mexico these forests receive up to five *metres* of rain per year, so are very humid, lush and verdant. Half of this water is absorbed, combined with vast quantities of atmospheric carbon dioxide – one of the reasons deforestation is so disastrous is that this gas is released, contributing to the greenhouse effect. This great ecosystem, containing more diversity of life than any other, obtains most of its nutrients from the thin layer of soil which it itself produces as leaves and epiphytes constantly fall and rot. Thus nutrients are continually returned to the soil, only to be immediately taken up again by a plant. Leaf litter that would take a year to rot in temperate climes can be totally broken down and reabsorbed in just six weeks here. Once the forest is felled, this thin layer of soil is rapidly washed away, leaving infertile land that is soon exhausted.

All plant life in the forest competes for sunlight. Trees grow tall and straight, branching out at the top to form the canopy which provides a separate sun-drenched world. Smaller plants (epiphytes or air-plants, including many orchids) grow on these trees, and other seeds wait to grow in clearings where larger trees have died and fallen. Animals (ranging from mosquitoes, frogs, crabs and snakes to monkeys and birds of all sizes) also live and breed up there, many never descending to the ground, relying on rainwater held in plants. There is always food here: in particular there are 900 species of fig worldwide, each fertilised by a different agaonid wasp at a subtly different time of year to provide year-round food for many birds and bats. Indeed fruit is so plentiful that some frugivorous birds can spend 90% of their time singing to attract a mate!

At ground level the forest is far from impenetrable because there is insufficient light for excessive growth; in fact it's only at the forest edge and where large trees have fallen (or where forest has been cleared for slash-and-burn agriculture) that truly "jungle-like" conditions occur. All tropical forests have a natural cycle, changing from primary or virgin forest to this secondary or succession forest and then gradually reverting (over a century or more) to primary forest as the canopy trees grow and and plants adapted to lack of light take over below them from the "jungle". Palms and treeferns dislike light and are very rare in secondary forest, providing a good indicator of undisturbed forest. There's an amazing diversity of species, with 160 plant species (excluding vines, epiphytes etc) found in a one-hectare plot at Bonampak; in Amazonia one hectare can contain 283 species! However, at ground level many look the same, with broad thick leaves, trunks covered with moss and lichen and vast buttress roots. Because the layer of nutritious soil is thin, trees have shallow root systems and the fin-shaped buttresses have probably evolved to help support them.

Typical trees in primary forest include oaks (*Quercus spp*; broad-leaved types are known as *roble*, small-leaved types – liveoaks – as *encino*), cedars (*cedro/Cedrella spp*), kapok or silk-cotton (*ceiba/Ceiba pentandra*) and mahogany (*caoba/Swietania macrophylla* and *S. humilis*); smaller trees below the canopy include the avocado and its relatives (*Persea, Nectandra* and *Ocotea spp*), *Chamaedorea* palms, *Cyathea* treeferns, and strangler figs (*matapalo/Ficus spp* and *Clusia spp*), which sprout on a branch in the canopy, then send roots down to the ground, which grow all around the host tree and eventually (after maybe a hundred years) choke it to death. Below these grow dahlias, magnolias, and other herbaceous plants and ferns.

In secondary forest up to 2,000m you'll find large quantities of cecropia (*guarumo/Cecropia spp*), easily recognised by the bamboo-like rings on its trunk and its large hand-like leaves. Heliconias, recognisable by their huge paddle-shaped leaves and the opposed red or orange lobster-claw bracts that hold the blossoms, *candelillos* (*Piper spp*), with their candle-like flowers, *capulín* (*Trema micrantha*), balsa (*Ochroma lagopus*) and *papelillo* (*Miconia argenta*) are also common in these areas.

Whereas rainforest is found in lowlands with a generous year-round supply of rain, **cloudforest** is located where warm air moving up a mountain mingles with the higher cooler air to condense as clouds (usually at 1,500m plus). Water collects in the sponge-like mosses that proliferate, so that even on a sunny day the air is very humid. Everything here is smaller than in the mighty rainforests, due to the effects of wind and fog. Oak trees are common, their gnarled limbs bearing such a burden of air-plants that they eventually break off under the weight. Liquidambar or sweetgum (*Liquidambar styraciflua*), characteristic of the eastern USA, is also widespread in secondary growth and along streams; its rough, grey bark is often cut for resin, used in soaps and expectorants. Even the creatures tend to be miniature: toucanets rather than toucans, hummingbirds, tiny jewel-like frogs and multi-coloured butterflies.

The northern Pacific coast, the northern part of the Yucatán, and the Cabos area of Baja California is naturally covered with **thorn forest**, low forest largely composed of spiny shrubs adapted to a drier climate. Many of these are in fact members of the bean family, notably the fifty-plus acacias, above all sweet acacia (*Acacia farnesiana/huizache*, or, in Los Cabos, *vinorama*), a 3m grey tree with thorns and yellow flowers. The thorns can make for pretty hellish hiking, but in many areas the forest has succumbed to clearance for farming. To a botanist the variety of closely related and almost indistinguishable species (above all in the Balsas valley) is fascinating, but otherwise it's not the most attractive of environments.

The eastern slopes of the Sierra Madre Occidental and some of the mountains south of Mexico City form the **pine-oak** zone; I phrase it in that way as much of the forest has in fact been cleared. What's more, you in fact tend to get oaks (and cypress and juniper) but no pines at lower elevations (up to 2,000m in the south, lower in the north), then a transition zone, then pines but no oaks at about 3,000m. Oaks are of course found in the tropical forests as well, and there's a bewildering variety of species here, at least 165 of them (or 350 including subspecies). Pines first developed in Mexico and then spread more or less all over the world, but there's a mere 69 species of them in Mexico. On the highest mountains, above all in the Transversal Volcanic Axis, you'll eventually move on up into fir trees (*oyamel/Abies spp*), with large tufts of bunchgrass (*Muhlenbergia spp*, known as muhly in the USA); above this there are alpine meadows of bunchgrass and fescue grass, with a few stunted shrubs, and above this rocks with lichen and moss, and then only snow and ice.

Much of northeastern Mexico is covered by grassland and a xerophytic *matorral* (drought-resistant scrub) dominated by **mezquite** (*Prosopis spp*); again, this is a thorny tree, just a couple of metres high, adapted to arid conditions, particularly by having roots that go straight down for up to 30m to find water. It's an important food source for many birds and animals, and it's also very useful to humans, producing fuelwood, gum and a rough flour.

Half of Mexico (about a million square kilometres) is covered by **desert**, although little of this is in fact bare sand dunes; in fact much of it is barely distinguishable by the lay person from the habitats described above. Most of Sonora and Baja California is technically desert, but you'll find vast expanses of cacti and other plants here; the most characteristic plant of the Mexican deserts is *gobernadora* (*Larrea tridentata*; known north of the border as creosote), which is the key to preventing widespread erosion. This has amazing powers of survival; some cloned plants are now 11,700 years old. It's a dense bush with trilobate leaves which smells strongly of camphor, particularly at dawn. There are about 6,000 species of desert plants, all highly specialised, and 90% of them endemic to the deserts of Mexico and the USA; it's a complex but fragile ecosystem.

There are four main deserts in Mexico: the Sonoran and Chihuahuan deserts are the big two, with smaller ones in Hidalgo/Querétaro and the Tehuacán-Cuicatlán Valley (Puebla and Oaxaca states). The Sonoran desert

INTRODUCED PLANTS

It's said that we now live in a global economy, but in a sense this has long been the case. It's well known that tomatoes, corn, potatoes and tobacco made their way from the New World to enrich our lives in the Old World, and that just about everything from Europe was taken to the colonies by nostalgic settlers. But beyond this, there have been many more movements of plant species around the globe, and I found it intriguing trying to work out where the various cash crops actually originated.

For the record, then, as far as is known, oranges come from Indochina (and actually came to the Americas with Columbus in 1493), mangoes from Burma and Assam, carrots from Afghanistan, rice from Southeast Asia, coffee from Ethiopia and Sudan, watermelons from tropical Africa, breadfruit from Tahiti and Indo-Malaysia, sugarcane from New Guinea, bananas from India and Burma, and cardamom from India. Coconuts seem to have originated somewhere in Oceania, but nobody's sure where, as they've quite successfully established themselves by natural means around the world, including both the Pacific and Atlantic coasts of Central America.

One of the most common trees in Central America now is the African oil palm (*Elaeis guineensis*), brought by slaves from Africa. Date palms (*Phoenix dactylifera*) were introduced to Baja California by missionaries, but olives were banned, in order to protect the Spanish producers; a few trees have survived nevertheless. Other African species are Guinea grass (*Panicum maximum*) and *jaragua* grass (*Hyparrhenia rufa*) which now dominate most of the savannas and fields of the region, growing very quickly but then becoming tough and inedible by cattle, necessitating annual burning. More recently, Macadamia nuts have come in from Australia, together with *Grevillea* trees, used to shade coffee, and *Eucalyptus* and *casuarina* trees, used in reforestation schemes.

Of the New World species, squashes were first domesticated both in the Honduras/Nicaragua area and in South America, maize likewise in Mexico and in South America, and beans in Mexico and Peru. Diego Rivera, in his mural in the National Palace, claims that just about everything originated in Mexico, but in fact many of these species (notably tomatoes, pineapples, cacao and sweet potatoes) had been introduced to Mexico from South America well before the Spanish conquest; however, commercial strains of the pineapple were developed in Britain and then re-introduced to the Americas. Chili peppers, pumpkins, papaya, vanilla, avocadoes, turkeys and one strain of cotton did originate in Mexico, and passionfruit, custard apples, potatoes and quinoa in South America; grapefruit and cashew nuts probably originated in the West Indies, and allspice there or in Central America.

Many ornamental plants also derive from the American tropics, notably fuchsia, mimosa, zinnias, dahlias, marigolds and *Cattleya* orchids; finally diosgenin, a key element in contraceptive pills, was derived from Mexican yams.

(which also covers most of Baja California) is very hot, with scattered rain in both summer and winter causing carpets of ephemeral flowers to appear; the saguaro cactus (*Cereus gigantea*), which grows to 14m in height, is found only here. The Chihuahuan desert, on the altiplano, is less hot, with summer rain only; there are no columnar cacti here but a greater variety with rosette leaves (such as *lechuguilla*), and fewer annual flowers and trees (with only *mezquite* and *huizache* in large areas).

There are over a thousand **cacti** in Mexico (including 134 of the 260 higher plants threatened in Mexico); they are perennial succulents, mostly with green photosynthesising stems, adapted for water storage, and contrary to widespread belief they do flower every year. Cacti breathe in carbon dioxide at night, keeping their pores closed by day to avoid evaporation; the carbon dioxide is stored chemically overnight, and broken down by day. Many of them are pollinated by bats, although birds, bees and moths also contribute. About seventy species are columnar, the classic cacti of the *Snoopy* cartoons, such as the saguaro, cardón (*Pachycereus spp*, found in Baja, up to 15m tall with up to thirty parallel branches, ten tonnes in weight and 200 years old), and *órgano* (in the Balsas and Tehuacán Valleys). The other main types of cactus are those with rosette leaves, barrel cacti (*biznaga/Echinocactus* or *Ferocactus spp*), and the (edible) prickly pears (*cholla, nopal/Opuntia spp*, with spiny beaver-tail leaves and *tuna* fruit). Agaves such as yucca and *maguey* (*Agave spp*, source of pulque, mezcal and tequila) are also succulents, but are not actually cacti; they're similar to the old-world aloes.

Mangroves (*manglares*) are trees adapted to grow in and beyond the edge of the salt water; their stilt-like roots form impenetrable barriers that hold silt until it forms first a mudbank and then solid land. Before this happens, a complex ecosystem develops in and around the mangroves, prime components being coastal birds and crocodiles. Sandy coasts also form complex and specialised communities of salt-resistant plants. Palm trees grow in many areas, not just along the coast, but you'll certainly notice cohune palms (*Orbignya cohune*) in the Yucatán, the corozo palm (*Scheelia spp*) in Chiapas, and fan palms (*Washingtonia* and *Erythea spp*) in the oases of Baja California; date palms have also been introduced to Baja.

Mammals

Mexico is home to such a variety of creatures that we can only describe those that you are most likely to see.

Howler monkey
(mono congo, saraguato/Alouatta palliata, A. pigra)
Howlers, in Mexico found mostly in Chiapas's Lacandón Jungle and the southern Yucatán Peninsula, are usually heard before they're seen. If you camp at the Mayabel campsite near Palenque, you may hear them each morning. The sound carries for miles; from a distance it can be mistaken for wind in the trees, but close to it defies description. If you're not forewarned, you may think the forest is haunted.

Howlers have rich chestnut-coloured bodies and black limbs. They live in troops, the leader of which is responsible for the dawn and dusk howling concerts, although others may join in. The male has a huge voice box, strengthened with cartilage, which enables him to project sound so impressively. Being the largest of the American monkeys also helps.

Spider monkey
(mono araña, chango/Ateles geoffroyi)
Although spider monkeys have no thumbs, their bodies are beautifully adapted to tree life, where they are the most efficient climbers and swingers of all the New World monkeys. It's a joy to watch them moving effortlessly through the trees, making prodigious leaps, and using their tails as hands; howlers also have prehensile tails, but they're less agile. In fact the spider monkey's tail has a hairless area on the underside which can feel as efficiently as a finger, so it really is a fifth limb.

Spider monkeys come in a variety of colours, black, chestnut, and light brown, but you'll always be able to identify them by their long limbs. Like howlers, they're only found in the southern forests.

Nine-banded armadillo
(cusuco, armadillo/Dasypus novemcinctus)
These endearing creatures are quite common in drier forests, and you'll often see them shuffling around in leaves or grass, hunting out insects and other small creatures, then digging frantically to reach the nest. With their noses so often buried deep in the ground, it's as well that they can hold their breath for up to six minutes. They have poor hearing and even poorer eyesight, but an excellent sense of smell. It's possible that the eleven-banded or naked-tailed armadillo (*Cabassous centralis*), native to Central America, has now moved into Chiapas.

Agouti
(guaqueque/Dasyprocta punctata, D. mexicana)
Agoutis have the misfortune to taste good, and in populated areas relentless hunting has driven these diurnal rodents into mainly nocturnal habits. They have two colour phases, reddish brown and black. The related *tepescuintle (Cuniculus/Agouti paca)* is the lowland paca; it's nocturnal and bears rows of creamy spots along its flanks.

The Raccoon family
The raccoon (*mapache/Procyon lotor*) is identifiable by its black face-mask and ringed tail, and is common near beaches and rivers. The kinkajou (*mico de noche/Potus flavus*) is as agile as a monkey, with a truly prehensile tail, and is popular as a pet; it looks nothing like a raccoon, but has soft brown fur (whence its other name of honey bear), large eyes (it is nocturnal) and low set ears. The ringtail (*cacomixtle/Bassariscus astutus, B. sumichrasti*), sometimes called the ringtail cat, in fact looks more like a squirrel with an even more strongly ringed tail than the raccoon. You are unlikely to travel far in backcountry Mexico without meeting a coati (*tejón, pizote/Nasua narica*), either in the wild or as a pet. They are playful and affectionate pets, but their long whiffly noses get into everything and they are very destructive. They live in tropical forests where they are particularly active in the early morning and evening, foraging in troops of up to 30, although the males may also be solitary (they were thought to be a separate species, the coatimundi or lone coati). They are excellent tree-climbers and may at first glance be mistaken for monkeys as they shin up trees in search of fruit or tasty insects.

Silky anteater
Unlike the big South American anteaters the silky anteater (*oso hormiguero/ Tamandua mexicana*) is a squirrel-sized creature, living in trees in the tropical forests of southern and central Mexico.

Collared peccary
(chancho de monte, saíno, javalina, jabalí/Tayassu tajacu)
Collared peccaries are related to pigs and live in a variety of habitats in the Americas (though not in Baja California), at up to 2,000m. They are highly gregarious and you may see groups of up to a hundred of them in protected areas. The slightly larger white-lipped peccary (*Tayassu pecari*) is found only in wetter areas along the east coast from southern Veracruz into the Yucatán, and is very sensitive to environmental disturbance.

Peccaries secrete musk from a gland in the middle of their backs, so you often smell them before you see them. Adults can be aggressive and are capable of inflicting a serious wound with their sharp tusks. A woodsman in Chiapas told Jim Conrad that of all the animals in the Lacandón Jungle he feared this animal the most because, he said, "it's so stupid". If you surprise one on a trail, it may try to escape by running right over you, slashing with its tusks, instead of running away.

Tapir
(danta/Tapirus bairdii)
These are large primitive creatures, related to the horse and weighing up to 300kg. You will be very lucky to see one, as they inhabit the dense forest of Chiapas, Tabasco, Campeche, and Yucatán, only coming out to feed at night; however, you may well see their large hoofprints and piles of dung along the trail. They are excellent swimmers and often take to the water when pursued.

Cats
There are six species of felines in Mexico: in descending order of size they are the jaguar (*tigre/Felis onca*); the puma/cougar (*F. concolor*), the ocelot or manigordo (*F. pardalis*), the margay or caucel (*F. wiedii*), the best tree-climber of this group, and the jaguarundi (*F. yaguarundi*), which looks more like a weasel with its short legs and long, slender body. From the Transversal Volcanic Axis to the north there's also the bobcat (*gato montés/ Lynx rufus*), which weighs about 10kg and preys on deer fawns and wild turkey. All are largely nocturnal and hard to see, especially as the bigger ones only need to hunt every week or so.

The jaguar is the largest of the New World cats, though the three Mexican races are smaller than those to the south, about 1.7m long and 64kg in weight (females weigh about 45kg). It needs a territory of at least 20km² of hot wet forest and thus is suffering badly from deforestation. You will read and hear more rubbish about this magnificent and retiring creature than about any other. No description of adventures in the jungle is complete without a hair-raising account of the terrors and dangers suffered by the author on account of "tigers". However, while locals used to say, "*Cuidado! hay tigres!*" and shake their heads in disbelief on hearing that you were about to venture into *la selva* (the jungle), nowadays the forest is so disturbed and degraded that the remaining jaguars stay well out of the way.

So let's get a few facts straight about the jaguar, even though you won't see one unless you're incredibly lucky. The jaguar is immensely strong, killing large animals such as the tapir with ease. A good swimmer and fond of the water, it often pursues its prey into rivers. Being such a good hunter, it is self-sufficient in the jungle and very rarely makes an unprovoked attack on a human. There is no authenticated account of one becoming a habitual man-eater, although naturally one will attack if provoked or threatened, or if injured.

The mountain lion, puma or cougar (*Felis concolor*) has the widest range of any American mammal, from Canada to Tierra del Fuego; in Mexico it's found above all in the western mountains (in Sonora, Chihuahua, Durango, Zacatecas, Michoacán, Guerrero and Oaxaca). It preys on white-tail deer, peccary and turkey, often hiding its leftovers under brushwood. Puma can weigh up to 110kg in Canada and Patagonia, but Central American specimens are about half this size.

Black bear
(oso negro/Ursus americanus)
Black bears can be found throughout the Sierra Madre Occidental from the US border south to Zacatecas state, and from the border south to San Luís Potosí in the Sierra Madre Oriental, although they used to range further south. They live mainly in the pine-covered mountains, where they hibernate from November to early May; cubs are born in mid-winter, and emerge in spring with a very hungry and belligerent mother. They're largely vegetarian, feeding on fruit, berries, nuts and wild honey, but also take the occasional lizard, chipmunk, ground squirrel or coati – skunks and porcupines are left well alone.

There's almost no chance of the Mexican grizzly bear (*Ursus arctos nelsoni*) still surviving in its last redoubts around the headwaters of the Río Yaqui and in Cerro Campana, and the Sierras Santa Clara and del Nido (in Chihuahua), although it's hard to be sure. Likewise, the Mexican timber wolf (*Canis lupus baileyi*), once found throughout the forested sierras to the north of the Valley of Mexico, is now almost certainly extinct in the wild, although some are captive in La Michilía Biosphere Reserve. In the 1950s the US Fish & Wildlife Service trained Mexican ranchers in wolf-poisoning; now, the FWS runs a captive breeding programme, including one of the Mexican subspecies, extinct in the USA since 1976.

Coyote
(coyote/Canis latrans)
The coyote (from its Aztec name *coyotl*) or brush wolf is one of those exceptional species that has benefited from mankind's intervention in the environment; its range is steadily expanding, and in 1995/96 it actually crossed the ice to reach Newfoundland. It is found throughout Mexico, having no specific habitat or diet; it'll eat fruit, mezquite beans, deer fawns, wild turkeys, peccaries and carrion, and also visits beaches to raid turtle nests. It's not hard to spot, being diurnal except where persecuted.

Deer and other herbivores
The most obvious species of deer is the **white-tail deer** (*venado cola blanco/ Odoceilus virginianus*), hunted by the million across North America. There are 14 subspecies living all over Mexico except peninsular Baja California, most in pine-oak and tropical evergreen forests, but also in the Sonoran desert; all are much smaller than the US races, a maximum of 100kg rather

than 135kg. In Mexico the males shed their antlers in April/May (apparently these are often eaten by porcupines) and replace them by September; they rut from October to January, and the young are born from June to August (as against May/June in Texas). In summer they have fine but dense red-brown fur, with longer woollier brown-grey fur in winter.

You might also, if lucky, see the red brocket deer (*tazama/Mazama americana*), a small deer with short prong antlers found in the tropical evergreen forests of the Gulf Coast and southern Yucatán. The mule deer (*venado burro/Odoceilus hemionus*) is so called because of its large mule-like ears. Of its seven subspecies, *O. hemionus eremicus* is found in Baja California and Sonora, and as far south as Guaymas, and the smaller, lighter grey *O. hemionus canus* in Chihuahua, Coahuila, Tamaulipas and San Luís Potosí. These reach a maximum weight of about 100kg, against 140kg north of the border. Their habitat is arboreal desert, although they may move up into forest in early spring, returning to lower altitudes in autumn.

Also in the northern deserts, the **pronghorn** (*berrendo/Antilocapra americana*) is now rare; this was heavily hunted from around 1909 until 1922, but has been protected since and has recovered slowly. It can move at up to 80km/h, outstripping wolves and coyotes, but its curiosity made it easy to shoot. It's sometimes misnamed an antelope, but in fact it's the sole species and genus of the pronghorn family. The **bighorn sheep** (*borrego cimarrón/Ovis canadensis*) is recovering more successfully from hunting, perhaps due to its perfect camouflage in the less accessible desert mountains of Baja California Norte, Sonora and Chihuahua. In addition there is a breeding programme on an island off Loreto. They rut in October (males ramming each other in *very* violent fights), then shed their horns in November; females have smaller horns, curving backwards.

Bats
In the tropical rainforests bats account for at least half of all mammal species; in Mexico as a whole the proportion is lower, with 133–143 bats in a total of 436–455 mammals, and just six endemic to Mexico. Perhaps only half of these are insectivorous, the others feeding on fruit, fish, animals, nectar, and even, in two cases, blood. One of these is the common vampire (see *Health and Safety*), and the other is similar, but feeds only on smaller animals and birds.

About 60 species live in caves, above all the Mexican free-tailed bat (*Tabarida brasiliensis*), which spends its summers in the southern USA, with 20-odd million living in Bracken Cave, Texas, the world's largest bat colony. These migrate south for the winter, and one cave in Durango houses about 100,000, eating an estimated nine tonnes of insects each month. Alas, five of the nine largest colonies in Mexico have been destroyed, thanks to their being mistaken for vampires.

In addition to disposing of insects, bats also play a crucial role in the pollination of many plants, such as maguey (so no tequila without bats!) and many other cacti, balsa, and ceiba. Bats are of great importance to the indigenous people of Mexico, with a bat god protecting maize in Oaxaca, and human sacrifices being performed by bats in Maya art.

Other vaguely familiar mammals include the Eastern grey fox (*gato de monte/Urocyon cinereoargentus*), silver badgers (*tlalcoyote/Taxidea taxus*), otters, rabbits, hares (jackrabbits to North Americans) and squirrels. In addition there are plenty of skunks (popularly thought to be venomous, because they can carry rabies) and rodents. In fact there are 215 species of rodents, 106 of them endemic, a quarter of these on tiny islands in the Gulf of California. Among the most primitive mammals in the region are the marsupials: the opossums (*tacuazin* or *tlacuache/Didelphis spp*) are the only ones in the Nearctic kingdom, although closely related species such as mouse-opossums are also found in southern Mexico.

Marine mammals are dealt with in the *Baja California* chapter.

Reptiles and amphibians

You're bound to see plenty of **lizards** wherever it's dry and sunny. These include spiny lizards (*Heloderma spp*, generally misnamed *escorpión*), skinks and green anole lizards; in addition, above 1,500m you may well see salamanders.

Some of them are pretty big, and of course the largest members of the lizard family are the **iguanas**: contrary to what you might expect, these like to live in trees, particularly along rivers, so are suffering from habitat loss. They are also widely hunted and so are at risk; there are imaginative schemes to breed them commercially, as they yield three or four times as much meat per hectare as cattle, and the trees are left standing. The *garrobo* (*Ctenosaura spp*) is like an iguana, but smaller and non-arboreal, and is said to be even tastier. A half-sized iguana, up to a metre long, may be a basilisk (*Basiliscus spp*); these essentially Central American creatures have dinosaur-like sailfin crests and the smaller ones at least (nicknamed "Jesus Christ lizards") can run on water, for up to 400m and at up to 12km/h.

Crocodiles (*Crocodilus acutus, C. moreletti*) can be found on both coasts of southern Mexico, as well as the smaller black caiman *Melanosuchus niger*.

You'll see (or at least hear) lots of **frogs**, some of which spend their entire lives in the forest canopy, breeding in pools of water in bromeliads.

Perhaps the best-known Mexican amphibian is the endemic **axolotl** (*ajolote/Ambystoma mexicanum*), which comes to the surface to breath but has otherwise lost the ability to live out of water. It was a major food-source for the Aztecs, but is now rare.

Turtles
Most of the world's marine turtle species nest on the beaches of Mexico; these have only been protected since 1990. It's estimated that 50,000 sea turtles were killed each year by shrimp boats in the Gulf of Mexico (of 150,000 worldwide), until the US government required the use of Turtle Excluder Devices on nets; at first these also freed 30-35% of the shrimps, but this has now been reduced to under 10%. Turtles are still threatened by people and animals plundering their nesting sites for eggs.

The Atlantic beaches are visited by five species: the Atlantic hawksbill (*tortuga carey/Eretmochelys imbricata*), the Atlantic loggerhead (*caguama/ Caretta caretta caretta*), the green (*tortuga blanca* or *parlama/Chelonia mydas*), the Atlantic/Kemp's ridley or parrot (*tortuga lora/Lepidochelys kempi*), and the Atlantic leatherback (*laúd* or *golfina/Dermochelys coriacea*). The most seriously threatened are the hawksbill, the green, and the ridley, which is the smallest Atlantic turtle (up to 80kg) and the only one with a circular shell. The ridley was thought to be a sterile hybrid of the green and the loggerhead until 1947, when a nesting site was found north of Tampico; the egg harvest was only halted in 1966, and in 1978 some eggs were moved to a safer beach in Texas. The hawksbill (c130kg) was caught for its tortoiseshell until it was saved by plastics, and in the 19th century the green, so called (in English) for the colour of its fat, was used for soup and almost wiped out. The green can stay underwater for five hours and dive to 1,400m, deep enough to escape sharks; it weighs in at about 270kg, and the Atlantic loggerhead at about 220kg. The leatherback is the largest marine turtle (up to 800kg), feeding entirely on jellyfish.

On the Pacific coast you may find the hawksbill, the leatherback, the Pacific loggerhead (*caguama/Chelonia agassizi*) and the Indo-Pacific ridley (*Lepidochelys olivacea,* which can also be found in the Caribbean, but doesn't nest there). At Mazunte, on the coast of Oaxaca, you can visit the *Centro Mexicano de Tortuga* to see turtles in breeding tanks. This area, the Playa de Escobilla, is perhaps the third busiest turtle-beach in the world, and was until 1990 a scene of horrific slaughter; now this has been replaced by ecotourism. Alas, the area is being developed as a beach resort for mass tourism, which may prove almost as harmful to the turtles.

Chiapas is the only state left with sizeable populations of freshwater turtles; of thirteen species, ten are commercially valuable, notably the Tabasco turtle or Central American river turtle (*tortuga blanca/Dermatemys mawei*), weighing up to 17kg. This is found only in water, from Veracruz to Honduras, at altitudes up to 200m. You may also see snapping turtles (*Chelydra serpentina*), mud turtles (*casquito/Kinosternum spp*), sliders (*Chrysemys ornata, C grayi*), and softshell turtles, such as the Guadalupe spiny shell (*Trionyx spiniferus guadalupensis*), best described as an "animated pancake".

In the northern deserts you'll see land turtles of the *Gopherus* genus (notably in the Mapimí Biosphere Reserve) and desert box turtles (*Terrapene spp*), not to be confused with terrapins (such as *Malaclemys terrapin*) which live in brackish waters along the Gulf Coast.

Snakes are dealt with under *Health and Safety*.

Birds

Europe has a little over 500 bird species, North America north of Mexico has in the vicinity of 650, but in Mexico itself you can see over 1,000. Obviously it's impossible here to provide more than a peep at Mexico's more colourful and interesting birds.

Visitors from the USA and Canada have an advantage over Europeans, as many species will already be familiar. Not surprisingly, many North American species (at least 338 out of 650) head south for the winter, just like many humans; some stop in Mexico and Central America, while others go all the way to South America, passing rapidly through Mexico or the Caribbean islands. Half a million raptors pass through Panamá in a few weeks, including Swainson's hawk (*Buteo swainsonii*), which breeds in northern Mexico and winters mainly in northern Argentina. Among the more amazing migratory feats is that of the ruby-throated hummingbird (*Archilochus colubris*), the only hummingbird to breed in eastern North America, which travels from Ontario to the Yucatán, including 800km non-stop across the Gulf in 20 hours, before moving on to Central America. The calliope hummingbird (*Stellula calliope*), which breeds in the northwestern US and British Columbia and winters in central Mexico, is the smallest in North America at just 7.5cm in length. Most North American swallows, flycatchers, thrushes, vireos, tanagers, wood warblers, and many raptors and waders, are migratory.

Other winter visitors which will be familiar to many include the Vaux's swift, sapsuckers, towhees, kinglets, bluebirds, American robins and many warblers. In fact, although we think of these birds as coming from the north, most of the New World's wrens, quails, towhees, woodpeckers, vireos and orioles have their origin in Mexico. Coastal birds naturally follow the coastlines, with a mecca for bird-watchers in the Mazatlán-San Blas area on the Pacific coast; the Caribbean coast is barely tidal, so with no inter-tidal feeding zone there are few shorebirds here. The brown pelican (*Pelecanus occidentalis*) is resident all year on Mexico's coasts, while the white pelican (*Pelecanus erythrorhynchos)* is a winter visitor; likewise Brandt's cormorant (*Phalacrocorax penicillatus*, in northwestern Mexico) and the neotropical cormorant (*P. olivaceus*) are resident, while the pelagic and double-crested cormorant (*Phalacrocorax pelagicus* and *P. auritus*) are winter visitors, as are the common and Pacific loons (*Gavia immer, G. pacifica*), North America's most magical birds.

Since river travel is leisurely and comfortable, there is ample opportunity for birdwatching and you will see far more species than during a walk in the jungle when they're all out of sight in the treetops, and your pack makes it difficult to look above you anyway. Most are migratory, but juveniles may be seen throughout the year. Any marshy area is full of **jacanas** (*combatiente/Jacana spinosa*). They have the longest toes (proportionally) of any bird, and yellow wings visible only when they fly. **Anhingas** or snake-birds (*Anhinga anhinga*), common along eastern rivers, are like greeny long-necked cormorants with white wing patches. Their snake-like neck is often the only part visible above the water's surface, but you're more likely to spot them as they stand motionless drying their wings in the sun. **Kingfishers**, notably *Ceryle alcyon*, the belted kingfisher, are easily recognisable, and **herons** (ten species) and **egrets** (four species) need no introduction. The cattle egret (*Bubulcus ibis*) has spread worldwide in a spectacular fashion in little more than a century, with very little direct help from man; it was first brought to South America by a storm in 1877 (and is still often seen passing through Ascension Island), it had spread through Central America and Florida by 1942, through Mexico to Texas by 1954, and reached Alaska by 1981.

Moving on to tropical forest, this is the habitat of a huge variety of birds, but you will need binoculars to spot them in the concealing foliage. **Parrots** (*loro*/mostly *Amazona spp*) are seen through much of Mexico and are easily recognised; they are basically green with other colours on their heads and wings. You are much more likely to see them as they fly home in the evening than in the trees where they noisily prepare for the night. Parrots usually fly in pairs, although larger flocks are also common, and you can recognise them by their rapid wing-beats and their habit of shouting at each other as they fly. A few parrots can even be found in the temperate conifer forests of the Sierra Madre Occidental; these include the thick-billed parrot (*cotorra serrana/Rhynchopsitta pachyryncha*), now found only in a small area where Chihuahua, Durango and Sinaloa meet, south of Guachochi, and the maroon-fronted parrot (*R. terrisi*), in the Sierra Madre Oriental north of El Cielo. The **parakeets** (*perico*) are similar but smaller. **Macaws** (*guacamaya, lapa/ Ara spp*) are larger and even noisier than parrots, and are unmistakable with their brilliant colours and long tails.

The **keel-billed toucan** (*tucán/Ramphastos sulfuratus*) favours humid tropical forests, whilst its smaller cousins the **emerald toucanet** (*tucancillo/ Aulacorhynchus prasinus*) and **collared araçari** (*Pteroglossus torquatus*) prefer cloudforests.

Trogons (*trogón* or *coa*) are widely distributed, although the most famous member of the family, the **resplendent quetzal** (*quetzal real/Pharomachrus mocinno*), lives only in a few cloudforests in Chiapas and to the south. Most trogons have bright green plumage and red or yellow breasts, but only the male quetzal has a golden sheen to its green feathers and that magnificent tail.

Most of the other birds in the tropical forests are drab and harder to spot, but you'll hear them. According to legend, the **solitaires** (*jilguero/Myadestes spp*) were the last to be given their colours and all the brightest ones had gone, so they were given the best voice instead; they're found in mountain forests. The chacalacas and guans are large birds with long tails: the **plain chacalaca** (*Ortalis vetula*) is a plain brown-grey bird with a call like a rattle or a firework going off; the Guatemalan black chacalaca or highland guan (*Penelopina nigra*) is in a separate family. The crested guan (*pava/ Penelope purpurascens*) is a big, ungainly wild turkey that I'm always surprised to see on a branch rather than on the ground; the great curassow (*ocofaisán/Crax rubra*) is brown with a striking black-and-white head and crest, and is very sensitive to disturbance and thus a good indicator of the state of the ecosystem. (The horned guan *pavón/Oreophasis derbianus* survives on a few mountains in Chiapas.) The cloudforest is also home to quail (*codorniz*) and four species of tinamou (or *gallinita de monte*), a sort of partridge.

As you move north the fauna becomes more and more familiar to North Americans; birds are of course highly mobile, so that there are relatively few endemics (only 125, ie little more than 10%) – these include no less than 38 endemic **buntings**. The general area of the isthmus marks the northern limit of many Central American genera, and the southern limit of many North American ones, such as the nuthatches, tits, larks and shrikes; the Yucatán sees many species of Caribbean origin, such as the grassquits, some now resident.

The **wild turkey** (*Meleagris gallopavo*) is Mexico's main contribution to carnivorism, having been domesticated by about 1300AD; the wild race weighs about 10kg and can still be found to the north of Michoacán and San Luís Potosí, roosting in pines; they mate in March and April, when the male's gobbling call can be heard up to a kilometre away. The ocellated turkey (*Agriocharis ocellata*) lives in tropical forest in Yucatán, Campeche and Quintana Roo, but is still hunted. Another domesticated species is the Muscovy duck (*Cairina moscata*).

Finally, birds that you'll see everywhere include the great-tailed grackle (*zanate/Quiscalis mexicanus*), somewhat like a blackbird but with a long broad tail, the groove-billed ani (*talingo* or *tajuil/Crotophaga sulcirostris*), similar, jet-black but with a large puffin-like beak, the red-winged blackbird (*Agelaius phoeniceus*), much as its name suggests, and the drabber melodious blackbird (*Dives dives*), in the east and south of the country. There are about 63 **flycatchers** in Mexico, mostly mousy in colour, although the social (or vermilion-crowned) and boatbilled flycatchers and the great kiskadee are all yellow-breasted, with a white throat and eyestripe and dark uppers.

There's a new Museum of Mexican Birds in Saltillo (at Hidalgo and Bolivar, three blocks south of the cathedral), in the old Colegio de San

Juan Nepomuceno; it's a collection of 670 species of stuffed birds, alas (Tues-Sun 10.00-18.00, free on Wednesdays and Saturday afternoons).

Insects
Invertebrates account for more than 90% of known animal species, and doubtless an even higher proportion of unknown ones, as they're small, hard to distinguish from each other, and usually cunningly disguised or hidden. Most national parks and so on don't even try to quantify them. The most interesting insects are, alas, detailed in our health section.

The most distinctively Mexican insect is the jumping bean, actually the larva of the moth *Carcocapsa saltitans*, growing in the pod of *Sebastiana palmieiri*, which can be found rustling in the undergrowth of the Alamos area of southern Sonora and northern Sinaloa from June to October.

There are between 2,200 and 2,500 species of butterflies in Mexico, which play an important role in pollinating many plants, especially cacti in the northern deserts.

Likewise there are probably over 2,000 species of bees, mostly in the northern borderlands; most are solitary, nesting in the ground and without castes. The European honey-bee *Apis mellifera* was introduced by 1530 at the latest.

Fish
There are 384 exclusively freshwater fish in Mexico, 375 in the relatively shallow waters of the continental shelf, and at least 1,350 oceanic species. Fifteen of the freshwater species are now extinct in Mexico, and there are 41 introduced species, some of which are causing serious disruption. There are endemic species in most major river systems and large lakes; the karst sinkholes of the Yucatán have been isolated for five million years, producing very specialised species. Just as with other types of birds and plants, there's an overlap between species of Nearctic and Neotropical origin, with Nearctic species reaching as far south as the Guatemalan highlands.

See the section on *Baja California* for more on sport fishing and marine mammals.

Chapter Two

The People

HISTORY

Humans first crossed into North America over the Bering Strait about 60,000 years ago, and headed south, crossing into South America around 15,000 years ago and reaching Tierra del Fuego approximately 4,000 years later. Some stopped along the way, living as small nomadic bands until some time between 7000BC and 2000BC, when the climate warmed and they learnt to farm corn (*Zea mays*) and beans (*Phaseolus vulgaris*), as well as squashes and root crops. This was the key to the development of the settled cultures of Mesoamerica (the region stretching from just north of Tampico and Guadalajara in Mexico to northern Costa Rica); in the drier lands to the north a nomadic hunter-gatherer lifestyle was all that was possible.

The Pre-Classic period began around 1600BC when the Olmec culture developed in what are now Veracruz and Tabasco states, on the Gulf of Mexico; appearing seemingly out of nowhere, they produced colossal sculptures and cities before declining around 175BC. The Classic period, from 300AD to 900AD, was dominated by the Maya culture, perhaps the most impressive of all, in the Yucatán peninsula; at the same time Teotihuacán, just north of the present Mexico City, grew to become the largest city in the Americas and the sixth largest in the world, with a population of around 100,000 by 600AD. It's a mystery who the people of Teotihuacán were or what became of them; likewise it's unknown why the Maya cities were abandoned, but the Maya people still live throughout southern Mexico and northern Central America. The Post-Classic period was marked by a succession of invasions by "barbarian" groups from the north, who settled in the cities they found but never achieved the same levels of culture as the earlier civilisations. The most notable of these were the Toltecs, who dominated central Mexico between 900 and 1200AD; the south of Mexico was ruled by the Zapotecs and then the Mixtecs. The Aztecs, a group of northern peoples led by the Mexica tribe, arrived in the late 12th century and by 1345 were able to found the city of Tenochtitlán on the site of the present Mexico City. After a series of vigorous military campaigns they soon ruled 15 million people, and sacrificed large numbers of them.

In 1518 the Spaniard Juan de Grijalva reached the island of Cozumel, and in 1519 Hernan Cortés landed on the mainland with 500 men, with guns and horses. Although it was touch-and-go several times, within three years they had brought down the Aztec empire and plundered huge amounts of gold. This was the governing principle of the Spanish viceroyalty for the next three centuries; the indigenous people were exploited terribly, quite apart from being ravaged by European diseases, which reduced their population by two thirds within just 50 years. There were revolts, but these were always crushed bloodily; it was the growth of a Hispanic population (of pure and mixed blood), which became rich but was allowed no political power, that brought about change. In 1810 Father Miguel Hidalgo led a revolt, which was soon defeated; however, a guerrilla campaign continued which Spain, greatly weakened by the Napoleonic Wars and the growth in power of Britain (and the USA), was unable to crush. In the end, in 1821, it was a loyalist general, Agustín de Iturbide, who brought about independence, to block the liberal reforms being introduced in Spain.

In 1822 Iturbide declared himself Emperor but was soon overthrown, ushering in a century of strife between liberals and conservatives. In 1836 Texas, Mexican territory but largely inhabited by settlers from the USA, declared independence; President Santa Ana captured the Alamo but was then captured himself and forced to accept Texan independence. In 1845 the USA annexed Texas, but deemed it to include the Mexican territories of Arizona, New Mexico and California. This led to war and the capture of Mexico City in 1847; in 1848, under the Treaty of Guadalupe Hidalgo, the USA paid US$15m for these states, and in 1854 the Gadsden Purchase (another US$10m) extended US territory to the Río Bravo del Norte (known to North Americans as the Río Grande), to allow construction of the Southern Pacific railway. Mexico lost 40% of its territory, but only about 10% of its population; this still rankles, but it could have been worse, as President Polk wanted to take all the land east of the Sierra Madre, as far south as Tabasco. What's more, "filibusters" (freelance colonialists) such as William Walker continued to seize Mexican territory, having to be driven out by force.

Liberals led by Benito Juárez, a Zapotec Indian lawyer who remains the country's greatest hero, came to power in 1855 and introduced reforms and a democratic constitution in 1857. The Roman Catholic church, which had immense wealth and power, supported the conservatives in further civil war; Juárez seemed to have won by 1861 and set about closing the monasteries and confiscating church property. However the economy was in dire straits, forcing him to suspend payment of foreign debts; France, with Britain and Spain, occupied Veracruz to force payment, but when it became clear that Napoleon III of France was plotting with the Mexican conservatives to put the Hapsburg Archduke Maximilian on the throne his allies withdrew. The French were nevertheless able to occupy Mexico City in 1863, but US support for Juárez and the growing Prussian threat forced withdrawal; Maximilian was defeated and executed in 1867, and Juárez managed to stay in power until his death five years later.

From 1876 until 1910 Mexico was ruled by a military dictator, Porfirio Díaz, who presided over a period of headlong industrial development, largely at the expense of the poorest people, who became virtual serfs. Again, however, it was middle-class dissatisfaction that led to rebellion in 1910 and Díaz's overthrow in 1911. His successor Francisco Madero gave some satisfaction to the middle class but did nothing for the landless peasantry, and was killed in 1913 by a general acting for US business interests. The revolutionary leaders Pancho (diminutive of Francisco) Villa, in Chihuahua, and Emiliano Zapata, in the southwest, took up arms once more, but again it was establishment figures with US support who took power. Zapata was murdered in 1919 and Villa in 1923, and peace was restored after the election as president of Alvaro Obregón in 1920.

Social reform gradually gathered way again, and most importantly the huge *haciendas* were transformed into communal communities known as *ejidos*; eventually 95m hectares were redistributed in this way. The church was repressed viciously, provoking another revolt between 1927 and 1935. Since 1929 power has been monopolised by one party, now known as the Party of the Institutional Revolution or PRI (pronounced Pree); the constitution is based on a six-yearly presidential term, with re-election forbidden but each president nominated by his predecessor and guaranteed election by a seemingly flawless party machine. Continuing reform and industrial development, with a huge public works programme (funded by oil revenues, nationalised by Lázaro Cárdenas in 1938) and total control of patronage did in fact ensure that the PRI was popular enough to win elections without much problem.

This benevolent corporate dictatorship was weakened by a proto-Tiananmen when hundreds of students demanding true democracy were massacred in the capital, in the run-up to the Mexico City Olympic Games of 1968. Between 1958 and 1970 economic growth had averaged 6.5% per year, with average inflation at just 3.6%, but this was not enough to keep up with population growth; in the 1970s corruption and incompetence led to the peso losing half its value, inflation over 100%, and a 250% growth in foreign debt, to US$86bn in 1982, when the oil boom ended. Miguel de la Madrid, president from 1982 to 1988, adopted a policy of economic austerity and began a process of structural reform; rampant inflation and mass unemployment led to increasing opposition and a steady decline in support for the PRI. The powerful earthquake that hit Mexico City in September 1985, killing between 7,000 and 20,000, accelerated this process, as it revealed the corruption, incompetence and self-interest of the government (a year later there were still 80,000 homeless). Grass-roots citizens' groups began to develop, and a right-wing party, the Party of National Action (PAN), began to win local elections, and in 1989 its first state governorship. In the 1988 presidential election, even after massive electoral fraud, the PRI's Carlos Salinas de Gortari only narrowly defeated a defector, Cuauhtémoc Cárdenas (son of the 1930s president), who united the leftist opposition as the Party of the Democratic Revolution (PRD).

Salinas took Mexico into the North American Free Trade Agreement (NAFTA, or in Spanish TLC) in 1994 and introduced radical neoliberal economic policies, with massive spending cuts and privatisations that slashed the foreign debt (from 50% of GDP in 1988 to 17% in 1994) and benefitted business but made life much harder for everyone else. The only employment growth has been in the *maquiladora* sector, duty-free assembly plants for foreign companies using cheap labour and low environmental standards.

Even so, it seemed that the PRI would as usual win the elections of August 1994, but a remarkable series of crises intervened. On 1 January 1994, as NAFTA came into effect, a guerrilla group known as the Zapatista Army of National Liberation (EZLN) seized five towns in the state of Chiapas, where powerful landlords have been blocking reform ever since 1917. Despite warnings in the *Latin American Weekly Report* since August, the army was taken by surprise and over-reacted appallingly. Salinas rapidly called it off and initiated peace talks. The EZLN issued a series of very witty and literary communiqués that led to their chief negotiator, Subcomandante Marcos, being voted Mexico's sexiest man without even removing his balaclava! The EZLN also uses the Internet to bypass the Mexican media. In March an agreement emerged, but after a painstaking process of community consultation, was rejected by the EZLN.

More crises erupted: in March the PRI's presidential candidate, Luis Donaldo Colosio, was assassinated, and in September the same fate befell

---

ECONOMICS AND REAL PEOPLE

In 1993 Mexico had the 11th largest economy in the world; in 1995 it shrank by 6.6%, but is expected to grow by 3% in 1996. In 1994 inflation was 7%, in 1995 it leapt to 52%, and is expected to be 27% in 1996. Unemployment was 3.2% at the end of 1994 and rose to 5.4% in 1996. It's estimated that 53% of people rely on the informal ("grey") economy, worth c20% of official GDP (as against c1.25% in Britain). Population growth is around 2% per year, and with 38% of the population under 15 years of age, 3% economic growth is needed just to keep up; but Mexican industry already seems over-staffed.

Of a population of 91m, 14m live in extreme poverty and half of rural children are malnourished. Around 9m lack all health care; health accounts for 4.8% of GDP (against 9% in Canada, and 12.7% in the USA). However, average life expectancy has risen from 41 in 1940 to 62 in 1970 and 69 in 1990.

the party's general secretary, José Francisco Ruiz Massieu. It's generally assumed that the killings were warnings by the "dinosaurs" of the PRI establishment for those in favour of reform and democratisation, but there are also very nasty links between drugs interests and the Salinas family; since leaving office Salinas has left the country as a virtual fugitive. Colosio is widely seen as a Gorbachev figure who might have taken apart the whole corrupt system. The new PRI candidate for the presidency, Ernesto Zedillo Ponce de León, was a protegé of perhaps the chief dinosaur, Hank González, but may in fact turn out to be something of a Gorbachev himself. The PRI in fact won the elections comfortably, but the governorship of Chiapas in particular was disputed by the opposition, and in December the EZLN began to occupy towns again. Zedillo was forced to devalue the peso (traditionally over-valued before elections but then devalued by the outgoing administration); due in part to the EZLN uprising there was a massive crisis of confidence and the peso plummetted, and interest rates, prices, unemployment and inflation all shot up. A US-led rescue package of US$50.8bn was laid on, and in some ways the economy has benefitted from cheap exports; however, most people are suffering, there are daily demos and disruption in Mexico City, the equivalent of "The Economist' is called "El Crisis", and in January 1996 255 of the 298 PRI deputies called for an end to neoliberal policies. Credit-card use fell by 50% in 1995, and uncollectable debt is put at US$7.9bn in all (164,000 farmers owe US$800m, and 164,000 coffee producers US$42m).

Negotiations with the EZLN resumed in April 1995 in the village of San Andrés Sacamch'en (or Larrainzar). These have been remarkably open and wide-ranging; there are hopes that they will, for instance, help protect the tropical forests of Chiapas and establish indigenous rights nationwide. Certainly they are fuelling moves towards political reform, not just in Chiapas (where it's almost impossible to understate the resentment and need for change), but also nationally. Despite regular walk-outs (most by the PAN) the main parties agreed a deal in July 1996 which would give the vote to expatriates (assumed to be anti-PRI), ban anonymous campaign contributions, remove restrictions on coalitions, introduce proportional representation in senate elections, and above all separate the Federal Electoral Institution from the government/PRI. There have also been agreements on reform at the state level, for instance in Guerrero.

Chiapas remains a near-feudal place, run by vigilante groups ("white guards") working for the landlords and, usually, PRI interests; in Chilón a group known as "Los Chinchulines" (The Chitterlings) attacked the PRD municipal government in May 1996, leaving a total of 17 dead or missing. (Things are done in a similar way in Oaxaca and Guerrero, where Mixteca and PRD leaders have been terrorised and killed by "Antorcha Campesino" or Rural Torch, and a new guerrilla campaign broke out in mid-1996.) In Chiapas, the army has been harassing indigenous villagers under the guise of searching for marijuana plantations, and in Rancho Nuevo, near San Cristóbal, it has trained villagers as paramilitaries, which is truly alarming given the precedents in Guatemala and Peru. Church and human rights workers are being intimidated, and in Mexico City two EZLN sympathisers were jailed after a faulty trial (though freed on appeal). As a result the EZLN pulled out of the peace talks in May 1996.

There's been no military involvement in politics since the late 1920s, and in general the army has been respected, while the police force has not (the drug squad has an especially bad human rights record). The level of political killings and "disappearances" has been rising recently, with 65 PRD supporters killed in 1990, and 500-plus during Salinas' term. Hank González' son, who is obsessed with smuggling rare animals and has been blamed for the murders of Cardinal Juan José Ocampo de Posadas and a campaigning Tijuana journalist, seems to be immune from prosecution. In June 1995 17 *campesino* demonstrators were massacred by police in Aguas Blancas (Whitewater!), Guerrero, and a video was doctored to show guns in their hands; the PRI state governor Ruben Figueroa Alcocer was dumped by Zedillo and forced to resign amid calls for impeachment. In April 1996 police killed a demonstrator in Tepoztlán at protests against golf-course development in a national park; sixty police were arrested, and eleven were even refused bail.

There is undoubtedly a huge involvement in narcocrime; 70% of the USA's cocaine passes through Mexico, and the trade is worth cUS$30bn a year, of which cUS$6bn stays in Mexico (cUS$500m of it as bribes). Heavy pressure from big brother north of the border (failing to deal with the demand for drugs at home) results in frequent searches on the main roads and the occasional arrest of a cartel boss followed by rapid extradition to the USA. Foreigners are unlikely to be harassed, unless they really are suspected of carrying drugs, and it's now most unlikely that they'll be pressured for a *mordida*, the petty bribe that was for so long a key component of Mexico's image abroad. Overall it seems that Mexico is in a transitional phase, with old habits dying hard but distinct signs of reform and modernisation in politics, economy and society. Even Fidel Velasquez, 96 years old and secretary-general of the Confederation of Mexican Workers for six decades, has announced that this will be his last term of office.

Chapter Three

Preparations

INFORMATION

There are Mexican Government Tourist Offices in Britain at 60/61 Trafalgar Square, London WC2N 5DS (tel: 0171 839 3177); in Canada at 2 Bloor St W, #1801, Toronto M4W 3E2 (tel: 416 925 0704); and in the USA at 405 Park Ave #1401, New York NY 10022 (tel: 212 755 7261); 2707 North Loop W #450, Houston TX 77008 (tel: 713 880 8772); and 10100 Santa Monica Blvd #224, Los Angeles CA 90067 (tel: 310 203 8191), and toll-free on tel: 1 800 44 MEXICO, 1 800 446 8277 or 1 800 482 9832.

Current affairs are covered by the *Latin American Weekly Report* (61 Old St, London EC1V 9HX, UK; tel: 0171 251 0012) (politics) and *Latin American Monitor*, 56-60 St John St, London EC1M 4DT, UK; (tel: 0171 608 3646) (business).

In Mexico tourist information is thin on the ground, except in the capital where SECTUR (the Ministry of Tourism, not to be confused with SCT, the Ministry of Transport) has an office at Av Masaryk 172 (at Hegel) in posh Polanco, reached by bus 32 (tel: 520 6230/255 8555/250 0151). They also have a booth at the airport. If your Spanish isn't yet great, it might be better to go to the city tourist office at Amberes 54 in the *Zona Rosa* (tel: 525 9380). You can ring the SECTUR helpline 24 hours a day on 250 0123 (in Mexico City) or 91 800 90392 (elsewhere).

If you have access to the Internet, there are some sites that deal specifically with ecological topics:
http://www.planeta.com
http://www.txinfnet.com/mader/ecotravel
gopher://ecosys.drdr.Virginia.EDU (ELAN – Environment and Latin America Netsite)
http://www.lanic.utexas.edu
http://www.uam.mx/INE (the National Institute of Ecology)
http://www.infosel.com.mx/elnorte/ (*Ecologia* on line daily), as well as rec.travel.latin-america.

GETTING THERE

Travelling to Mexico is inexpensive for North Americans, while Europeans benefit from low transatlantic fares, particularly from London to Miami. This may change, but the chances are there'll always be a reasonably cheap flight to one of the American gateway cities, and nowadays you can transit without having to pass through US immigration.

From Europe, the most economical route at present is to Miami and from there to Mexico City, or to Cancún or Mérida in the Yucatán. Both United and American Airlines have hubs in Miami, and British Airways flights link here with those of Aeromexico (who fly direct from Paris and Madrid, but not London). If you want to see a bit of the USA, American also has a hub at Dallas/Fort Worth, and Continental at Houston (from where there are buses to Monterrey); Delta's hub at Atlanta, Georgia, is less useful. Alternatively fly to California (San Diego or Los Angeles) and continue across the border by land, or by Mexicana's *Moonlight Express* from LA to Mexico City. In 1996 British Airways introduced daily flights to San Diego via Phoenix: from Phoenix, America West fly to Los Cabos, Mazatlán, Vallarta, Manzanillo and Mexico City. BA also now flies non-stop (in 11 hours) three times a week from London to Mexico City; it's always worth checking their fares; KLM, Iberia and Aeroflot are also reasonable. Shop around: there's bound to be something affordable, or at least a cheap flight to one of the US gateway cities. In 1996 the best fares were around £260 one-way/£350 return from London to Mexico City.

It is possible to take a through bus from points in the US into Mexico, but we would advise buying a ticket only as far as the border (or at most to Monterrey), then getting off and buying another ticket onwards. That way you'll be travelling at Mexican prices, not US ones. Once across the border, there are luxury and first-class buses to Mexico City; you'll need to change again there to reach the south.

In Britain, agencies specialising in travel to Mexico include:

Journey Latin America, 16 Devonshire Rd, Chiswick, London W4 2HD (tel: 0181 747 3108, fax: 742 1312), and in Manchester
South American Experience, 47 Causton St, Pimlico, London SW1P 4AT (tel: 0171 976 5511)
Steamond, 23 Eccleston St, London SW1W 9LX (tel: 0171 730 8646). For tours, 278 Battersea Park Rd, London SW11 3BS (tel: 0171 738 0285)
Passage to South America, 41 North End Rd, London W14 8SZ (tel: 0171 602 9889)
STA has offices nationwide (London tel: 0171 937 9921)
Trailfinders, 48 Earl's Court Rd, London W8 6EJ (tel: 0171 938 3232/938 3939/938 3366)

In North America:

CIEE/Council Travel Services, 205 East 42nd St, New York, NY 10017 (tel: 212 661 1414, fax: 972 3231)
STA, 5900 Wilshire Boulevard, Los Angeles, CA 90036 (tel: 1 800 777 0112, fax: 213 937 2739)
TravelCUTS, 171 College St, Toronto M5T 1P7, Canada (tel: 416 977 3703, fax: 977 4796)

Charter flights

From North America there are frequent scheduled services to all major cities in Mexico, and an increasing number of charters. This is especially the case from Canada, with companies like Regent, Fiesta and FunSun offering flight-only deals with AirTransat, Canada 3000, Sunquest SkyService and Royal Air (from C$500 plus tax), as well as packages.

From Britain there are five charter flights a week in the summer of 1996, and less frequent flights in winter: First Choice operate from Gatwick and Manchester to Puerto Vallarta; Thomson from Gatwick to Puerto Vallarta; Caledonian, Kuoni, Thomson and Cosmos from Gatwick to Cancún; and Cosmos from Gatwick and Manchester to Cancún. Most flights are in Boeing 767s, taking 12-13 hours; flight-only prices range between £338 and £482.

From continental Europe a number of companies offer seats on charters to Mexico:

Globetrotter Travel Service, Rennweg 35, Zurich (tel: 211 7780)
Hajo Siewer Jet Tours, Martinstrasse 39, 57462 Olpe, Germany (tel: 02761 924 120)
Nouvelles Frontières, across France (Paris tel: 01 4141 5858)
Uniclam-Voyages, 63 rue Monsieur-le-Prince, 75006 Paris (tel: 01 4329 1236)

Group Tours

Few companies offer organised hiking trips, but there's any number of overland packages, which include day-walks in some reserves. For hiking, try:

Explore Worldwide, 1 Frederick St, Aldershot GU11 1LQ, UK (tel: 01252 319 448, fax: 343 170); with **Adventure Center**, 1311 63rd St, #200, Emeryville CA 94608, USA (tel: 1 800 227 8747, 510 654 1879, fax: 654 4200) and **Trek Holidays**, 8412-109 St, Edmonton T6G 1E2, Canada (tel: 1 800 661 7265, 403 439 0024, fax: 433 5494). They offer a 15-day trip, with eight days hiking from Oaxaca's Sierra Madre del Sur down to the coast (from £1,095/C$1,570).
Baja Discovery, PO Box 152527, San Diego CA 92195 (tel: 1 800 829 2252, 619 262 0700). Their "Transpeninsular Trek" (8 days for US$1,295) is a series of day hikes; also whale-watching.

Other ecotourist trips:

The Natural World, Crusader Travel, 57 Church St, Twickenham TW1 3NR, UK (tel: 0181 744 0474, fax: 744 0574)
Backroads, 1616 5th St, Berkeley, CA 94710-1740, USA (tel: 510 527 1555, fax: 527 1444)
Baja Expeditions, 2625 Garnet Ave, San Diego, CA 92109, USA (tel: 1 800 843 6967, 619 581 3311, La Paz 53828, fax: 619 581 6542, email: 72234.1520@compuserve.com)
Esprit International Adventures, USA (tel: 1 800 596 7238) (rafting in Veracruz)
Tread Lightly, 1 Titus Rd, Washington Depot CT 06794, USA (tel: 1 800 643 0060)
Wildland Adventures, 3516 NE 155th St, Seattle WA 98155, USA (tel: 1 800 345 4453, 206 365 0686, fax: 363 6615)

Overland trips (Yucatán, Baja and Copper Canyon):

Journey Latin America (see above)
Dragoman, 94 Camp Green, Debenham, Stowmarket IP14 6LA, UK (tel: 01728 861 133, fax: 861 127); with **Adventure Center** (as above)
Encounter Overland, 267 Old Brompton Rd, London SW5 9JA, UK (tel: 0171 370 6845, fax: 244 9737)
Exodus, 9 Weir Rd, London SW12 0LT, UK (tel: 0181 675 5550, fax: 673 0779).
Adventures Abroad, 20800 Westminster Hwy #2148, Richmond BC, V6V 2W3, Canada (tel: 1 800 665 3998, 604 303 1099, fax: 303 1076; email: adabroad@infoserve.net)
GAP, 264 Dupont St, Toronto M5R 1V7, Canada (tel: 1 800 465 5600, 416 922 8899, fax: 922 0822, email: gap@inforamp.net)
Globus Tours, 1061 Eglinton St West, Toronto, Canada (tel: 1 800 221 0090, 416 787 1281)
Green Tortoise, PO Box 24459, San Francisco, CA 94124, USA (tel: 1 800 227 4766, 415 821 0803)
Journeys International, 4011 Jackson, Ann Arbor MI 48103-1825, USA (tel: 1 800 255 8735, fax: 313 665 2945)
The Adventure Center, 25 Bellair St, Toronto, M5R 3L3, Canada (tel: 1 800 267 3347, 416 922 7584, fax: 922 8136); with **Trek Holidays** (as above)
Trek America, Trek House, The Bullring, Deddington, Banbury OX15 0TT, UK (tel: 01869 338777, fax: 338846); with **Premiere International Corp** (dba TrekAmerica), PO Box 189, Rockaway, NJ 07866, USA (tel: 1 800 221 0596, 201 983 1144, fax: 983 8551)

Colonial and heritage trips:

ACE Study Tours, Babraham, Cambridge CB2 4AP, UK (tel: 01223 835055).
Bales Tours, Bales House, Junction Rd, Dorking, Surrey RH4 3HB, UK (tel: 01306 885 991, fax: 740 048)

Cathy Matos Mexican Tours, 61 High St, Barnet EN5 5UR, UK (tel: 0181 440 7830)

Cox & Kings Travel, St James Court, 45 Buckingham Gate, London SW1E 6AF, UK (tel: 0171 834 7472, fax: 630 6038)

Hayes & Jarvis, Hayes House, 152 King St, London W6 0QU, UK (tel: 0181 748 5050).

Trips Worldwide, 9 Byron Place, Clifton, Bristol BS8 1JT, UK (tel: 0117 987 2626, fax: 987 2627)

Specialist trips for wildlife and bird watching are easily found in specialist magazines; a few operators are:

Animal Watch, Granville House, London Rd, Sevenoaks TN13 1DL, UK (tel: 01732 741 612)

Neotropic Bird Tours, 38 Brookside Ave, Livingston, NJ 07039, USA (tel: 1 800 662 4852)

Royal Adventures, Canada (tel: 1 800 453 4754)

Voyagers International, Box 915, Ithaca, NY 14851, USA (tel: 1 800 633 0299)

Wildlife Worldwide, 170 Selsdon Rd, South Croydon, Surrey CR2 6PJ, UK (tel: 0181 667 9158).

Botanical trips are run by **David Sayers Travel**, UK (tel: 0181 995 3642)

BUDGET AND FINANCE

How much your trip will cost is anyone's guess, but let us reassure you that you can live and travel quite comfortably on US$15 a day, particularly if you're spending time in the wild. Day to day expenses will depend how much time you're spending in towns and cities, and how much time in buses, which can also eat up your cash. One thing we've learned is that hitting a capital city after backpacking for a couple of weeks can be a pretty heady experience and can blow apart a perfectly good budget. Everything looks so delicious, so comfortable, so splendid, after weeks of rice and beans, thatched shelters and school buses; and after all, backpacking costs next to nothing. So we over-indulge ourselves and money just spins through our hands. We've made it a rule never to cash more than US$50 on such occasions. When that's gone we usually get a grip on ourselves.

The US dollar is the only currency to carry in this part of the world, although you'll find a few branches of Lloyds and other European banks which may change sterling and other currencies. Take your dollars partly in travellers cheques and partly as cash (some in small denominations). If you carry American Express or Thomas Cook travellers cheques you can change them in their respective offices without commission; otherwise you'll pay about 2% (either declared as a commission or just massaged from the exchange rate), as well as the 1–1.5% paid when you bought the cheques. If buying cash in Britain, Thomas Cook offices give a notoriously bad rate.

Cash machines (ATMs) are appearing even in fairly small towns, allowing you to withdraw cash from your bank account; both the issuing bank and VISA take a fee of 1-2%. The real advantages are in being able to get cash at any time, without queues and with English instructions, and in small quantities, just to last you to the border. You can also use them to draw cash on your credit card, but this is horrendously expensive.

If you want to have money sent out to you, plan this in advance with your bank, which will have a partner bank in Mexico. Then all you have to do is cable your bank and wait for the cash. It will take a few days, and actually collecting the cash is invariably a hassle, but it works. Citibank (US) and Lloyds (British) have quite a few branches in the region, and Western Union can also cable money to branches there.

The New Peso introduced in 1993 is now officially called the Peso; you'll come across the odd 100 Peso coin, equivalent to 10 New Centavos, but otherwise you'll only come across Old Pesos on postage stamps and in *very* remote indigenous villages.

WHAT TO TAKE

As Saint-Exupéry said, "He would travel happily must travel light"; you should take the standard 20kg airline allowance as your absolute maximum, bearing in mind that you gain a kilogram when you put a litre of water into your bottle. Start by disposing of as much packaging as you can before departure; I find that a 60ml Body Shop plastic bottle carries enough shower gel for a month or two, and if you want solid soap as well this can be carried in a film cannister.

Specifically for hiking, you should remember the six essentials of map, compass, matches (and maybe a firelighter) in a waterproof box, first-aid kit, extra food and extra clothing. A knife, spoon and plastic mug or bowl are also pretty important. Wood fires are becoming environmentally unacceptable nowadays; if you want to cook, take a stove. Kerosene and white gas (Coleman fuel) are usually available, and it's getting easier to find Camping Gaz. Personally I don't bother for three- to five-day trips in warm climes. There's no need to spend a fortune buying special lightweight saucepans for backpacking, as perfectly suitable aluminium ones are sold throughout Mexico.

With regard to clothing, you will usually be dressing for hot conditions, so won't need heavy clothes unless you plan to go high. Even so, the key principle is that of layering; tee-shirts are light and comfortable but expose you to sunburn, so you should take a bandana and some long-sleeved shirts to protect you from the sun and insects. You should also take an insulation layer (a light pullover or a fleece jacket) and a shell layer (waterproof jacket and trousers). In the rainy season an umbrella can also be useful. A hat is essential, a cotton one being more practical than a straw one. It's very refreshing to fill the hat with water, then plonk it on your head!

Shirts and trousers (pants) should be mostly cotton; jeans are not suitable, as they're heavy, hot, hard to wash, and take ages to dry. (However, pure cotton doesn't dry well and can rot surprisingly quickly in tropical climates.) Nor is army-surplus wear appropriate if you're going to Central America, with its enduring civil conflicts. Khaki and camouflage patterns are out: you're safest in brightly coloured clothes, and remember that mosquitoes are attracted to dark clothing. It's always been inadvisable to dress outlandishly in Latin America: officials generally treat travellers who look dirty and penniless with suspicion and hostility, and if you look (to them) like a drug user you may have drugs planted on you. So short hair and trimmed beards for men, and reasonably conventional clothing for women are sensible.

Mexico is Roman Catholic and it is offensive to the local people to wear shorts in churches, or for women to be conspicuously bra-less. In addition the latter invites attention from all those macho men. If you prefer to go without a bra because it's cooler, you'll find that a man's shirt with breast (sic!) pockets handily hides your feminity. Bear in mind the problems of getting to your money-belt if you're wearing a dress.

Few of these hikes require heavy boots, although good ankle support and shock absorption are essential. If hiking on volcanoes, "Vibram" soles or the like are the only ones that won't be cut up by the lava. Canvas jungle boots are ideal for jungle hiking, as they drain and dry out quickly; you may need to look for these in army surplus stores rather than hiking shops. Basketball boots are recommended for fording rivers, and these or trainers are handy to change into at the end of the day. Rubber thongs or sports sandals are also good to have, but be careful and never go barefoot. Take a spare pair of bootlaces, and use them as a laundry line. You'll also need to waterproof your boots from time to time.

To carry all this you need a backpack or rucksack – above all make sure you have a padded hipbelt, and preferably a so-called internal frame (meaning only that it's better hidden away than the old-fashioned external frame!). This is less likely to be caught on jungle creepers, and is handier for travelling on trucks and buses. At airports wrap the hipbelt backwards around the pack, do it up in reverse and tuck away or tie up any strap ends, both to stop them getting caught in conveyor belts, and to delay anyone wanting to sneak a look inside; a small padlock is also useful, although more as a deterrent than as a real barrier (and for some hotel rooms). No rucksack is ever totally waterproof, so you should keep clothes and the like in plastic bags. Ideally you should carry 50% of your load on the hips – any more and you slip out of your shoulder straps, even with a chest strap. Nowadays there are also likely to be straps to adjust the balance of the load for uphill or downhill work, away from the body going uphill, and closer to the body downhill.

You're also likely to need a tent, and don't wait till you get there to buy one. It'll need to be bugproof and waterproof, and as light as possible – no more than 2.5kg for a two-person tent. Ventilation is important; if your tent is inadequate in this respect, you might wish to cut windows in the front and rear and face them with mosquito netting. In fact it's easy enough to make a basic tropical tent entirely out of mosquito netting, using a tarpaulin as a fly.

Many people prefer a hammock to a tent. They are very comfortable, and often it's easier to find two trees suitably spaced, or hammock hooks in a jungle hut, than to clear an area for your tent. However, remember that two hammocks can weigh more than a light two-person tent, and you must be able to rig up netting so that no insects can get inside. Excellent hammocks can be bought in Mérida, while some army surplus stores stock jungle hammocks which are a combination of hammock, mosquito netting and a waterproof roof. We haven't put them to the test but they seem ideal.

While on the subject, did you know that there's a right way and a wrong way to lie in a hammock? If you lie diagonally acros it, your body and legs are more or less horizontal, not sagged into a "U" position which is uncomfortable for a whole night. If you're particularly tall or heavy you'll probably resort to sleeping on the ground in any case after a night or two in a hammock.

You won't need a particularly warm sleeping bag, and the tropics are too damp and humid for down to be ideal as a filler. A very light artificial filler is preferable (as light as possible), as a "bivi-sac" cover will add a lot of warmth at high altitudes and can be left behind for hiking in warmer areas.

Some sort of insulation and protection from the cold hard ground is essential in the mountains; closed-cell "ensolite" foam mats are the most efficient, providing good insulation and tolerable comfort even when less than a centimetre thick. The most comfortable mat of all, though, is the combination of air-mattress and foam-pad made by Thermarest, available in three-quarters or full length.

Rather than a conventional flashlight, use a headtorch, which frees your hands and is ideal for cave exploration and for putting up your tent after dark. Remember a spare bulb; alternatives are a candle-holder or a Camping Gaz-fuelled lantern.

See *Health and Safety* for the contents of the definitive first-aid kit. Other useful items include a sewing kit (with heavy thread and needles for tent repairs), safety pins, pencils or ball-point pens, a notebook and paper for writing home, travel alarm clock, penknife (preferably Swiss Army type), plastic bags (preferably the "zip-loc" type), a universal bath plug (or punctured squash-ball), clothes-pegs, scrubbing brush, dental floss (excellent for running repairs, as well as teeth), toilet paper, and a Spanish dictionary or phrasebook.

It's very useful to bring a small daypack; you can leave things in a hotel while you're backpacking, and in any case you invariably end up coming home with more luggage than you started with. A lightweight nylon bag with a lockable zipper is ideal, or a stuffsack (with compression straps) can double up.

A camera should be as robust as possible (I have destroyed several in the past by travelling on rough roads; remember not to sit behind the rear axle of a bus). Simple work-horses are the best in tropical climates, above all mechanical Nikons and Leicas, if you can afford them. It may be worth taping over flash and motordrive sockets, when not in use. It's also worth remembering that sun shining directly into the lens can warp delicate camera innards – keep that cap on ... Nature-lovers will probably want a macro lens for close-ups of all those wonderful flowers and insects, and also a telephoto lens for shots of birds and animals (the latter can replace binoculars or a telescope), but otherwise a 35mm compact camera is most practical; even those incorporating a small zoom lens are now pretty affordable. You will need a spare battery for a long trip, and plenty of film; it's expensive in Mexico and there is a limited range. Slide film is hard to find, as is film of ASA 400 and faster, which you'll need in the jungle, as there's little light there. Humidity may also be a problem in the jungle, so keep your camera in a plastic bag, together with a small sachet of silica gel.

Insurance

Baggage insurance is well worth having. With all the care in the world you can lose something, and it does ease the grief somewhat if it's insured. Read the small print carefully. If something is stolen you must report the theft to the police and get a copy of their report. Often a time-consuming and expensive process, since some police won't help without a bribe.

Documents

Check current visa requirements with embassies or with the Foreign Office, State Department or your equivalent. If planning to head further south, be sure to work out which countries require you to have a visa (as opposed to a tourist card, obtained at the border), and get them either before leaving or in the first capital city you visit. Consulates tend to be situated in the suburbs and to keep strange hours (often something like 10.00-12.00 a couple of days a week). If you are planning to pass through a country twice (ie returning the way you came) ask for a multiple-entry visa, which should cost less than two single-entry visas. This may require a passport photo, so carry some of these with you.

It's a good idea to keep a strong rubber band around your passport to hold all those papers that countries require you to keep during your stay. (In Mexico your tourist card is more important than your passport, and should be with you at all times.) Another idea you might try is to stick a coloured dot of paper (such as you can buy in stationery shops), or even a gold star, onto the front of your passport. That way you'll recognise it when it has to be taken from you and given back by calling out an unintelligible version of your name. Your passport, air ticket, most of your travellers cheques and so on should be kept in a money belt.

If heading south overland, remember that many countries have requirements for an onward ticket or a minimum level of funds; I've never been asked a single question at any Central American border, but if you are student age or have a nose-ring or half your head shaved, you can expect some tough questions. There is no charge to enter or leave Mexico, but the Central American countries charge about US$2. Don't change all your money until you've completed the emigration procedure, or else you'll have to pay in dollars at a bad rate; the same applies when you move on to immigration. There are always money-changers around (those at the borders are much safer than those in cities, although you should still be aware of possible problems), and you can always spend what's left on a few oranges or a drink. In a way it's more straightforward than in Europe, where you rarely stop at borders, can never find a money-changer, and have to contend with varying exchange and commission rates when you do.

Chapter Four

Health and Safety

GENERAL HEALTH

It's advisable to be vaccinated against typhoid, tetanus, TB, poliomyelitis and yellow fever before travelling. The gamma globulin injection against hepatitis A has now been superseded by the *Havrix* vaccine, which offers full protection and is well worth having. Cholera vaccination is largely ineffective, but given that the major outbreak of 1990-91, which started in Peru, has now spread as far as Mexico you may wish to have some protection.

A week or so before reaching any malarial area it is essential to start a course of prophylactic pills. For up-to-date details on the most effective, phone the Malaria Reference Laboratory in the UK (tel: 0891 600 350) and in America the Center for Disease Control in Atlanta (tel: 404 332 4559). (See *Mosquitoes*, below, for more information.) It's also wise to have your teeth checked before leaving. Your best protection is to be fit and well before you set out on a hiking trip. Carry your prescription if you wear glasses and, finally, be sure to take out medical insurance.

Virtually any medicine can be bought over the counter in Mexico, but you would be best advised to bring all your normal medication (and contraceptives) and a first-aid kit from home: anything bought in a *farmacia* may be well past its expiry date or may not have been refrigerated properly.

If you become ill, head for a hospital or clinic, or failing that, see a private doctor. Although the experience may be somewhat alarming, remember that these local doctors have a more intimate acquaintance with tropical diseases than does your GP back home. There is a reasonable supply of English-speaking doctors, and in the capital cities your embassy can recommend a good doctor.

It's also worth knowing about the *análisis clínico* laboratories found all over Mexico. If you are pretty sure of your diagnosis but want it confirmed you can take a sample of urine or faeces to the lab and they'll give you the results of the analysis a few hours later.

There are some excellent books on the market which supplement the necessarily skimpy health information we have space for. Some are listed at Appendix Two.

Suggested Medical Kit
- Elastoplast (Band-aids)
- butterfly closures
- micropore tape
- bandages
- tubular bandages
- Melolin dressings
- vaseline (for cracked heels and tick removal)
- "moleskin" (for blisters)
- antifungal foot powder
- scissors
- safety pins
- tweezers
- earplugs
- sterile hypodermic needles
- drugs:
  malarial pills
  aspirin or Paracetamol/Tylenol (for fever and toothache)
  a more powerful pain-killer/anti-inflammatory such as ibuprofen (Nurofen/Advil)
  diarrhoea medicine (Diocalm, Imodium)
  antihistamine tablets such as terfenadine (Seldane)
  antibiotics (ciprofloxacin, tetracycline, ampicillin)
  antiseptic and wipes
  travel sickness pills.

COMMON MEDICAL PROBLEMS

Many of the ailments that beset travellers are caused by poor toilet practice, eating contaminated food and drinking unclean water, so you can do much to avoid illness by taking a few simple precautions: wash your hands after using the toilet (to remove other people's germs, not your own), don't eat raw vegetables, salads or fruit you haven't peeled yourself; boil water or purify it with chlorine (Sterotabs, Puritabs or Halazone) or better still with iodine (which kills amoebae). Compact water purifiers are now available, which filter out and kill amoebae, viruses and bacteria. Tea and coffee are usually made with hot rather than boiling water, and ice is also unsafe. But don't spoil your trip by never eating in wayside restaurants or from street stalls. Just be cautious at first while your system adjusts, and don't eat food that's been sitting around cooling.

Diarrhoea

Montezuma's Revenge is caused by the bacterium *Escherischia coli* which everyone has naturally in his or her intestines. The trouble is that each geographical area has its own strain of *E. coli*, and alien strains may cause inflammation of the intestine and diarrhoea. On a long trip you'll acquire a nice collection of the local *E. coli* in your gut and will be troubled no more. The first few weeks can be tough, though. Everyone has a favourite remedy (see *Natural Medicine*) but most people agree that it's best to let nature take its course rather than bunging yourself up with strong medication. Drink lots of liquid but don't eat any greasy or fatty food for 24 hours, then for a few days stick to a bland diet with plenty of mashed potatoes or rice, papaya and bananas. Avoid alcohol, fatty and spicy foods and milk products and take plenty of fluids, and you should be OK. Replace the lost salts and minerals by sipping a solution of half a teaspoon of salt and four teaspoons of sugar or honey in a litre of water; if possible add baking soda (½ teaspoon) and potassium chloride (¼ teaspoon) as well, or a little lemon or orange juice. You can buy or make up some of this rehydration or "electrolyte replacement" formula before leaving home.

There will be times when you'll want to block the symptoms of diarrhoea: before setting off on a long bus journey, for instance, or when you're camping in heavy rain. Probably the best "chemical cork" is loperamide (Diocalm or Imodium), but Paracetamol/Tylenol (acetaminophen) is an effective codeine-based bum-blocker and pain-killer.

Dysentery

If you have diarrhoea with a fever, bad gut cramps and blood in your stool you may have bacterial (bacillary) dysentery. Amoebic dysentery is similar but starts more gradually, and the diarrhoea is persistent but not dramatic. Get your stool analysed and take the result to a doctor, who will probably prescribe a week's course of Flagyl (metronidazole or tinidazole) for amoebae, or an antibiotic such as ciprofloxacin for the bacterial variety.

Fever

If you develop a fever for any reason you should rest and take aspirin or Paracetamol/Tylenol. You should also bring with you a supply of antibiotics, such as ciprofloxacin or tetracycline, in case you are struck by some more serious infection in a hopelessly remote place. If this happens, take antibiotics as instructed on the packet and see a doctor within four days. For gut infections taking ciprofloxacin for three days should suffice, but otherwise you should finish the course (usually seven days).

Injury

Be prepared. If you're not familiar with first aid carry a booklet on the subject, and pack an appropriate medical kit. Wash and treat even minor cuts and sores since they easily become infected in the tropics.

When there are only two of you and one has an accident, the other should stay with the injured one and wait for help to arrive. The temptation is to rush for help, but being injured, worried and alone could have a disastrous effect on the patient. So, except for the rare cases when you know the trails are little used, wait for someone to come along, and keep the injured person warm and comfortable.

On some of these hikes serious injury would be one hell of a problem, so be careful. Don't hike when you're tired, and don't take risks.

Heat-Related Problems

The very humid conditions that prevail in southern Mexico cause problems because not enough perspiration can evaporate for the body to be able to cool itself sufficiently. After a week or two your body becomes acclimatised and begins to sweat more freely while losing less salt in the process.

You can help your body by drinking lots of water, avoiding alcohol and taking extra salt in your diet. Avoid hiking during the hottest part of the day and don't wear or carry too much. Dehydration occurs faster at altitude, and can be brought on even by travelling in air-conditioned buses or on the back of a wind-swept pickup truck.

Heat exhaustion

This is caused by over-exertion when the body cannot dissipate its heat quickly enough: blood rushes to the skin depriving the brain and other vital organs of oxygen and producing symptoms of nausea, florid complexion, stumbling, lack of alertness, cramp and eventual collapse. It tends to affect those unaccustomed to being outdoors in extreme weather, the old, the unwell and convalescents; it's not life-threatening but is a clear warning to rest in the shade, sip cool, salty drinks and munch a high-energy trail snack.

Heat stroke

This is far more serious and is the result of a complete breakdown of the body's cooling mechanisms; if untreated this results in brain damage or even death. The symptoms are feeling generally ill, a very high body temperature, and (usually) flushed hot, dry skin where sweating has ceased. This may be followed by splitting headaches, loss of coordination, confusion or even aggression, and ultimately delirium. Resting in the shade is not enough: the victim's body temperature must be brought down by any means possible. If there's a river handy, that's dandy, but heat stroke is more likely to hit in waterless areas. Remove the victim's clothing and sponge him or

SUNGLASSES AND SUNBURN

Ultraviolet radiation from the sun causes sunburn and increases the risk of cataracts. A broad-brimmed hat reduces eye damage to a certain extent, but sunglasses should also be used, especially at altitude or when light is reflected off water or snow. Together they can cut UV exposure by 95%; buy sunglasses advertised to block 95% to 100% of UVB rays and at least 60% of UVA rays. The ability to absorb UV radiation is not determined by lens colour or darkness, although they should be dark enough for you not to see your eyes in a mirror; nor are mirror lenses any more use than ordinary ones. Grey and green lenses distort colours least; brown-amber improves contrast in haze or fog but causes other colour distortions. Check for shape distortion by moving your head around while looking at a rectangular shape; if its sides bow in and out the lenses are causing distortion. Polarised lenses reduce reflected glare off glass and water but have nothing to do with UV protection. The best sunglasses are large, curved to fit the face and with opaque or UV-blocking side-shields.

Remember that on hazy or cloudy days you can still receive 70% to 80% of a clear day's radiation. Prevent sunburn by using sunscreens, which come in two main kinds. Reflectors, such as zinc oxide and titanium oxide, which are white pastes, reflect and scatter UV wavelengths; because they are thick and messy, they are used only in high-risk areas such as the nose and lips. Absorber sunscreens, such as PABA (para-aminobenzoic acid), cinnamates, benzophenones and parsol, absorb UV waves.

Soak mild to moderate sunburn in cold water, give ice massages, and take painkillers if needed. Solarcaine and other anaesthetic creams may cause allergic reactions. Severe sunburn with blisters should receive medical treatment. This leads to rough, sagging skin with liver spots, wrinkles and increased skin-cancer risks; these effects are cumulative, irreversible, and begin at an early age – by the time wrinkles appear, the damage is done.

Prevention is the name of the game.

(*With thanks to Dr Bob Vinton.*)

her with water from your bottle or canteen, then fan vigorously. Massage arms and legs to divert blood to the extremities, and keep it up until temperature is normal. Then abandon the hike and look for a doctor; if you press on, a recurrence is likely.

Fungal infection

Fungi, flourishing in the humidity of tropical rain forests, are a common problem, especially for your feet. To avoid infection, wear loose clothes of natural fibres, wash them and yourself frequently and dry well. If infected, wash and dry the affected area regularly, and sprinkle it with an anti-fungal powder such as Tinaderm (easily found). If you have a persistent and itchy rash, this could be a type of fungus that can only be killed by antifungal drugs.

Another type of fungus lives in tropical rivers and can infect bathers' ears: it's best not to submerge your head.

Prickly heat (Miliaria)
This is an irritating rash caused by the blocking of sweat glands, particularly when acclimatising to the tropical climate. Loose-fitting cotton clothes will help prevent it, and washing with cold water and a solution of soda bicarbonate will help to clear it up. Don't use creams which will further clog the pores.

MOUNTAIN HEALTH

Altitude sickness
Quite a few hikes in this book take you into mountainous country and to heights of over 5,000m, where you may fall victim to altitude sickness or *soroche*. Most people will need to do little more than rest for an hour or two for the usual symptoms of thumping heart and gasping breath to pass; however some will experience hangover-like symptoms including headaches, fatigue, dizziness, loss of appetite and nausea. If this fails to clear up overnight, consider descending at least 500m and then returning in shorter stages. If there is no time for this, you may choose to take acetazolamide (Diamox) for five days, starting two or three days before the ascent, to counter the symptoms. Take lots of fluids and carbohydrates (up to 70% of your diet).

Two dangerous varieties, cerebral oedema and pulmonary oedema, cause a rapid collapse with coughing, frothing and blue lips; the only solution is immediate and rapid descent. The key symptom of both varieties is a loss of coordination, accompanied in the case of cerebral oedema by illogical thought processes, loss of interest in events and surroundings, and even hallucinations, and in pulmonary oedema (water in the lungs) by a dry cough, breathlessness and a rapid heartbeat.

Hypothermia
In the midday desert you will long for a touch of hypothermia, but you should take it seriously on some of the high exposed walks. The danger is that since most of the trips are tropical, you may be tempted to skimp on warm clothing. If you're going above 2,000m or so, bring a good sleeping bag, a light sweater or fleece jacket and, most important, a thoroughly waterproof jacket. It is the combination of wet and cold that kills, with fatigue often a contributory factor; temperatures can easily drop below freezing, and the unimpeded wind of the high mountains can make it far colder. As soon as it gets dark the temperature plummets; be sure to camp in good time.

The symptoms of hypothermia are lethargy, shivering (initially only), numbness (especially of fingers and toes), staggering, slurred speech and irrational perceptions and behaviour. Above all get the victim out of the wind and into dry warm clothing, or even a sleeping bag, and give high-energy food and warm, non-alcoholic drinks.

NATURAL MEDICINE

Indigenous people, of course, have always used medicinal plants (and animals), and their knowledge has benefitted modern medicine in many instances. If you become ill while you are among Indians (or *mestizos*) you are well advised to try any remedy they offer. Don't be too enthusiastic, however, as dosage is hard to measure and even natural medicines have side-effects. You can also try the following products of nature if you're stuck without medicine while off the beaten track.

Papaya
The fruit of the papaya speeds up the healing of cuts or sores, soothes diarrhoea and stomach upsets – and tastes good. It has been reported that the seeds (which are strongly alkaline and taste disgusting) kill intestinal parasites; chew them thoroughly on an empty stomach.

Honey
This excellent cure for persistent sores is now used (externally) in some hospitals.

Urine
Yes, it really is good for you, and it's certainly always available! Burns, cuts and sores all seem to clear up more quickly if covered with a urine-soaked dressing; it's said to be a particularly good treatment for scorpion and jellyfish stings. It's said to be a beneficial drink, too, but we don't expect anyone to rush behind the bushes with their little cup.

Ginger
This has found a modern use as an antidote to travel sickness: it can be taken in capsule form as well as in food.

Charcoal
This is the traditional treatment for diarrhoea, and it still works. If you habitually make a camp-fire you'll have medicine galore; take it mixed with water several times daily.

Other plants that the locals may unleash on you include the bark of *Spondias spp* trees (*cimarron*) for wounds, *Larrea tridentata* (*gobernadora*) or *Arctostaphyllus pungens* (*manzanita*) for stomach upsets, and *Bixa orellana* (*achiote*) against dysentery and scarring, as well as a mosquito-repellent body paint and food colouring.

Do let us hear of any other interesting ones.

FANGS AND STINGS

By Hilary Bradt, with additions by Tim Burford

Certain members of the animal kingdom are definitely hazardous to the health. Not the ones you may be thinking of, such as jaguars and snakes, so much as disease carriers like vampire bats and a multitude of insects. Knowing the life cycle and habits of these creatures will help you to avoid them, or to understand, forgive and even like them! You'll need to devote just as much attention to avoiding the spines and thorns of cacti and other plants, although the agony is transient without longterm consequences.

Pumas and jaguars

Pumas (mountain lions or cougars) are still found in the mountains of Mexico, and in some low-lying areas. The only time one might pose any danger to a hiker would be if it were injured and/or cornered. Like the jaguar, pumas do prey on livestock, however, and are the scourge of some villages.

Snakes

It will surprise many readers to learn that far from being snake-infested, jungles harbour relatively few of these reptiles. The reason is simple: snakes, being cold-blooded, need sunlight to raise their body temperature, and there's precious little sunlight in a tropical rainforest (other than in the canopy, where some snake species spend their whole lives). But there's no denying that snakes are a danger, especially in cleared areas, and for the backpacker venturing into these places, our best advice is not to get bitten. Most of you probably know that snakes attack only when provoked or cornered, so don't give them that excuse. If you keep to the trail, watch your feet, and never put your hands where you can't see them, nothing will happen to you. You may see snakes, but they will be in a hurry to get out of your way. Wearing good boots and thick socks is a wise precaution. Most snakes hunt at night, so you should move cautiously after dark and make sure your tent or hammock is snake-proof. It's also a good idea to shake out your boots in the morning in case a snake thinks it's found a marvellous new hidey-hole.

   Snakebite is certainly an alarming prospect, but if you or your companion are bitten, take comfort in the fact that more than half the victims of snakebite receive minimal or no poisoning, even from venomous species, since snakes tend to use little if any poison in self-defence. The most venomous snake in Mexico is the coral snake (*corál/Micrurus nigrocinctus*), a small land snake striped in red, black and yellow, but this is nocturnal, very timid and often too small to bite a human; the false coral is similar but harmless. Others to watch out for are rattlesnakes (*cascabel/Crotalus spp*), eyelash vipers (*bocaracá/Bothrops schlegelii*) and the fer de lance (*terciopelo* or *barba amarilla/Bothrops asper*), identifiable by a diamond pattern on its back; this can be found in undergrowth and often lies on warm roads at night. It's up to 2m long and is less timid than other species. Boas (*boa/Boa constrictor*) can bite, although of course they kill by constriction; they may be up to 6m in length and can kill ocelots and young deer.

One of the first symptoms of poisoning may be tingling in the mouth, and a metallic taste, followed by swelling, pain and numbness at the site of the bite. Sweating, nausea and fainting may be a symptom of shock rather than of poisoning.

Views vary on how to treat snake bite in remote areas, but doctors agree that you should *not* make razor cuts around the fang marks or try to suck the poison out. You should merely gently wash the surface of the wound to get rid of any sprayed venom which could subsequently enter the wound. A crepe bandage (rather than a tourniquet) should be applied to the whole limb (assuming the bite is on a limb) to slow the blood flow, and released for one minute in every ten; the limb should be kept below the level of the heart. The victim should be kept quiet and calm.

And if you're days away from medical help, that's all you can do. Hospitals hold stocks of serum; these are specific to the exact species of snake, so do what you can to help accurate identification. Any snake is known as a *serpiente*; venomous snakes are *viboras* and non-venomous ones are *culebras*.

Vampire bats

These rather endearing little creatures (we'll tell you why in a minute) are definitely dangerous, because of all the animals listed here they are the only ones to actively seek you as a prey, and because they're carriers of rabies. However, the dangers of vampire bats have been exaggerated, as studies show that only one in 200 carries the rabies virus. But with a disease that is invariably fatal once established, you don't want to take any risks, so always sleep under a mosquito net. Completely under a mosquito net – we met a rather sheepish looking Indian in the Darién Gap with a bandaged foot: he'd found the night too hot for his liking so had stuck his foot out under the netting to cool off. A nice treat for a passing bat.

Now a little about the habits of vampire bats (*vampiro/Desmodus rotundus*), which are different in many ways from those of other bats. Vampires can stalk their prey "on foot". They have specially elongated legs and arms that enable them to walk on the ground, and they usually attack the feet or legs of their warm-blooded victims. Domestic animals such as horses, donkeys and cows are frequently attacked, but chickens are often victims of the smaller *Diaemus youngii*. The animal feels no pain from an attack: if the vampire strikes while flying it lulls the animal with its rapidly beating wings, and its saliva may contain an anaesthetic which makes the bite painless. Certainly it does contain an anticoagulant. Contrary to popular opinion these bats don't suck blood, nor do they have hollow teeth. They make a slashing cut with their razor-sharp canine teeth, and lap up the blood with the help of a groove on their lower lip. They drink their own weight in blood, so that they can barely fly away, and then don't feed for several days. Because of the anticoagulant the victim continues to bleed copiously after the bat has left, and several vampires may feed successively from the same wound, so that many animals eventually die from blood loss.

So why does Hilary find them so endearing? Well, apart from their nasty feeding habits, vampire bats are social animals with impeccable family values. The gestation period is a remarkable seven months, and the infants are suckled for nine months. While the mother is out feeding, the young are left in the care of "foster parents" which may also suckle them. On her return, the mother and baby recognise each other's calls. Vampire bats keep themselves and each other immaculately clean, and this can lead to their downfall. One method of destroying a colony is to catch one and paint it with a sticky mixture containing strychnine before releasing it to return to its cave. The other bats crowd around to clean it and are poisoned.

Rabies
Rabies may also be carried by any warm-blooded animal that bites – most obviously dogs. As ever, prevention is the key, so you should avoid dogs that seem to be behaving erratically and consider carrying a stick or hiking pole. Most dogs will keep clear if you throw stones, or even pretend to pick up stones. If bitten, or even scratched, scrub the bite at once under running water for five minutes with soap and then with iodine or a 40-70% alcohol solution; it's been shown that this alone reduces the risk of contracting rabies by 90%. Then head for a doctor: the traditional advice about catching the beast and hanging on to it for ten days to see if it develops symptoms is a waste of precious time if you're in the back of beyond. Ideally you should start a two-week course of jabs within a week of being bitten, but if the wound is on an extremity (bats often bite on the toes – wear socks in bed!) you may have a couple of months before the virus reaches the brain, from which point death is certain within twenty days.

An alternative to the expensive course of injections after being bitten is the only slightly less expensive three-jab course of vaccinations before travel; this should be enough to keep you safe, but if bitten you should still have a booster.

Bugs
Understanding the habits of man-loving mites and insects can help you to outwit them. And if that fails, we have suggestions below on how to deal with the misery they inflict.

Prevention is always better than cure, and a good insect repellent is the best preventative. The two main active ingredients are Deet (diethyl-metatoluamide), on your skin, and Permethrin, on your clothing. Deet is present in concentrations from 30% up to 95% in the leading brands of repellent. The higher the concentration, the longer protection lasts, but it's neurotoxic and 95% concentrations may cause rashes or seizures in children; nor is it suggested during pregnancy. Some people find that 100mg of vitamin B1 (thiamine) taken daily will stop mosquitoes and other insects from biting, alhough there's no scientific evidence for this. You can also sleep under a mosquito net; the ones with their own frame that you can set up on top of a bed (or anywhere else) are best, as few budget hotels provide hooks for tying up the conventional nets. It should also be impregnated with permethrin; if not, you can get a DIY kit from MASTA. Permethrin is available in the USA as Duranon or Permanone, but not in Canada; it should stay active through four or five washings. In a tent you'll certainly need ventilation, but make sure that any opening is covered with fine-gauge netting. Sprays containing pyrethrum can zap any beasties inside your tent or ones that have just attached themselves to your body, and mosquito coils (which give out an insect repellent odour as they burn) last all night and are very effective in a closed room.

Experience shows us that, although in theory you can do a lot to deter insects by wearing long-sleeved shirts, long trousers tucked into long socks, and so on, in practice it's difficult to do so in hot humid jungle, at least during the sweltering days. You're lulled into a sense of false security by the fact that you're not usually aware of the mites and insects that are busy feasting. Probably the best advice is to spray like crazy during the day, and wear bite-proof clothing at night when the malarial *Anopheles* mosquito is doing her rounds. Bite-proof means closely woven material; a nylon "shell" jacket does the trick but is sweaty. You should still spray your clothes, of course, but not the nylon which will disintegrate. Don't forget that washing whenever you cross a stream will dislodge some bugs before they've settled in.

Once you are bitten, calamine lotion or an analgesic cream or spray containing mepyramine (antihistamine) or benzocaine can help soothe the itching, while hydrocortizone (tablets or cream) reduces the swelling. Aspirin or paracetamol may help (after all, an itch is just a specialised form of pain). Toothpaste (applied externally) is said to have a soothing effect, as may anaesthetic cream. Scratching may not help but it feels awfully good. Let's be honest, it's one of life's supreme physical pleasures, isn't it?! But be careful and keep your nails short; if you break the skin apply antiseptic, as the bite can easily become infected.

Mosquitoes (*zancudos*)

Above all these carry **malaria**; symptoms of this potentially fatal condition include flu-like fever, headaches, shivering, sweating and chills. It is on the increase throughout the world as malaria organisms become resistant to drugs such as chloroquine, and mosquitoes to pesticides. Most areas below 2,500m are affected, and in low-lying regions mosquitoes also carry **dengue fever**: this virus produces fever, headaches and musculo-skeletal aches, followed by a rash, and should pass within a week, although in very rare cases it can kill. In Panamá mosquitoes also carry yellow fever; they can also carry bot fly eggs. Thus the emphasis should be on avoiding mosquito bites rather than on medication.

Before we discuss this, however, you should recognise your enemy. Of at least 2,600 species of mosquito, and 400 species of *Anopheles* mosquito, only about 60 can carry a malarial parasite, and of the 100 or so species of malarial parasite only four commonly affect man. In Mexico the main risk is from *Anopheles albimanus* which feeds at night; however *Aedes aegypti*, which carries dengue fever, prefers daylight, so you can never relax altogether. As with other types of mosquito, it's only the female who sucks blood, which she needs for egg production, and she has a definite preference for women in dark clothes. The *Anopheles* is under 1cm long, rests with her tail end in the air and lacks that high-pitched hum so characteristic of most mosquitoes. In towns and hotels you'll usually be confronted with the (relatively) harmless *Culex quinquefasciatus*.

In addition to the preventive measures above, you should take antimalarial drugs. These do not prevent the disease, but kill the parasites in your system. You must take the medication regularly, starting a week before arrival in a malarial region, throughout your stay there, and for six weeks after leaving it. Chloroquine (sold as Avloclor, Malarivon, Nivaquine, Aralen or Resochin, and taken weekly) is still the best in most cases. If you contract malaria, you can treat it in the short term by taking four chloroquine tablets (600mg) followed by two more six hours later and then two daily.

Assassin bugs (*vinchuca*)

These carry **Chagas' Disease**, a nasty complaint which kills 50,000 persons a year throughout Latin America. Also known as the reduviid, cone-nosed, kissing or barber bug, it is an oval brown insect (*Triatoma dimidiata*) with a long thin head which lurks in crevices and between palm fronds, notably in thatched roofs, at up to 1,500m (South American species go up to 3,600m). It emerges at night to feed on the blood of vertebrates, including humans: it is likely to bite on the face, feeding for at least twenty minutes, and leaving faeces containing *Trypanosoma* parasites. These enter through the bite and reproduce inside fat cells which burst and release them. In some victims a hard violet swelling appears at the site of infection after about a week, and soon the parasites invade organs such as the heart, brain and liver. Symptoms are fever, vomiting, shortness of breath and a stiff neck. An acute form of the illness can kill you within three months, but it's more usual for victims to show no symptoms after a month or two, but then to die of a weakened heart up to 20 years later. It has been speculated that Charles Darwin died of Chagas' Disease.

If bitten on the face, see a doctor; a blood test after six weeks will show if the disease is present. Benznidazole and nifurtimox are effective against most strains of the parasite in the first six months of infection, but it is better by far to avoid being bitten. Avoid sleeping under palm trees or palm roofs, use insect repellents and a mosquito net, and check for hidden insects.

It should be stressed that this is a disease of poor villagers and extremely rare among travellers.

Wasps, bees and hornets
Some people are allergic to the sting of *Hymenoptera* or membrane-winged flies, as this group is called. If you already know you're allergic, you'll presumably carry a sting kit with you.

Generally these stinging insects are not a problem in the jungle, but Hilary once inadvertently shook a branch which was the nesting site for some small blue wasps. Furious at this apparent assault, they pursued her, tangled in her hair, and she ended up with her head in the river trying to get rid of them. No fun, so be careful not to disturb nests in any way and don't even go near them if you see any activity. If attacked, stay calm and don't flail about.

Scorpions (*escorpiones* or *alacranes*)
As a rule scorpion stings just hurt for four hours or so, but eight of the 25 Mexican species are dangerous. These are the bark scorpions (*Centruroides spp*), 5-8cm long with a long thin body, and are found in Guerrero, Morelos, Nayarit and Durango states. They can cause serious, possibly fatal, systemic reactions, especially in young children; anti-venom is available. Like other scorpions, they are timid and nocturnal, and become aggressive only when disturbed. Don't move stones, timber, or mess around in leaf litter unless you can see what you're doing. If you need to clear a site, use your boots and a knife rather than your hands. If your boots really must spend the night outside the tent, be sure to shake them out before putting them on in the morning. In cheap hotels, check around the bed and under the toilet seat.

If stung, treat the place with a topical anaesthetic cream, and take pain killers and plenty of fluids. Don't confuse scorpions with spiny lizards (*Heloderma spp*), often called *escorpión*.

Bocones
I don't know the English name for these tiny blood-sucking beetles, but their bite itches a lot for a few minutes, then eases off. They only bite during the day.

Ticks (*garrapatas*)

These are plentiful and persistent in jungle areas and savannah grasslands. You may finish a walk with hundreds of these crawlies. If removed before they dig in and start sucking your blood, they're harmless, but there are few things less conducive to a peaceful night than to feel hundreds of ticks crawling around on you. And once established they cause an itch lasting several days. They may also carry typhus, a fever which requires medical attention; in this case there's usually a large painful swelling around the bite and nearby lymph nodes will be inflamed.

Keep ticks off your skin by tucking trousers into socks and tops into trousers, and spraying them (but not bare skin) with a repellent such as Permanone. Inspect your body periodically for ticks (some are so small as to be practically invisible) and remove them with masking tape, by far the best way of trapping the creatures. At the end of the day wash thoroughly (Neko soap, available in tick countries, is very effective) and change your clothing. Before going to bed inspect yourself carefully, sharing the job with a friend if possible, and be sure to check those warm clammy areas so dear to a tick's heart. Yes, that's when you learn who your friends are!

Once established, ticks must be removed by firmly pinching them as close to your skin as possible and steadily pulling at right angles to the skin; tweezers and kerosene, alcohol or vaseline may help.

Chiggers (*coloradillas* or *coloraditos*)

The secret life of chiggers (*Eutrombicula spp*) was revealed in an article by E F Rivinus in the *Smithsonian* magazine of July 1981, and it's so fascinating we can't resist going into some detail. Apparently these creatures have long been misunderstood. No, it's not that they're nicer than we thought, it's that they're even nastier, and all the traditional cures such as killing the beastie by painting nail varnish over the spot are quite futile. It's going to itch like hell for about ten days and there's nothing you can do about it.

But to begin at the beginning. First, the chigger is not an insect, but the larval stage of a mite, about a millimetre long. Second, they don't suck blood, and third, they don't burrow under your skin. What happens when you pick up a chigger (more likely a hundred chiggers) in long grass is that it bites into your skin and liquifies the tissue with its saliva. In reaction to this your tissue creates a hard tube called a stylostome, which makes a handy drinking straw for the chigger. After about four days the fat and happy chigger leaves, but the stylostome remains, and you will go on itching for ten days or so, because your skin goes on reacting against the stylostome.

Mr Rivinus has a sensible and scientific explanation for this behaviour:

"First there's no love in a chigger's life (no sex, I'm sorry to say, and no parent/child relationship) ... so it's obviously inappropriate to expect them to show a mite of compassion towards their hosts ... secondly, the adult has a blind gut and is consequently unable to defecate. Anything that spends its entire adult life in a constipated state is bound to develop a pretty nasty nature, and that may be reflected in its offspring."

So, once the stylostome has begun to form you'll just have to put up with it. As usual, prevention is better than cure, so use lots of repellent (sulphur powder may help) and keep away from long grass, especially if there are cows there. Or don't lounge around in it, anyway. The itch can be somewhat relieved with analgesic ointment, and of course if you scratch hard enough you may rip the stylostome out. If so, use antiseptic to prevent infection.

Jiggers (*chigoe*)
Not to be confused with a chigger, a jigger is a flea (*Tunga penetrans*) which burrows imperceptibly into your toes and remains there to enjoy its pregnancy. It can grow to the size of a pea, but you should use a sterile needle to hook it out before it gets to this stage. Treat the resulting hole with antiseptic. Don't go barefoot. That's also the way to pick up hookworm.

Bot fly larva (*colmoyote*)
This creature deserves a proper description and I'm grateful to Linda Rosa of the South American Explorers Club for this information. The adult bot fly (*Dermatobia hominis*) is a harmless insect which doesn't even have mouth parts, but its larva is parasitic on humans and other warm-blooded animals. The bot fly attaches its eggs to the abdomen of a blood-sucking arthropod such as the *Psorophora* mosquito which conveys them to the host. As the mosquito has its meal, the bot fly eggs hatch and the larvae burrow into the skin through the mosquito bite or a hair follicle. Here they prosper and stay, maturing in 40 to 60 days by which time one may measure 2cm in length. The grub is all body, with no head or legs, but has an effective mouth and strong oral hooks which, with the spines which encircle its body, keep it firmly anchored. It breathes in a most undignified way through its backside, and its unfortunate human hosts, who can't tell a face from an arse, mistakenly talk of the creature "poking its head out".

A cyst or hard mass forms around the grub and this often becomes infected, so you should deal with the creature as soon as it makes its presence felt. In a follow-up to Linda's article in the *South American Explorer* magazine, Barb McLeod writes:

"Graced with the dubious distinction of having extracted more than forty of the beasties from myself and other people over some ten years in Belize, I thought I should pass on a tried and true remedy: cover the breathing hole generously with Elmer's Glue, or better (unless your skin is sensitive) Duco cement or other non-water base glue. Place over this (it need not dry) a circular patch of adhesive tape, 1-2 cm in diameter, depending on size and location of cyst. Along the edge of the tape, apply a second seal of glue. Allow this to dry well, being on the lookout for lymph leakage around the edge – that is the larva's devious means of forcing a new breathing channel. Leave on overnight; the next day the suffocated beast can be easily squeezed and tweezed out.

Before I arrived at this method I'd tried: glue alone, peanut butter, toothpaste, nail polish, lard, Sno-Seal and nicotine extract. None but the last killed the larva – they only induced (at best) the critter to poke its rear end out. Grabbing it alive is inadvisable; not only will it dig in painfully with its spines, but accidental rupture could also cause a serious allergic reaction as well as infection. Nicotine extract will send the beast into convulsions for fifteen minutes – most distracting to the host. The recommended method is painless and 100% effective *if* the second seal is carefully applied.

I've noted, in myself and others, lymphatic complications (swelling of face, tenderness of nodes) whenever the larvae locate in the neck or head. Normally they hook directly into the lymphatic system and feed from it.

Considerable lore has accumulated around this exotic affliction – even stories of hosts lonely or curious enough to keep their worm as a pet until nocturnal twinges begin to keep them awake at night."

Sandflies (*Phlebotomus spp*)

These feed only at night, and the females carry the parasite *Leishmaniasis* which, if left untreated, can lead to disfigurement or even death. Again, you can avoid them by sleeping under a permethrin-impregnated mosquito net. Here's a cautionary tale sent to us by Barbara Clark of New Hampshire:

"Staying in a cheap hotel in Guatemala City, I awoke with my hands covered with hard bites. These went away, but after we'd been home about a month, a sore appeared on my arm and one on my back. These gradually got bigger and uglier. My doctor sent me to a surgeon, who removed the smaller one on my back. It reappeared. Finally I went to a dermatologist, and here I was in luck, because he happened to have studied and treated a form of the disease. I was approaching the time when the disease could appear in the nose and throat area, which it would start eating away. The doctor treated the disease with antimony injections, and the sores went away like magic and without any side effects."

Don't let a doctor excise these sores, which serve as a useful barometer of treatment.

For some reason as yet unknown to science, Avon "Skin-So-Soft" works wonders in repelling sandflies; it also repels mosquitoes, but only for short periods.

Sandfleas

You'll meet swarms of these creatures biting your ankles on some tropical beaches. They are very unpleasant at the time, but the effects are short-lived.

Blackflies (*mosca negra*)

Clouds of viciously biting blackflies (*Simulium spp*) can make hiking a misery, as anyone who's hiked in the eastern USA or Canada knows. Fortunately, they are less common in Mexico and the irritation of their bites doesn't last long. Near the Guatemalan border they can carry *Onchocerciasis* or river blindness.

Crabs and lice (*piojos*)

Travellers sleeping in cheap hotels are liable to catch these. If in your hair, you can deal with them by using a shampoo containing *gammabenzene hexachloride*.

Stingrays

These are the most commonly encountered venomous marine animals. They lurk in the sand, so do the "stingray shuffle" to let them know you're coming. When poking around in corals or wading, wear gloves and shoes or booties. After being stabbed you'll have to deal with both a laceration and an injection of venom, which causes immediate and intense local pain, swelling and bleeding that usually peaks in 30 to 60 minutes. Fragments of the stinger, or sheath, may be left behind and should be removed. To relieve the pain, soak the affected area with water as hot as you can stand for 30 to 90 minutes and repeat as necessary. If severe pain persists or if spines or stingers possibly remain in the wound, or if there is any sign of infection, seek medical attention.

The **sea urchins'** spines are less troublesome, dissolving in about a week.

Jellyfish (*medusa*)

Most stings occur between July and September; effects are usually mild and disappear in two or three hours, though a rash may persist for a few days. If a jellyfish's tentacles latch on to you, try to remove them without using your hands. Wash the affected area with cold salt water (don't use fresh water and don't rub it with sand). Then soak it in vinegar for about 30 minutes, apply a paste of baking soda, wet sand or shaving cream, and leave in place for several minutes before scraping off and washing with salt water. If itching is a problem, a steroid cream or antihistamines may help. If vinegar isn't available, use rubbing alcohol, bleach, distilled liquor, meat tenderiser or ... urine.

Finally some happy news. There are no leeches in Mexico. Few insects will bother you above 2,000m (and in this area there's no malaria above 1,500m), so if you're thoroughly put off by this section, keep high and you'll be alright. In any case, the dry season is far healthier than the wet; avoid the dampest parts of the Caribbean coast and you'll have few problems.

ON BEING A *GRINGA*

Wendy Dison

There is an ambiguity about the status of women in Mexico: on the one hand they are seen as sex objects and on the other is the revered mother figure of the Catholic church. The Virgin Mary is displayed alongside a pin-up over the bus driver's seat and no-one thinks it odd. These attitudes are reflected in the way you will find yourself treated in Mexico – one moment with lack of respect, the next with old-fashioned chivalry.

Being a foreign woman makes the situation even more confusing. Stereotypes exist about Western women and a woman travelling alone is often assumed to be "available". Dressing modestly helps to avoid unwanted attention, but as a *gringa* you will never escape it entirely. Not frequenting bars and other male-dominated places is also a good idea, yet often there is no choice when you want a meal or a drink. I have at times been made so uncomfortable by stares and comments that I've wished to disappear into my bowl of beans. Restaurants where families are eating are likely to have a more pleasant atmosphere.

Harassment usually takes the form of whistles and hisses. This is the *ladino's* way of paying you a compliment and many local women seem to expect and even welcome it. But while being whistled to like a dog can make your blood boil, it generally isn't threatening and the best thing to do is to ignore it.

However, meeting people is one of the reasons for travelling and you need to distinguish between unwanted advances and friendly approaches. Use your intuition, but also use your discretion. Making friends isn't difficult as there is a lot of curiosity about foreigners, but it is harder to meet other women, particularly indigenous women, who are very shy. Long bus journeys offer a good chance to meet and talk, and I enjoyed getting to know women who run guesthouses. Questions about husbands and children always came first and, instead of pitying me for having neither (which is a common reaction in many other countries), I found that generally women were envious of my freedom.

Women travellers have some advantages, too: we pose less of a threat than men do and I'm sure I'm invited into people's homes more often than men are because of this. There still exists in Mexico a chivalrous attitude to women and should you need help, or even appear to need it, men are ready to pitch in.

The world is an increasingly dangerous place, but the mountains are safer than the cities. The further off the beaten track I go, the safer I feel. In the mountains of Central America the friendliness and hospitality I have met have been humbling. Once, I lost my way and had to beg shelter for the night. An elderly couple, both farmers, welcomed me and shared their food; when I left in the morning they refused my offer of payment. This was in a remote area of Guatemala, near Todos Santos. Other places are not so safe, especially where there are many tourists, and I would strongly advise women walking alone to seek local advice. Robbery, assault and even rape are not unknown. Local people will have information that is more up to date than that in guidebooks. In some places walking with a friend may be safer.

I have given a lot of warnings, but it is important to keep things in perspective. Don't ruin your trip by being paranoid; be aware – but don't let it stop you from travelling. The world is full of wonderful people and you won't meet them if you stay at home.

CRIME

Theft

Robberies always figure prominently in travellers' tales, and certainly
Mexico has its share of skilful thieves. Fortunately, violent robbery is very
rare (though a real danger on some overnight buses in Michoacán and
Nayarit), and theft is almost unknown in rural parts. Travellers are most
likely to be parted from their possessions unawares, particularly in towns
or areas frequented by tourists. John Hatt's *The Tropical Traveller* has an
excellent section on safety (see Appendix Two), but here are a few do's
and don'ts.

- Do keep your valuables in a money belt, neck pouch, or secret pocket.
  John Hatt suggests using a tubular bandage (such as Tubigrip) to secure
  his valuables to his leg. This comes in various sizes so you can choose
  the most comfortable and practical place to wear it. Bear in mind that it
  can be embarrassing to be seen with your hand deep inside your trousers.

- Don't carry a handbag or any type of shoulder bag into known danger
  spots. That means markets, fiestas, crowded buses and trains. A leather
  bag is easily snatched or slit.

- Do be wary of performing chivalrous acts. A standard trick is for some
  poor old lady on a bus or train to ask a gringo to lift her bag on to the
  luggage rack. Meanwhile his own bag disappears. If you agree to help,
  make sure your own luggage is safe. Equally don't let yourself be
  distracted by someone sitting in your reserved seat or telling you about
  dirt on your back.

- Do select a hotel room which has bars on the window or one that can't be
  entered from a neighbouring room. Lock your valuables in your luggage
  when leaving your room.

- Do bring a combination lock (harder to pick than an ordinary padlock) to
  secure your hotel door or luggage. A chain is a useful and versatile
  addition.

- Don't leave your money in your clothes when you go swimming.

- Don't camp in an urban area unless well guarded.

- Don't become paranoid. As a backpacker in rural areas you will experience
  incredible honesty and generosity in the face of grinding poverty. It's a
  humbling experience. In any case, the more alert, open and friendly you
  seem, the less likely you are to be a target.

There's always the problem of whether to carry your passport with you at
all times or to leave it in the hotel strong box. It's often better to leave it

behind but to carry some other form of identification. Something impressive-looking with a photo and a number (a student card might do) will usually serve just as well as a passport. Carry a photocopy of the key pages of your passport. Keep this and the numbers of your travellers cheques, plastic cards and air ticket separate from your valuables, so that if they are lost you can more easily replace them. Divide your money and travellers cheques between at least two different places, in your baggage and on your body.

Officials

You will be up against petty bureaucracy time and again, and it's great training in the art of public relations. However frustrating the situation, however corrupt the official, you must remain calm and pleasant. This is particularly important if you are arrested. Providing you keep cool you'll almost certainly be released within a few hours (assuming you haven't actually committed a crime). Try to assume an air of authority and quiet confidence, but don't do anything to threaten the ego of the official in question. Often a potentially awkward situation can be defused with jokes and a friendly gesture such as the offer of a cigarette or some chocolate. Don't resort to money bribery unless you know what you are doing; it's best to wait for the suggestion to come from the other side.

Chapter Five

On the Road

TRANSPORT

Mexico is big, and you'll spend a lot of time travelling, unless you just stick to one locality. There's an excellent transport infrastructure, with a full range of possibilities.

Top of the hierarchy is **air**; since deregulation in 1991 there are no less than fifty private airlines operating a good network of routes (although you have to go via Mexico City for many journeys). The two largest are Mexicana and Aeromexico, both privatised and now owned by the same holding company (Mexicana having been saved from bankruptcy in 1994) but still separate and competing. Mexicana owns the regional airlines Inter, Aerocaribe, Aero Cozumel etc, while Aerolitoral is part of Aeromexico. The third largest airline is Taesa, serving 30 destinations, mostly in the north, while Aerocalifornia covers all of Mexico north of the capital and Aviacsa covers the southeast. Most flights are operated by reasonably modern jets; fares are around US$100 from Mexico City to Guadalajara or Monterrey, and US$160 to Cancún.

The main form of inter-urban transport is now **bus** rather than train; the rail system is more or less defunct as an effective form of passenger transport. Second-class ("regular" or "local") buses serve local routes (usually with a Mexican-built DINA vehicle, generally known as a *camion*), while for inter-urban travel you'll normally have to take a first-class bus (Mercedes-Benz etc); various types of luxury or *ejecutivo* services also operate on major routes, but they actually offer little extra. Even second-class buses now often have first-class features such as reclining seats, videos, seat reservations or checked baggage, though never all at the same time. All buses are now limited to 95km/h (60mph); second-class buses will stop anywhere, but first-class buses take "15 minute" mealbreaks which last 30 minutes, so even if you do have a choice there's relatively little difference in time at the end of the day (but the price differential is so little that you should always go first class if you have a choice). In the south of

Mexico, in particular, you'll frequently find separate first- and second-class terminals at opposite ends of town, and in Baja each company tends to have a separate office, so you'll probably just stick with whichever one you're at. In the centre of Mexico most towns have a big new *central camionera*, used by all companies; there may seem to be hundreds of them, but if you look closely you'll often find that they form just a couple of big cartels. Thus the *Sistema Estrella Blanca*, for instance, includes Elite, Caballero Azteca, TNS, Futura and many local companies; and if two companies claim to have six services each at the same price to the same place, they probably in fact run three each.

The system works pretty well, even if you don't speak much Spanish. The bus number or departure bay is usually written on your ticket, and the destination is usually painted on the windscreen with a wipe-off spray. Staff are helpful and professional; no-one wants to risk losing such a good job, so you can be sure that they won't let anyone make off with your luggage. Even so, you may prefer to sit on the right-hand side, to keep an eye on the lockers. Some things, of course, remain a bit third-world: there may not be a single clock, even in a new *camionera*, and computers don't seem to have improved your chances of getting on a *de paso* (passing through) bus until it's already due to have departed. Don't sit at the rear: it's a rougher ride, the toilet can get pretty smelly, and the air-conditioning can pump out a considerable quantity of heat, even when it's too cool at the front. First-class buses currently cost about £2/US$3 per hour's travel.

Buses go to most places, and most other roads (including some dirt roads) are served by shared minibus-taxis known as *combis, colectivos* or (in Mexico City) *peseros*. On any other road you'll be able to get a ride on a *camioneta* or pickup truck; in some areas you'll have to pay, but in the northwest and Baja California rides are always free. On back roads in these areas the first vehicle to pass will usually pick you up, but conversely they'll almost never pick you up if you try to hitch on a bus route.

In Mexico City *peseros* currently cost N$1 (one peso) up to 5km, N$1.50 to 12km, and then N$2. The **Metro** costs N$1 for any distance and is considerably faster. Therefore it gets very crowded and at peak times you'll be prevented from entering with heavy baggage; take all usual precautions against pickpockets. It's French-built, so runs on rubber tyres and has colour-coded routes known by the terminal stations and magnetic tickets sold in *carnets*, just like Paris! It's improved by using pictograms to match the station names, but for some reason there are no ticket machines; queues can be lengthy. It claims to be the world's third busiest metro system, carrying over five million passengers per day.

There are a few **trolleybus** routes, which are particularly useful for north-south journeys through the city centre; elsewhere there are buses and even a few cycle-rickshaws. The city also swarms with **taxis**; most of them are VW Beetles (known as *sedans*), and even with the front seat removed it can be hard to get a big rucksack in. Most Mexico City taxi-drivers believe that they are immune to the normal laws of physics and can safely turn right from the left-hand lane as long as they have their hazard lights flashing at all times. There's no need to tip taxi-drivers (but on the other hand it's usual to tip at filling stations).

It's getting easier to travel in Mexico by **car**, although there's little point for most purposes. US insurance is not valid, and there's plenty of other paperwork if you're going more than about 30km from the US border. About 6,000km of new *autopistas* have been built, and another 6,000km are planned to complete ten main axes. At the moment the main routes are from Mexico City to Veracruz, Oaxaca, Acapulco, Guadalajara, Aguascalientes and San Luís Potosí; to the north of Guadalajara and Aguascalientes there are some gaps before you hit the *autopistas* to the border, but there's a bigger gap between San Luís Potosí and Monterrey. These mostly have two lanes in each direction, but some are only one lane each way; they're also expensive, so not surprisingly they're under-used and the concessionaires are demanding subsidies to cut tolls. They also make excellent cycling routes (no-one bats an eyelid), but take plenty of water. At the other end of the spectrum, a *terraceria* is a dirt road of a pretty decent standard, while a *brecha* is much worse, although pickups still manage, especially those with *doble tracción* or 4-wheel-drive. Lead-free fuel (*Magna Sin*), is now available, from green pumps, and in 1996 accounts for 56% of sales; you'll normally need cash, rather than a credit card, to fill up. There's a free breakdown service for tourists, known as the *Angeles Verdes* (Green Angels; tel: 250 8221/0123).

Mexican driving is not as bad as the myth would have it (except for *colectivos* and Mexico City taxi drivers); they hoot a lot, but often actually stop at the flashing green light, which comes before the yellow and red! You should not drive at night in the Sierra Madre Oriental between Sinaloa and Guerrero states, and should exercise caution elsewhere. Three things to look out for are *topes*, four-way-stops and checkpoints. *Topes* (or *vibradores*) are the fearsome speedhumps found in every settlement and *usually* well signposted; take them very slowly, especially if following a bus which might take the opportunity to drop off a passenger. Four-way-stop signs are possibly the most inefficient form of traffic regulation (a car produces ten times as much pollution when stopping and starting as when moving); they work relatively well in the USA and Canada, but here they are less well marked, so you can't be sure whether it's a four-way-stop or a junction with a major road. One day perhaps they'll be replaced by traffic calming and mini-roundabouts, but it'll be a very long time. Checkpoints waste time, but are not now a major hassle; a policeman or soldier will board a bus, check some poor *indigeno's* ID or search his bag, and get off.

As for the **railways**, passenger services are incredibly inefficient, with just one train a day on most routes, or separate first- and second-class trains, usually running many hours late and often conveying goods vans as well as passenger coaches. They are far slower and cheaper than buses, and as a rule they're not worth the trouble. The government's solution is privatisation, but this has been delayed; the first in line is likely to be the Chihuahua-Pacific line, perhaps in 1997. This and the main lines to the US border are the only potentially profitable parts of the system, and US companies such as Union Pacific, Railtex and Kansas City Southern are forming consortia to bid for 50-year concessions for them. The railways still carry 20% of freight, but only 1.5% of passenger traffic, which will be subsidised by the government.

ACCOMMODATION

There are, of course, all classes of hotels throughout Mexico, and prices are currently no higher than in Central America. If you're not on a tight budget you'll find some wonderful *posadas* in the colonial cities, particularly just to the north of Mexico City. These are much better value than international chain hotels, such as Hilton, Hyatt, Holiday Inn and Marriott, which are expanding into the main business centres. In northern Baja you'll find US-style motels, which are a useful option for car travellers; Mexican-style motels are basically sex-stops. All-inclusive deals are common, and good value, in the new resorts. At the lower end are cheap hotels and *hospedajes* (a *pensión* is for cars, not people) which charge around £3/US$5 for a single. These are fairly basic, but usually provide soap, paper and a towel, and loads of atmosphere. The *Rough Guide* tends not to list the cheapest dives.

The best value for money is found at a *villa juvenil*, one of the youth hostels run by the *Comision Nacional del Deporte*, generally found in sports centres in major towns and resorts; they cost about £2/US$3, except for the slightly pricier ones in La Paz and Cancún. A youth hostel membership card is not necessary, but gives you a discount. They are very clean and usually quiet, unless there's a large teenage sports team in.

There are few campsites as such, but you can usually camp among the RVs (camper vans, or trucks really) in the trailer parks. Camping wild is not a problem, but be very aware of security risks, especially on touristy beaches. Many beaches also have *cabanas* (beachhuts) and *palapas* (thatched shelters) in which you can hang a hammock, and you'll probably be able to rent the hammock too.

FOOD

Generally speaking, you'll get better food in an independent restaurant than in a hotel, and the best value of all tends to be in and around the markets. Each market has an area for *comedors*, where hot food is prepared;

you'll see what each stall has and pay the lowest prices. Always ask the cost of a dish before ordering it, however, and if in doubt just ask for the set lunch (*comida corrida* or *paquete*). Breakfast (*desayuno*) is usually served until around 10.00, lunch (*comida*, the main meal for most people) from 13.00 to 16.00, and dinner (*cena*) from 20.00 to 22.00. Lunch times in particular are very variable, and workers often pop out for a snack mid-morning, so it's best to make appointments to see people.

Mexican food is far more interesting and varied than in Central America, and bears little relation to the Tex-Mex pap served as Mexican food abroad. The only *chile con carne* I ever came across was in Los Cabos airport. It's a myth that Mexican food is unrelentingly hot; as a rule the *salsa* is on the table (in a bowl if it's homemade, as it should be), so you add just as much as you want. The most distinctively Mexican dish is *mole*, above all the *poblano* or Puebla version; this is a sauce of 32 ingredients, dominated by the unlikely blend of chile and chocolate. Obviously the best is home-made, but it may take up to a week to prepare; fortunately you can also buy it ready-made. In Yucatán there is a fantastic blend of Spanish and Mayan influences, with dishes such as pork in banana leaves with achiote sauce, and (especially in Mérida) New Orleans ties; in northern Baja there are Chinese restaurants on almost every corner.

Restaurant food in particular is unremittingly carnivorous, and if you're **vegetarian** you'll find yourself eating a lot of scrambled eggs (*huevos revueltos*). One solution is to concentrate on snacks (*antojitos*), such as *tamales* (dumplings of steamed corn wrapped in corn leaves), and what is for me one of the greatest achievements of Mexican culture, the *torta*. This is a bread roll overstuffed with salad, avocado, meat or cheese and chile, and toasted (a *sandwich*, however, is a limp imitation of a toasted sandwich). Leave the salad out if you are unsure about the local water or your stomach's ability to adapt to it. The quintessential *antojito*, however, is the *taco*, a *tortilla* (a round of unleavened bread) rolled around a filling of meat or beans (or anything else); a northern version, of wheat rather than corn flour, is called a *burrito*. The standard version is *al pastor*, filled with meat cut from a vertical kebab-style spit with a pineapple on top. A baked version is an *enchilada*, a crisp toasted *tortilla* piled high with (as a rule) meat and salad is a *tostada*, a *quesadilla* is filled with molten cheese, a *taco dorado* is deep-fried, and a *gordita* is a tortilla slit open and stuffed rather like a pitta.

For hiking and camping, you can pick up supplies in the markets; if you're not cooking you'll have to buy ready-made snacks in *abarrotes* (groceries) shops or (in major cities or more generally in Baja California) US-style supermarkets. Healthfood stores (*tiendas naturistas*) are widespread, but they're more into ginseng and royal jelly than serious food such as hummus or granary bread. There are vegetarian restaurants in most cities, but they often serve fish, and soya/germen is always made to look like meat.

The quintessentially Mexican **drinks** are fruit juices and *licuados*, fruit juices blended with water or milk; orange juice is omnipresent, but *licuados* can be made from almost anything, from alfalfa to *zanahoria* (carrot) via *rompopo* (a mix of nuts); in the south they often have granola added. You usually get a top-up, so don't drain your glass and rush out. As for bottled drinks, Coke, Pepsi and Fanta are omnipresent, if you must have them, but the grapefruit-flavoured Fresco and Kas (produced by Coca Cola and Pepsi-Cola, respectively) are far more refreshing. Milk (other than *chocomilk*) is only available in litre packs or larger, and these are not usually resealable. In the north, folk seem obsessed with ices (*neves*), which always seem to be from Michoacán.

Compared to most beers north of the border, Mexican beer is pretty good; it's in the Germanic lager tradition, although it's always worth asking for *cerveza oscura* or dark beer. The basic brands of Corona, Cuauhtémoc, Carta Blanca, Sol, Tecate and more local breweries are sweet, watery thirst-quenchers; there are more interesting Pilseners (Bohemia, Superior) and reddish Austrian-style beers (Dos Equis, Indio Oscura).

There's a variety of alcoholic drinks produced from the maguey cactus; the basic one, a milky beer, often home-made, is *pulque*; *mezcal* is a distilled spirit made from several species of maguey; and *tequila* is a more refined version made only from *Agave tequilana*.

Mexican bars are chauvinist male-only haunts, but there are a few ladies' bars in tourist areas; these, and bars in tourist resorts, are about the only places where you'll find "Mexican" cocktails such as margaritas. Tequila and beer are most widely available in shops; the best place to try pulque is in the bars off Plaza Garibaldi in Mexico City.

COMMUNICATIONS

Mail to be collected at post offices should be addressed c/o *Lista de Correos*, the equivalent of General Delivery or *Poste Restante*. At the central post office in Mexico City letters received are listed on a clipboard that you can read through yourself, but you should still instruct your nearest and dearest to write your last name in capitals or to underline it. American Express offices will hold clients' mail and are more reliable than post offices, although the hours during which you can collect mail are often restricted. To use this service you must have either AmEx travellers cheques or an AmEx credit card; American Express can send you a list of their Mexican offices.

There are more high-tech ways of keeping in touch nowadays: faxes are common and some agencies will hold faxes for you. Some provide the same service for e-mail. Phoning home is also a lot simpler nowadays with the arrival of services such as USA Direct, BT Direct and so on, which put you straight through to an operator in your home country and bill your home number or the person you're calling. It's wise to enquire before departure, as there are many variables regarding the types of phones you can use, whether you have to deposit a coin or wait for a second tone and so on.

Telmex was privatised in 1990 and will lose its monopoly in 1997; already there are many private *casetas* or phone offices (those in bus stations are particularly pricey). On the streets, coin- and card-phones marked LADA (*Larga Distancia Automatica*) can be used for long-distance calls; they accept Mexican credit cards, but not as a rule foreign ones. The long-distance code is 91, or 92 for collect (reverse charge) calls; for Canada or the USA dial 95, or 96 collect; and for the rest of the world 98, or 99 collect.

Direct access numbers:

AT&T Access	95 800 462 4240
MCI	95 800 674 7000
Sprint	95 800 877 8000
Canada Direct	95 800 0101 990
BT Direct	*791

ECOTOURISM

In case you hadn't noticed, you are a consumer in the world's largest industry – tourism. In 1995 this accounted for 6% of world GNP (US$3,500bn, generated by 567m tourist journeys) and 127m jobs (7% of world employment), and is predicted to keep growing by 8.7% per year. This affects Mexico as much as anywhere: in 1929 just 20,000 tourists visited the country, from the late 1940s Acapulco became fashionable and tourism revenues tripled, and from 1969 the state began to develop megaresorts such as Cancún. In 1974 FONATUR (the National Fund for Tourism Development) was set up, and by 1989 had financed the building of 128,000 new rooms, and had an annual advertising budget of US$30m. In 1976 there were 3 million visitors a year, in 1986 4.5m, in 1990 5m, and in 1995 7m. Of these, 85% come from the USA and just 70,000 a year from Britain, although with the introduction of charter flights this is expected to double. In 1986 tourism generated 2.6% of GDP, and in 1995 6%, and 1.8m jobs. Cancún accounts for 30% of this turnover, but FONATUR is developing other megaresorts such as Zihuatenejo (Guerrero, northwest along the coast from Acapulco), Bahías de Huatulco (Oaxaca), and Los Cabos (Baja California).

Mass tourism has brought many problems, such as environmental, social and cultural degradation, unequal distribution of the profits and the spread of disease. Many tourists come, of course, to lie on beaches, but in addition there's this year's Unique Selling Proposition, "ecotourism", or more accurately nature tourism. This tends to involve groups visiting Mayan ruins, nature reserves and hot springs and taking rafting trips, while still travelling in air-conditioned buses and staying in hotels with satellite television, and is little more than a variant on tourism anywhere else. It brings money in to the local economy, and some of that may end up helping to protect wildlife and habitats. It also helps convince governments and tour companies of the value of the reserves.

Of course, the inescapable paradox of all tourism applies: if a rarely visited destination becomes popular, the crowds of visitors, and the infrastructure which mushrooms to serve them, diminish and then ruin the thing they've come to see. While recognising this, we make no apology for publicising isolated, little-known locations in this book. This is because all through the region attractions are being destroyed at a phenomenal rate, and not principally by tourism. Ruins are looted, wetlands drained, sprawling urban slums appear along pristine rivers, steep mountain slopes succumb to slash-and-burn farming and then erosion, and immense areas of lowland forest are converted to weedy cow pastures. The decision is not between keeping some place wonderful and unvisited, or diminishing its charm by encouraging ecotourism; it *is* between doing nothing as everything lovely is destroyed, or at least trying to save something through the ecotourism route. Time and again it's become apparent that simply declaring natural areas to be reserves is not enough; biosphere boundaries mean little to a man needing the money that selling a baby monkey can bring. But if the man's friends and neighbours tell him that those monkeys need to be left alone because gringos come to see them and leave hard cash in the community, then that's a powerful influence working on behalf of the monkey and the entire ecosystem, including the local human community.

This is relatively unproblematical (if you accept the waste of fossil fuel inherent in any kind of travel not powered by sails) as long as a few **basic**

rules are observed: leave no garbage (especially plastic and other non-biodegradable materials) in a reserve, buy no products of endangered species of plant or animal, including coral jewellery and woodware, keep nothing you catch from the sea (unless you plan to eat it), don't leave TVs, lights or showers on when not needed. In addition you can choose hotels (and ships) that don't dump their waste and that use solar heating, automatic light switches and recycled water for watering lawns and golf courses. Don't eat agouti, turtle or iguana (unless you know it's farmed), and suggest that the restaurant ceases to serve it and indeed advertises the fact that it *doesn't* serve it. Avoid over-crowded resorts and seasons, and choose operators that only take small groups, that support community projects, and that use local goods and staff.

So far, so good. However this is essentially inward-looking tourism, in which the vacationers are concerned purely with resting and having fun. True ecotourism is *not* just to make the tourist feel good, but should also be about education, consciousness-raising (for both the tourist and the local populace) and actually making a difference somehow. Basically, things get complicated once you're dealing not only with animals but with indigenous peoples too. They are not to know that ecotourism is their best hope for avoiding the destruction of their habitat and the survival of their traditional lifestyle – to them ecotourism is something that just arrived unasked, something that's happening *to* them. There is danger in an unhealthy economic dependency on tourism, which could collapse in response to many outside factors. "Ecotourists" also bring whisky and marijuana, and the injection of cash into a largely cash-free economy has led to resentment and quarrels. Western thought tends to separate man from his environment, that is, to focus on species preservation at the expense of indigenous peoples; it's more important to see both as part of the same ecosystem and equally entitled to respect and to a sustainable and secure future. Local participation is vital, not just in profits but also in planning and decision-making.

The Chiapas Tourism Department defines ecotourism well as "any activity which promotes the conscious relationship between man and nature without altering the state of the environment being visited, generating economic and cultural benefits for the population. What is an ecotourist? Any person who travels with the intention of establishing a direct contact with nature to enjoy it and learn about it, while promoting community development." This can be summed up in three key criteria: is it sustainable (environmentally, socially, economically)? Is it educational? Is it locally participatory and beneficial?

Do as much research as possible before departure, learn some Spanish, and allow yourself plenty of time and a flexible schedule (if you don't have much time, consider restricting the number of places you'll see). For hikers there are more specific requirements: keep quiet, stay on the trail (in single file) even if it's muddy, never take shortcuts, don't cut live trees, if possible don't make fires from dead wood either, and erase signs of fires afterwards. Camp and wash (with biodegradable soap) 50m from water, wear lightweight shoes in camp. Burn toilet paper, bury your waste, and remove all litter. Take something for park staff, even it's just a pack of biscuits or a newspaper from the city.

Ecotourism is still nascent in Mexico, but if you want an organised ecotour, contact AMTAVE, the Mexican Association of Adventure Tourism and Ecotourism, at Av Insurgentes Sur, 1971-251, Col. Guadalupe Inn, 01020 México DF (tel: 661 9121, 663 5381, fax: 662 7354, email 74174.2424@compuserve.com). The *Asociación Nacional de Guías en Ecoturismo y Turismo de Aventura* (National Association of Ecotourism and Adventure Tourism Guides) is based in the Mar de Cortéz tour agency at Nicolás Bravo and Marcelo Rubio, CP 23000, La Paz BCS (tel: 112 52277, fax: 58599); it's involved in training, but also operates the best land-based tours of Baja California. The best-established operators are probably Ecogrupos, at the same address as AMTAVE (tel: 1800 874 8784), and Trek Mexico (Havre 67, #605, Col. Juárez, CP 06600 Mexico DF (tel: 525 5213, fax: 525 5093, email 104164.30@compuserve.com).

ENVIRONMENTAL ISSUES

Most species become extinct because they lose their habitats and cease to breed rather than through being actively killed. Although all natural habitats are at risk, the rainforests of the tropics contain a far higher variety of species than any other habitat in the world. One aspect of this high biodiversity is that distinct species can develop in remarkably small areas, and thus can be rendered extinct very easily, often without ever having been identified. In Mexico these forests are still being lost at a dizzying rate, despite laws that protect them on paper. Officially 300,000ha are deforested per year, and just 25,000-100,000ha reforested, but actual **deforestation** is nearer 1.5m ha per year. Over half the Lacandón Jungle has been lost since 1980 to logging and cattle-grazing, despite much of it being officially protected. Up to 70% of Mexico's forest is theoretically under the control of *ejidos* or indigenous communities, but thanks to trade liberalisation most of them are making a loss. In any case the forests are being plundered by armed outsiders. Two-thirds of wood-cutting is in fact for fuelwood, an undeniable need of poor *campesinos* which has caused an ever-widening ring of devastation around most towns, where every tree has been either savaged or cut down. In Oaxaca state each family uses about 12 cubic metres of fuelwood per month, or about 12kg a day.

In addition to habitat and species loss, this deforestation produces many other problems, such as soil erosion and low water levels in streams flowing out of the forest; in Mexico 210,000ha is desertified each year. In fact

Mexico has quite a long history of environmental degradation; the Maya culture may have collapsed due to overpopulation and consequent soil exhaustion or deforestation and erosion. The Mezquital valley had been made desert by sheep (introduced by the Spaniards) by the end of the 16th century, and in the early years of the next century the cartographer Henrico Martinez warned of the danger of eroded soil filling lakes and causing floods. Alexander von Humboldt (in some ways the first ecotourist) gave a similar warning in the 19th century, and it's surprising that disaster did not in fact strike sooner.

In fact the most pressing problem Mexico now faces is that of chemical **pollution**; this is so serious that when BMW bought a factory in Toluca they found that the magnesium and aluminium in the soil were worth more than the factory itself. There is widespread chromium pollution, particularly in Guanajuato and other industrial areas near the capital. In Mexico City itself it's been found that 25% of vegetation is contaminated by heavy metals, and blood lead levels are four times those in Tokyo, with a quarter of babies being born with high enough levels to cause permanent brain damage. Pesticides worth US$2bn are imported each year from the USA, at least thirty types being banned in the USA itself; in Mexico they cause widespread illness and death among poor farmworkers with no protective gear.

The area that most concerns the US is of course the **border zone**, which is crucially important as a water source but is increasingly filthy, largely due to businesses from the USA setting up plants on the Mexican side specifically to exploit lax environmental standards and low wages. The *maquiladora* plants produce 20m tonnes of hazardous waste a year, of which only 1% is returned to the USA as required. In fact an estimated 8m tonnes a year of toxic waste is illegally imported from the USA and dumped. In 1983 the USA and Mexico signed the Treaty on Cooperation for the Protection and Improvement of the Environment in the Frontier Zone (a strip of 100km on either side of the border) and part of President Clinton's package to persuade Congress to accept NAFTA was the US$368m Border Environment Project. Some efforts are being made, but even so waste emissions into the Río Bravo del Norte (known in the US as the Río Grande) from US-owned companies in Matamoros are 100,000 times US limits, there's said to be a 50% risk of an explosion in the Río Bravo at Piedras Negras due to Pemex oil leaks, and 100m gallons of raw sewage a day goes into the Río Bravo. At the western end of the frontier, the Río Tijuana carries 12m gallons a day of raw sewage, and the New River, which flows from Mexicali into California, is polluted by PCBs and 28 viruses (including typhoid, cholera, hepatitis, meningitis, dysentery, and polio). Fortunately the treaties cut both ways, so the Mexican Ecological Movement can protest against a proposed nuclear waste dump just 32km over the border. In addition a Commission for Environmental Cooperation in North America was set up under the NAFTA treaty, with jurisdiction over the whole of the signatory states, and is now investigating pollution in Guanajuato that killed 40,000 birds in December 1994.

Mexico City has the unenviable reputation of being the world's most polluted city, due to a thermal inversion that traps air in the city basin in winter, and the fact that it's home to 22% of Mexico's population, 45% of its industry and to at least 3 million cars, 200,000 buses and 35,000 taxis. Air pollution was within acceptable limits on just 31 days in 1993, and 20 days in 1994, and ozone levels are hazardous on 80% of days. However, as in many other places worldwide, it seems clear that the city's most serious environmental problem is its water supply. As its population has exploded, the water table has dropped by 32m, and the city itself has subsided by 7m since 1940; some parts are still sinking by 40cm/year. The city currently uses 63.5m^3/second, 80% of it groundwater (double the natural recharge rate), and this is expected to be 100m^3/second by 2000. Already consumption is double Swiss, Japanese or German rates, even though 14m people have no running water; this is because a third of the water supply is lost in leaks due to the subsidence – a circular problem (but little worse than in Yorkshire). The other 20% of the city's water comes, at great cost, from the Lerma and Cutzamala rivers, 100km to the west and 1000m below. 350,000 toilet cisterns have been replaced by smaller models, saving enough water for 250,000 people, but much more needs to be done. As for waste water, in 1900 the *Gran Canal del Desagua* or Great Sewage Canal was driven through the hills to the north, but as the city sank gravity ceased to do the job and eleven pumping stations had to be built. Now the *Sistema de Drenaje Profundo* (Deep Drainage System) is being built, with 120km in use and another 30km needed by the end of the century.

The city's *hoy no circula* (no driving today) rule, by which cars are banned (according to the last digit of their number plate) from driving on one day a week, is well known; this does apply to foreigners, but not to taxis, and in winter it may be extended to two or even three days a week. By the end of 1997 all filling stations in Mexico City will have new nozzles to prevent carcinogenic gases from being released, at an extra charge of one centavo per litre. Emissions testing is also being introduced.

Nuclear issues are not of great concern here: the Mexican Alfonso García Robles won the Nobel Peace Prize as the driving force behind the Treaty of Tlatelolco, which declared Latin America a nuclear weapons-free zone in the 1950s. There is one nuclear power station (at Laguna Verde, Veracruz), which environmental groups would like to see closed. Mexico was affected by Chernobyl, due to contaminated milk (between 42t and 50,000t, depending on whom you believe) bought from Ireland.

The first protected area was the island of Guadalupe, off Baja California, established in 1928, followed by the first National Parks in the 1930s. By 1996 there were 78 National Parks, National Marine Parks, Biosphere

Reserves, and Special Biosphere Reserves, and 2.5% of the national area was theoretically protected: but in fact only 0.8% was effectively protected, due to lack of cash and of political will. There is superficial public knowledge and approval of environmentalism: taxis are painted green with the sign *EcoTaxi*, litter-bins are marked *Deposito Ecologico* (perhaps a pun on the more common *Deposito CocaCola*), and there's a series of postage stamps showing twenty endangered species. There are two "green" political parties, the PVEM and PEM, the masked wrestler Super-Barrío Gómez campaigns on ecological issues, and the government has created the Federal Attorney-General's Office for the Environment (Profepa), which is working to stamp out the trade in protected species, with inspection booths at the infamous Sonora market in Mexico City and at all 98 border crossings – a belated conversion, as Mexico only signed the CITES convention in 1991, but better late than never. Beach-cleaning projects are popular, and not just where there are many *gringos* in residence. Population restraint is a key area of the government's 1995-2000 plan, with more sex education needed to boost contraceptive use and reduce population growth to 1.4% by 2005.

These are hopeful signs, but the scale of Mexico's environmental problems are immense. Don't let this put you off visiting, however.

ENVIRONMENTAL ORGANISATIONS

Border Ecology Project, PO Drawer CP, Bisbee, AZ 85603, USA.
Consejo Nacional de la Fauna, Apdo 41-631, 11001 México DF (tel: 540 7390/1).
Conservation International, 1015 18th St NW, Suite #1000, Washington, DC 20036 USA (tel: 202 429 5660).
Fondo Mexicano para la Conservación de la Naturaleza AC, Poseidón 18, Col. Crédito Constructor, 03940 México DF (tel: 661 9217/661 5591, fax: 662 2661).
Friends of Mexican Development Foundation, 165 East 72nd St, Suite #1B, New York, NY 10021, USA.
Instituto Nacional de Ecologia, Av Revolución 1425, México DF (http://www.uam.mx/INE).
Naturalia, Apdo Postal 21-541, 04021 México DF (tel: 674 6678, fax: 674 5294).
Pronatura (*Asociación Mexicano por la Conservación de la Naturaleza*), Av Nuevo León 144, Col. Hipódromo Condesa, México DF (tel: 286 9642).
Friends of Pronatura, 240 East Limberlost Drive, Tucson, AZ 85705, USA (tel: 602 887 1188).
Wildlife Conservation Society, 4424 NW 13th St, Suite #A2, Gainesville, FL 32609, USA (tel: 352 371 1713, fax: 373 6443, wcsfl@afn.org).

HIKING

There's a huge variety of landscapes and habitats in Mexico, although if you want to experience them all you'll spend a great deal of time travelling. In the south the remaining tropical forests are now largely protected, to a greater or lesser extent, and the volcanoes are all national parks too, and thus recognised as hiking territory; in the north, however, you can find worthwhile hiking almost anywhere. Mexico has a dense network of microwave stations, marked on many maps and signposted on the roads, and if you want a simple walk through thorny vegetation to a viewpoint, then the solution may be to walk up the dirt road to the nearest microwave tower. Access to *ejidal* (communal) lands is almost never a problem, although it's polite to ask anyone you come across in the fields if you can use the path (a useful way of checking you're going the right way, and of learning about country life).

However, certain areas are heavily into marijuana growing (and worse), and people may take a very dim view of intrusions, so if you receive warnings or just get bad vibes, it's best to steer clear or at least stick to the main dirt roads. This applies above all to the Sierra Madre Occidental from Michoacán to Sinaloa states, although there are also plenty of rumours in the Copper Canyon area. Camping wild can be risky if lots of people have seen you passing and it's obvious where you're going – a Maya ruin, or the only water source for miles around. However it's not hard to be discreet and camp where you'll not be found.

National Parks have existed since the 1930s, but most of them are less than exciting; in particular, many of those around Mexico City now have *no* natural vegetation left, being planted with eucalyptus and casuarina; they serve a useful role as places for families to have a day out, but in ecological terms their value is low. The more important sites are protected as Biosphere Reserves or Special Biosphere Reserves, and these are far more interesting. This book describes most of these, at least in outline, but the hikes described should in most cases be seen as starting-points for your own explorations rather than definitive itineraries.

Hiking in the rainy season
By Rob Rachowiecki

Many people have vacations during the northern summer and so are obliged to hike during the wet season. Don't worry! The rains are highly variable and usually only amount to heavy but isolated showers or storms in mid-afternoon. The northern deserts and Baja California receive hardly any rain at all, but the south can be very sticky with humidity. Chiapas and Veracruz are the wettest areas, but even here you can still enjoy hiking in this season. Your senses are heightened, everything is green and you can almost see things growing, and huge storm clouds make for spectacular sunsets and sunrises which you can almost touch and smell.

Set out early, and aim to finish by mid-afternoon. You won't want to tramp through humid mountain forests sweating profusely in waterproof clothing, but there are several solutions. You can use breathable rain gear (Gore-Tex remains the leader) which allows most of your perspiration to escape. You can wear your rain gear over underwear, or swimsuit, while your clothes stay nice and dry in a bag inside your pack. You can wear a rain poncho which is loose-fitting enough for you not to perspire greatly. If you're sure you won't be exposed to high winds and cold temperatures, you could dispense with rain gear and have one set of "wet" clothes and one of "dry" clothes. Remember that wool keeps its warmth even when wet, but cotton doesn't. The same distinction applies between down (useless when wet) and synthetics such as Polartec or dacron (warm when wet). The best clothing for cold, wet weather is artificial pile or fleece, which is ideal for the volcanoes, where you can be hit by rain or hail storms at any season. Bring a wool or fleece hat and if you get chilly, wear it (70% of heat loss is from the head, although this includes the breath). Finally, if you don't want to be scrambling in and out of rain gear every time it showers, bring a collapsible umbrella! The combination of an umbrella over your upper body and waterproof trousers over your lower body works well in all but the most severe rain.

In the heat of the tropics, wet clothes mildew very fast, so at the end of a hike, wash and dry your clothes thoroughly. Your tent must be completely waterproof. Some new tents are sold without sealed seams, so you may have to buy some sealant (from any good camping store) and do it yourself, or else it'll leak like a sieve. The same applies to raingear. Allow plenty of time for this before leaving on your trip.

In damp weather using a stove is far preferable to trying to light a fire, but if you must have a fire, bring fire-starting ribbon, which is available in toothpaste-style tubes. Remember those waterproof matches, or keep ordinary ones safe in a film canister.

Insects can be a problem during the wet season, so bring plenty of repellent and apply frequently and thoroughly.

Finding your way

Topographical maps are produced by INEGI, the *Instituto Nacional de Estadistica, Geografia y Informatica* or National Institute of Statistics, Geography and Computing. They're all pretty old, and therefore don't show many roads; nor are they highly accurate: for instance, the 1:250,000 map of Colima doesn't show any road at all into the sizeable town of Tuxpan, and shows the main road from Cuidad Guzmán to Colima as dirt, and the dirt road via El Fresnito as asphalt. These maps don't show national parks, reserves or tourist sights, so you have to work out their location for yourself. You'll also find that it's impossible to settle on a definitive altitude for any peak. Sectur produces a highways map for the whole of Mexico, which, surprisingly, does show many national parks and reserves. International Travel Maps (345 West Broadway, Vancouver BC, V5Y 1P8, Canada; available through Bradt in the UK) produce a fine map of the country at 1:3,300,000, which shows most archeological sites, caves and other tourist sights; their 1;1,000,000 maps of Baja California and the Yucatán are even better. They also have a very useful map of the South Coast, which includes Mexico City, Puebla and Veracruz.

INEGI has an office in every state capital, which as a rule have a reasonable stock of maps of that state, but not of other states; even so you may end up with a photocopy or a geological map, or a map at 1:250,000 scale instead of 1:50,000. Its HQ is in Aguascalientes (Av Héroes de Nacozari 2301 Sur, Fracc. Jardines del Parque, 20270 Aguascalientes; tel: 49 181 948/800 49042, fax: 49 180 739), and in the capital its main shop is at Av Baja California 272 (at Culiacán), Col. Hipódromo Condesa, 06100 México DF (tel: 722 5500), with others at the airport (shop 61; tel: 786 0212), below the roundabout at the Insurgentes metro station, at Francisco Sosa 383 (at Salvador Novo) in Coyoacán (tel: 658 4814), and at Patriotismo 711 (Tower A ground floor), Col. San Juan Mixcoac (tel: 598 8935, 563 9935, fax: 563 9935). If you want to look but not buy (maps cost N$20, currently US$3) try the Patriotismo shop or specified libraries such as the *Biblioteca del Congreso de la Union* (Tacuba 29), the *Biblioteca del Palacio Legislativo* (Av Congreso de la Union, edificio B, 3rd floor) or the *Biblioteca Daniel Cosio Villegas del Colegio de México* (Carretera al Ajusco 20). INEGI has a website (http://www.inegi.gob.mx), but this is unlikely ever to carry actual maps.

Limited information on National Parks and Biosphere Reserves can be had from SEDESOL, the Ministry of Social Development (formerly SEDUE, the Ministry of Urban Development and Ecology), which has just moved from Calle Río Elba 20 to Av Revolución 1425 (south of Barranca del Muerto metro). In the same building you'll find the National Institute of Ecology (INE), for more general information on conservation. Their publications can be obtained from the Libreria Bonilla, near their new offices at Francia 17, col. Florida. A guide to the National Parks (3/e 1995, N$20, in Spanish) is published by *Ediciones Jilguero* (Monte Pelvoux 110, planta jardín, Lomas de Chapultepec, 11000 México DF; tel: 202 6585, fax: 540 1771; or PO Box 371 656, San Diego CA 92137, USA), who also publish *México Desconicido*, an ecotouristic magazine. *Ecosistema 2001* (published by *Editorial Bios 2000 SA*, Eje Lázaro Cárdenas 13-602, Col. Centro, Deleg. Cuauhtémoc, 06050 México DF; tel: & fax: 512 2130) is a magazine concerned with ecology rather than tourism.

Incidentally, where I give compass bearings, these are uncorrected for magnetic variation, ie as they appear on the compass rather than as they should be on the map. The left bank of a stream is to the left as the water flows, ie to your right as you head upstream.

ACTIVITIES

Caving

About 35% of Mexico's area is composed of limestone, with the entire Yucatán peninsula and much of the Sierra Madre Oriental being karst, so it's not surprising that there's a great variety of caves in the country. Some are weird and beautiful tourist caves, while others are difficult and dangerous systems that still have huge potential for exploration. The latter include the world's eighth and ninth deepest cave systems, the Sistema Huautla (1,353m), and the Sistema Cuicateca (1,242m), both in Oaxaca; the twelfth longest is the Sistema Purificación, in Tamaulipas, at 71,583m.

The bell-shaped Sótano de las Golondrinas (the Swallows' Basement) is the world's largest freefall cave, with an entry 60m in diameter and a vertical drop of 310m to the base, 300m in diameter. This is in the southeastern corner of San Luís Potosí state, 7km southwest of the village of Aquismon (between Ciudad Valles and Xilitla). Other caves in this group, known as the Galerías de la Huasteca, include the Sótano del Cepillo (similar but with a mere 100m drop, and a lake at the bottom), and the Sótano (or Hoya) de Guaguas (with 150m of freefall, then a sloping passage 80m across to one of the world's largest chambers, 250m high, with natural lighting). Also in San Luís Potosí are the Sótano de Tlamaya (454m deep), and the Sótano Huetzmolotitla (245m).

Perhaps the most exciting caves for the "average ecotourist" are at Cacahuamilpa, 8km north of Michapa (Guerrero), which is 30km west of Amacuzac, just off the *autopista* from Cuernavaca to Acapulco; buses leave Cuernavaca every 20 minutes for Cacahuamilpa. The entrance (21m high and 45m across) is at 1,105m in the Limotilán valley, on the southeastern side of Cerro de la Corona; it's open from 10.00 to 17.00, for guided tours covering 2km (of an estimated 16km). You can also take some steps down to the twin opening through which the underground rivers Chontalcoatlán and San Jerónimo emerge to form the Amacuzac, which flows into the Río Balsas. Companies such as Trek Mexico operate trips with rafts and "floating backpacks" on both rivers, camping underground from February to May.

As part of the government's privatisation plans, the caves were to have been granted as a concession to a Canadian businessman; this was cancelled after a row over his dubious record, but doubtless someone else will soon be found to take over.

Also in Guerrero is the Juxtlahuaca cave, perhaps the most beautiful in Mexico; you need to turn east off the Acapulco highway just south of Chilpancingo to the village of Colotlipa. There are large chambers with an underground lake and transparent stalagtites and stalagmites, and Olmec paintings between 1,500 and 3,000 years old. Nearby are the Oxtotitlán caves, northwest of Chilpancingo off the highway to Chilapa.

In Yucatán, the best-known tourist caves are probably at Balankanché, by the highway just 4km east of Chichén Itzá, with hourly tours. The Loltún caves are near the Labná ruins, just a few kilometres south of Oxkutzcab; they also have fine formations and Maya paintings and carvings, and extend for at least 7km. The caves are closed on Mondays, and can be reached with a pickup from Calle 51, near the market in Oxkutzcab. Near Labná, but just over the state line in Campeche, at km180 on the Mérida-Hopelchén road (3km south of Bolonchén de Rejón) is the cave of Xtacumbilxunan (or Ixtacumbil), one of the largest systems in the Yucatán peninsula. Here there are seven cenotes, 150m deep, with blind fish living in them. There are plenty of other caves which are not open to tourists, such as Waybil Actún ("the bewitched cave of Yucatán"), which has maybe the most beautiful concretions in Mexico, and Actún Cot, and flooded caves such as Nohoch Na Chich and Naranjal.

On the highway from Tehuacán to Oaxaca, the Coxcatlán, San Marcos and El Riego caves are of archeological interest, containing the bones of animals extinct since the Wisconsin glaciation, such as *Ursus americanus* (the cave bear), *Canus dirus, Camelops hesternus* (related to the llama) and *Eremotherium rusconi* (the giant land sloth), and an archaeological sequence from 5000BC to 1500AD, including seven generations of maize and its predecessors.

Up north, the most famous tourist caves are the Grutas de García, in Nuevo León.

Climbing

You probably know the old story about Mexico resembling a piece of crumpled paper because it's so mountainous; what's more, it also has lots of canyons (*cañón* is the Spanish word), which offer a huge range of possibilities for climbing. One of the best-known areas is the El Chico National Park, in the Sierra de Pachuco (Hidalgo state), where the fir forests are punctuated by lots of weirdly eroded rocks such as Las Monjas (The Nuns), La Muela (The Molar), El Conejo (The Rabbit), and Las Goteras (The Leaks). In Querétaro state the Peñas Cargadas are 110m "candles", and Peña Bernal is a 300m sugar loaf, said to offer the best rockclimbing in Mexico.

The best mountain climbing in Mexico (for intermediate climbers) is on Popo' and Ixta', notably El Abanico on Ventorillo. There's also ice climbing here in winter, particularly in the Cañada de Nexpayantla, from 2,670m to 4,500m above San Pedro Nexapa.

The *Club de Exploraciones de México AC* or CEMAC (Apdo 10134, México DF; tel: 578 5730), founded in 1922 on the summit of Volcán Ajusco, is based on the Sierra Club and meets most evenings at Juan de Mateos 146, Col Obrero (northwest of Chabacano metro); it has chapters in ten other cities. The *Club Alpino de México* (tel: 574 9683) is at Córdoba 234, Col Roma (metro: Hospital General) and has social meetings on Fridays at 19.00. During the day you can call at the *Aguayo Deportes* sports shop around the corner at Coahuila 40 (same phone number), where you can buy or hire equipment including iceaxes and crampons. They are involved in mountain rescue (tel: 581 6402) and also in clean-ups on Popo' and so on.

Cycling

Cycling is renascent in Mexico City, thanks to traffic congestion; bikes are adapted to deliver ice, cola, newspapers and even people. Pollution is of course a problem and it's reckoned best to cycle at about 10.00, after the morning rush but before the day gets too warm.

The capital has a *velódromo* (by the metro station of the same name), where in 1984 Francesco Moser set the world one-hour record that stood until 1993, and there's a very good 11km cyclepath from Cancún town to about halfway through the Hotel Zone. Otherwise, apart from some half-built cycle lanes to the university in La Paz (BCS), I've seen no cycle facilities in Mexico. Nevertheless, many highways have good shoulders, and you even can cycle on the new *autopistas*, although you'll need to take plenty of water. There are plenty of thorns on the roads, so heavy duty tyres are a good idea. Boxed bikes can be carried on buses and planes.

Trek-Mex (tel: 1800 335 6776 (USA), 415 25011, fax: 25505) run day-trips, with sag waggon, from US$20.

Boating

Given the ambient temperatures, much of Mexico is a paradise for boating. The Gulf of California has the most beautifully fresh, clear, warm water, and is ideal for sea kayaking; outfitters include *Baja Expeditions*, several companies in California, and *Discover the World* (29 Nork Way, Banstead, Surrey SM7 1PB, UK; tel: 01737 218 800, fax: 362 341). Open-cockpit kayaks are more stable and easier for beginners to handle, but chillier in the wind than closed models. You'll need a boat permit only if fishing. The Gulf Coast is rather less attractive, but it's fun to read Don Starkell's "Paddle to the Amazon" (Prima, Rocklin CA, 1989), about a marathon trip along this coast.

Rafting is catching on fast: many operators are active in the Xalapa area of Veracruz. One of the best in the capital is *Trek Mexico*, which operates in Veracruz and also on the Río Amacuzac, near Taxco (Guerrero); this is a daytrip, only possible from June to October. It starts at the Cacahuamilpa cave (see above) and runs down through impressive canyons and Class III rapids to Huajintlán.

By kayak you can make your way down the Río Santa María, which passes just north of Xilitla in a region known as the Huasteca Potosina. Starting from a bridge on the Jalpan-Río Verde highway, just south of the village of Concá, it takes up to five days to pass through four canyons to Puente de Dios or Tanchanchín, southwest of Ciudad Valles (SLP). The first canyon is Class IV, dropping at 3.2m/km; the others are Class IV+

with quite a few portages, and are not navigable at all in the rainy season. You can also see the 100m Tamul waterfall where the Río Gallinas joins the Santa María.

Wind surfing is also popular in Baja, especially the eastern Cape. Equipment can be rented in most resorts, but the best place is the Baja Vela Centre (tel: 800 223 5443) at Las Barrillas, where the wind can reach 30 knots at any time of year.

ON GETTING LOST
By Hilary Bradt
It looked like a perfectly simple bit of bushwhacking; our trail had suddenly ended and the pine forests dropped away sharply. On the other side of the valley we saw patches of cultivation indicating a village nearby, and decided to descend through the trees, expecting to find a road or trail on the valley floor. What we hadn't taken into consideration was the effect of altitude on vegetation. After about 300 metres our nice pines became a subtropical rainforest and our nightmare began. Everything was damp, furry-green and rotten. The ground gave way beneath our feet, branches we grabbed for support turned out to prick or sting. It was also incredibly steep. Our descent was faster than we'd intended, with plants or branches that we grabbed to break our slide simply accompanying us down. "Be careful, that's a long drop!" called George helpfully as I glissaded past him hugging a loose tree. "I'm not doing this on purpose!" I said through my teeth, landing with a thump on my backpack.

The lower we dropped the denser the vegetation became, until we finally reached the bottom. Relief? No, it was a river. The patches of cultivation that had tempted us down from the top were no longer in sight. All we could see was trees, trees, and more trees. And the river, which we decided to follow downstream.

We made our way down the river for several hours before camping for the night. The next morning George persuaded me that we must climb up the almost vertical canyon side since he was pretty sure he had located those cultivated milpas. We climbed. It was a repeat of the previous day, except that this time we were sliding backwards. We had to grab any handhold available, relying on luck and balance when there wasn't one. As we got higher the vegetation turned into dense scrubby thorn bushes through which we had to force our way. Just as I'd reached the conclusion that death was preferable, we entered a clearing. A milpa! An old one, but a definite sign of civilisation. We soon found a weak trail, then an abandoned house, and finally an inhabited house with a clear trail leading up over the mountain.

Our ordeal had come to an end; it had lasted for about eight hours, which was quite long enough. Looking back on the experience we realised how stupid we'd been to make the initial decision to bushwhack. When you think of the basic rules of jungle hiking, like never putting your hands or feet in places you can't see, or not taking undue risks in remote areas, we were extremely lucky. Had we been bitten by a snake, or fallen and injured ourselves, the chances of survival would have been slim.

We hope our readers will profit from our experience. It takes more courage to turn back than to continue on, blindly.

Part Two

HIKING GUIDE

MEXICO CITY

Chapter Six

Mexico City

It's a bit of a myth that Mexicans don't know what you mean by Mexico City; certainly they are in the habit of simply calling it "México" or "el DF" (pronounced "el Day-Ef-ay"), and newspapers may refer to it as "la capital azteca", but it is increasingly common to call it "la ciudad de México". In English it's generally known as Mexico City, without the accent, and for simplicity's sake this is the form I use. Its citizens, incidentally, are known as *chilangos*.

Mexico City was founded in 1325 when the wandering Aztec tribes arrived from the north and founded the city they called Tenochtitlán ("Place of the Cactus"); the story is told of a pilgrimage until they found a golden eagle perched on a cactus eating a snake (now depicted on the state seal), but it was probably more of a barbarian invasion. The city was built on Lake Xochimolco, and as the Aztecs mastered the art of farming on "floating gardens" (see below) the city grew until it had a population of 300,000 by the time the Spaniards arrived in 1520. The lakes were drained from 1789, when a canal was dug through the Guadalupe hills to the north, and the canals were covered and replaced by sewers by 1794 (although they can still be traced, for instance beside the Supreme Court). Now 99% of the lakes and 75% of the forest that used to fill the Valley of Mexico have disappeared. Lake Texcoco, which once covered 14,500ha, finally vanished in the 1970s after the completion of the Deep Drainage System, leaving a lunar landscape which is too salty to be of use: three-quarters of it have now been planted with the salt-resistant *pasto salado* (*Distichlis spicata*), to combat erosion. On a more positive note, many bones of mammoths (*Mammuthus imperator*) have been found in the lakebeds.

The city has of course expanded over the lakebeds, and it is now one of the world's largest cities (and one of its most polluted: see p.72 for more on this). Immigration to the city peaked in the late 1980s (those leaving the land now tend to head for the *maquiladora* plants of the north), but it's still growing by 300,000 pa (a rate of 1.85%). The population density is double that of New York, and four times that of London. Although this may surprise many visitors, Mexico City has a reputation for innovative and imaginative urban planning. Certainly traffic congestion is not as bad as one might expect, and there is a very efficient Metro which is steadily being expanded; it currently carries 5.3m passengers per day, and line B, now under construction, is specifically intended to cut contaminant emissions by 50 tonnes a day. The 1985 earthquake, and the city's US$3bn debt, produced political repercussions too, and in the 1988 elections the PRI lost in the capital. However, mayor Manuel Camacho Solis (who has now defected to become one of the leading critics of the PRI) acted decisively, closing the March 18 refinery in the north of the city, and in 1989 banning cars from driving on at least one day a week; this reduced traffic by 500,000 vehicles a day at first, but as the economy recovered the middle classes simply bought second cars to get around the ban, and fuel consumption in fact rose by 30% between 1988 and 1991. By 1991 3,500 buses had been replaced or refurbished, and all pre-1985 taxis had been taken off the road; in 1992 emissions testing was introduced. In 1996, after wide consultation, the government released a further plan to tackle pollution, but Greenpeace-Mexico and the Mexican Environmental Movement claim their ideas have been ignored. The mayor is to be directly elected, and anything between 15m and 119m trees are to be planted.

It does seem amazing that as recently as 1957 Carlos Fuentes could entitle his first novel, set in Mexico City, "Where the Air is Clear"; in those days the volcanoes Popocatépetl and Ixtaccíhuatl were clearly visible to the south; this was the case again after the 1985 earthquake, when almost every vehicle and factory in the capital came to a halt, but otherwise they are always hidden by a pall of smog. This is worst between December and May; the lack of oxygen at 2,240m (23% less than at sea level) combines with the pollution to make unacclimatised visitors feel rotten, so it's wise to spend time at altitude before arriving in the city, if possible. The lack of oxygen also makes cars work less efficiently, of course.

Despite everything, it's well worth spending time in what is a very attractive and lively city; there are beautiful colonial buildings throughout the centre and in the southern suburb of Coyoacán, and great museums.

There are quite a few so-called **national parks** and ecological areas within the Federal District, which are of importance for recreation rather than ecology; some are in fact wholly planted with alien eucalyptus and casuarina.

The best-known park in the city is the **Bosque de Chapultepec**, which may have 100,000 visitors of a sunny Sunday; not surprisingly it is little more than battered grass and ornamental trees. However, its lakes are of interest, hiding an endemic fish, the *sardinita* (*Girardinichthys viviparus*) as well as axolotls (*Ambystoma mexicanum*) and other rare creatures. The eastern part of the park is the oldest, containing the superb National Anthropology Museum, zoo, "castle" and other museums; the second section or *Nuevo Bosque* lies to the southwest, beyond the *periférico* (Blvd Adolfo Lopéz Mateos) and railway, and is somewhat wilder. This contains the Museums of Natural History and Technology, which are well worth a visit. Further on down Av Constituyentes, beyond a cemetery, is the third and most recent section, known as the *Parque Nacional Molino de Belem*, which is little visited.

Also very crowded, especially at weekends, but probably more rewarding to the visitor, is **Lake Xochimilco** ("Place of Flowers") on the *periférico* to the south of the city (take the metro to Tasqueña and then the tram), which has been badly affected by water extraction and pollution, especially by phosphates. However it is famous as the site of the last remaining "floating gardens" or *chinampas*, great mats of reeds and branches piled with earth and long since anchored to the bottom by the roots of the plants grown on them. This system of farming in fact dates back to c500AD, long before the Aztecs arrived. In 1987 Xochimilco was declared a World Heritage Site and in 1993 it became an Ecological Park as part of a US$250m project to rescue the area; this also includes an award-winning water supply system, to prevent further pollution, and the planting of one million trees and shrubs. In contrast to the bad times of the 1970s and 1980s, when only 3,000-4,000 people a year visited, there are now 500,000 to 800,000 visitors a year, and boat trips in particular are very big business. If you visit midweek and tackle your boatman tactfully, you should be able to persuade him to show you *las chinampas veraderas*, along the 200km of canals that still exist behind the main tourist channels. There used to be very many axolotls in the lakes of the Valley of Mexico, a major source of food over the centuries; even now population levels here are still c300/ha.

Four parks in the immediate vicinity of Mexico City may be worth a visit. **Volcán Ajusco** (3,926m) is the most obvious of the peaks south of the city, and it offers good views over the Federal District and the big volcanoes. It's been a national park since 1938, covering 920ha of pine, fir, cypress and grassland, and other glaciated crags such as Santo Tomás (3,710m) and Pico del Aguila (3,880m). Wildlife includes volcano rabbits, squirrels, raccoons, coyotes, foxes, bats and raptors. Below the national park, the Coactetlán Ecological Zone of Controlled Development is being reforested with Mexican conifers such as *Cupressus lindleyi* and *Pinus montezumae*; there are plans for a larger Ajusco Metropolitan Park. Buses run from the Aztec Stadium on Calzada Tlalpan to the village of San Miguel Ajusco, 10km east of the park.

The **Desierto de los Leones** lies to the southwest off the main route to Toluca; "desert" was the name given by the Carmelites to their monasteries, and here you can visit a monastery built in 1602-11 and abandoned in 1780. It's damp and spooky, and there are tunnels and hermits' cells nearby. It's set in a beautiful forest, largely of timberline pine (*Pinus hartwegii*), which is suffering (as in Ajusco) from ozone and photochemical pollution. The park is a very popular escape from the city, and Mexico's superb marathon runners train here too. You can get here by taking a La Venta bus from the Observatorio metro station, or drive via Highway 15 to km25 (the La Venta toll booths) and then south for 5km. Immediately to the west, but in Mexico state, is the Insurgente Miguel Hidalgo National Park, famous more as a battle site, but also an attractive pine-fir forest (used for motocross events); it's reached via the La Marquesa junction of the Mexico-Toluca *autopista*.

To the northeast, just beyond Texcoco on the road to San Miguel Tlaxpan, is the **Molino de Flores National Park**; this is only 55ha, and partly planted with eucalyptus, casuarina, and other trees, but the 17th century mill is very beautiful, in a lovely setting by the Coxcacuacos river.

You may well visit the **Guadalupe Basilica**, in the northern suburbs, which is the country's leading shrine. Since 1937 the hill has been protected by the El Tepeyac National Park; again it's largely planted with introduced tree species, but you can see 70 species of birds (including the Montezuma quail, white-necked nighthawk, common screech-owl and greater roadrunner) and there's an attractive colonial aqueduct too.

The National University, **UNAM**, is often visited by tourists interested in the Mexican muralists and modern architecture: the core (by the Rectorate and library) is still impressive, but much of the rest now seems what it is – a 1950s project built in a hurry. The science area in particular is a badly-signed maze of arbitrary fences, and there are many other Third-World touches, such as padlocked fire-escapes and a total lack of facilities for the disabled or cycles. Still, it's the only university in the country with a really solid research base (see the huge range of books and journals in the *Fomento Editorial* shop by the museum) and you may find its libraries useful. The *Universidad* station is convenient for the Science area (including Geography), but otherwise you should use *Copilco* (from where it's 10 minutes walk to the campus, 15-20 to the library), or a bus on Insurgentes Sur, if you have time; taking the metro from Hidalgo and walking to the library should only take 40 minutes in all.

To the south of the Ciudad Universitaria and the Olympic stadium lie the *jardín botánico exterior* (with a fine collection of cacti) and the **Reserva Ecologica de Pedregal**, to the east of the exclusive suburb of Jardines del Pedregal. This is an area of lava fields deposited by the eruption 2,300 years ago of Volcán Xitle, now largely built on; the UNAM reserve covers just 124ha (1.24km²). However there are 58 species of birds to be seen here, including 21 *Emberizidae* (buntings), and 136 in the Pedregal area as a whole. To the south of here is Cerro Zacatépetl, and beyond that, across the *periférico*, is the Pedregal National Park.

EL CRUCERO
CHAMULA
Y CRUZCHEN
TENEJAPA
CHIS.
22.5.94

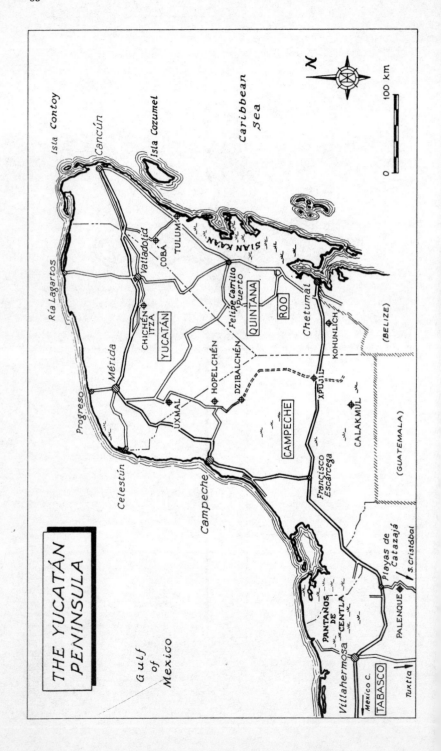

THE YUCATÁN PENINSULA

Chapter Seven

The Yucatán Peninsula

The Yucatán is special because of its ancient Maya ruins; Chichén Itzá, Uxmal and Tulum are the most famous, but throughout the peninsula there are literally thousands of other ruins that are seldom or never visited. The Yucatán's main roads are like tourist pipelines: at peak season it's just mind-boggling to see the numbers of tourists flooding along the Mérida-Chichén Itzá-Cancún-Tulum routes. It's hard to draw the boundary between Maya tourism and ecotourism; if you do it right (avoiding over-visited sites and putting your money into the local economy) it's ecotourism, but if you travel in a bus laid on by a multi-national tourism company it certainly isn't. The famous ruins are well worth seeing, but there's plenty of back-country Yucatán available for calm nature- and archaeology-oriented exploration. If you can nudge yourself off the main tourist routes, the Yucatán's small towns and countryside are as pleasant as any in Mexico.

Biological orientation

The Yucatán peninsula is one huge slab of limestone, mostly laid down in the Tertiary, although its northern edge is from the Quaternary, our present period. Its most characteristic feature is the *cenote*, a sort of sinkhole which is the most widespread source of surface water in the Yucatán; you'll find virtually no rivers or streams here, and the northwestern corner of the peninsula is virtual desert. The northeastern corner, north of Cancún, is wetter (up to 2m rain per year) due to the meeting of two wind systems.

Off the northern coast of the Yucatán is a 200km-diameter crater, left by the largest meteorite to hit the earth, which caused the second mass extinction, when 75% of all species (half of all animals) were wiped out by catastrophic climatic shifts. These included the dinosaurs, allowing the rise of mammals and birds. In the same area, in an anticline formed in the Cretaceous period (which ended with the meteorite strike, about 65m years ago), is the Cantarell complex, which contains 20,000m barrels of oil and is likely to be Mexico's most important oil field in the future.

Medium sub-evergreen forest covers two-thirds of the peninsula, with a strip of deciduous forest across it at the level of Chichén Itzá and Cancún, and thorn forest along the coast to the north of this. Most of this is fairly drab to the layman, but the wetter areas to the south do shelter interesting species such as felines, tapir, both types of peccary and the ocellated turkey *Agriocharis ocellata*. Armadillos, rabbits, ringtails, raccoons and skunks are found throughout the Yucatán.

QUINTANA ROO

Cancún

You're likely to fly in to **Cancún**: almost two million tourists do so each year. Though the resort does provide jobs for local people, it's estimated that 70-90% of profits leave the area. Cancún is not exactly what we have in mind when we speak of ecotourism and its sustainable, non-destructive philosophy. Nevertheless, there is a good bus service through the *Zona Hotelera*, as well as the only real cycle-track I've seen in Mexico, both leading to the "old" town, which remains a real Mexican town despite the tourist influx.

Cancún was originally an area of mangrove wetlands and tropical forest with just 117 inhabitants; now it has a population of about 30,000. The resort was supposed to be a model of green development, but inevitably much has been sacrificed. In 1972 there were two reserves on Cancún island – the Hotel Camino Real now stands on one, and the Club Med on the other (at Punta Nizuc). The Nichupté and Bojórquez lagoons were once ringed by mangroves on all sides – there are none left on the island, now known simply as the *Zona Hotelera*. Bojórquez lagoon was deteriorating by 1977, due to delays in building the "permanent" sewage plant; but Cancún is now unusual in not simply pumping everything out through an ocean outfall. There are still some Postclassic Maya ruins to be seen here: at El Rey (km18), where there's also a colony of fairly tame iguanas, and just north, San Miguelito, on the 12th green of the Pok-ta-Pok golf course. It's worth taking a look at the museum (closed Monday, free on Sunday), which is now in the Cultural Centre, by the old Convention Centre, at the north end of the Zone; it has a bookshop which is only open Monday-Friday 08.00-15.00.

Of course, the big attractions here are in the sea: there are 500 species of tropical fish, including snapper, bass, marlin and sailfish. Snorkelling and scuba diving are widely available; the best is at Punta Nizuc, at the southern tip of the Hotel Zone (access via the *Westin Regina Resort*). In addition, two submarines offer trips to see the reef fish – one, the *Atlantis*, can dive to 50m, but the *Subsee Explorer* in fact merely submerges its passenger cabin just below the surface. You can also choose among cheaper glass-bottomed boats, kayaks, speedboats, waterskiing, parasail and floatplanes (not to mention *Rollermania*, at km10).

One way to escape and find somewhere to decompress is to head south along the coast, either from the bus station or directly from the airport, which is about 4km off the highway south. The first major stopping point is **Playa del Carmen**, served by buses every quarter-hour or so. This is the main ferry port for the island of Cozumel and also has fine beaches itself; thus it has seen some hectic development in the last few years. Nevertheless it remains fairly laid-back and has more budget hotels and restaurants than Cancún (where the only affordable beds for those not on a package are in the youth hostel, 3.2km down Av Paseo Kukulkán, heading from town towards the hotel zone).

Isla Mujeres and Isla Contoy
Off the coast just to the north of Cancún, Isla Mujeres is no longer the idyllic resort you may have heard of, damaged both by mass tourism and by Hurricane Gilbert. The most interesting thing for ecotourists is the El Garrafón National Park, towards the southern end of the island, where you can snorkel amidst huge shoals of amazingly coloured and totally tame reef fish. At the island's southern tip there's a lighthouse and the tiny Maya temple in which the female idols that gave the island its name were found.

You'll arrive by boat from Puerto Juárez (a northern suburb of Cancún) at the town at the north end of Isla Mujeres, and from here boats also head north to **Isla Contoy**, a wildlife reserve since 1961. You're not allowed to land without a SEDESOL permit, but from the boat it's possible to snorkel and to see many of the 60-plus resident species of marine birds, including grey pelicans, white-bellied and brown boobies, magnificent frigatebirds, cormorants, and giant herons; four species of turtle can also be found here. Half of the island's 176ha is covered with mangroves (four species), and the rest is a mix of medium semi-evergreen forest, shrubs and cacti. The trip will also probably take in a reef to the east of Isla Mujeres where nurse sharks doze in underwater caves.

South of Cancún

Heading south on the main coastal highway, the first town you'll come to (20km from Cancún) is Puerto Morelos, from where the car ferry sails to Cozumel; about 2km north is *Crococún*, a crocodile farm, where you can see the rare Morelet's crocodile (*Crocodilus moreleti*); just south of Puerto Morelos is the Dr Alfredo Barrera Marin Botanical Garden, and at km49 at Rancho Loma Bonita (tel: 875 465/423, between 08.00 and 13.30) you can arrange horse riding and jungle tours.

Isla Cozumel
Archaeological orientation
The Spanish first set foot on Cozumel in 1518 when Juan de Grijalva was sent to explore the Yucatán area (discovered the year before by Francisco Hernández de Córdoba, who had been searching for slaves for Cuba's plantations). In his *True History of the Conquest of New Spain*, Bernal Díaz tells us of wild pigs, which he insists bore their navels over their backbones (probably collared peccaries, with musk glands on their rumps), and of an abundance of beehives and *patatas*, which were probably cultivated sweet potatoes.

The next year he visited Cozumel again, this time with Captain Hernán Cortés; this was the start of the gold-robbing expedition that eventually took them all the way to Tenochtitlán, the Aztec capital, and led to the collapse of the Aztec Empire. They came across Gerónimo de Aguilar, who in 1511 survived a shipwreck off the coast of Jamaica and drifted in a small boat for 13 days before being washed ashore on Cozumel, where he was enslaved by the Maya. His knowledge of the Mayan language proved of immense value to the conquistadors after they found a woman, Malinche, who spoke both Aztec and Mayan; to speak to the Aztecs, Cortés could speak in Spanish to Aguilar, who would speak in Mayan to Malinche, who would then translate the words into Aztec.

Of course this is only a tiny part of the whole story; for a quintessentially ecotouristic experience you should really read the *True History* yourself while sitting on a Cozumel beach! By the way, if you can't find this book, Fray Diego de Landa's *Relación de las Cosas de Yucatán*, penned in 1560, relates the Cozumel episode in Chapters 3 and 4 (he calls Cozumel "Cuzmil"; it means Swallow Island).

Biological orientation
As is often the case with sizable islands that for millenia have been separated from the mainland, on Cozumel you find organisms that have evolved into unique forms – species found nowhere else on earth. These include the Cozumel coati (*Nasua nelsoni*) and the Cozumel raccoon (*Procyon pygmaeus*), and birds such as the Cozumel thrasher (*Toxostoma guttatum*) and the Cozumel vireo (*Vireo bairdi*), and subspecies of the great curassow

(*Crax rubra griscomi*) and green jay (*Cyanocorax yncas cozumelae*); likewise, there's a white-throated form of the bananaquit, which elsewhere has a grey throat.

All these birds are fairly common on the island. The Cozumel vireo is particularly susceptible to the *shhh-shhh-shhh* sound that birders often make to coax curious birds closer for a good look. Its voice is rather like the white-eyed vireo's, and, at least to Jim Conrad, seems ventriloqual – the bird is in one place, but its voice seems to be in another! The Cozumel thrasher looks remarkably like a small edition of the long-billed thrasher of northeastern and central Mexico.

Several of Cozumel's birds are more typical of the Caribbean islands than of mainland Mexico. For instance, the grey kingbird (*Tyrannus dominicensis*) and the white-crowned pigeon (*Columba flavirostris*) reside mostly in the West Indies and southern Florida; the stripe-headed tanager (*Spindalis zena*) is found mainly in the Bahamas and Greater Antilles, and in Mexico only on Cozumel; the Caribbean dove (*Leptotila jamaicensis*) is found on Jamaica, Grand Cayman, St Andrew, and here and there in the northern Yucatán Peninsula; the Caribbean elaenia (*Elaenia martinica*) in the Lesser Antilles and islands off Yucatán; and there are others.

Practicalities

Ferries from Playa del Carmen (68km south of Cancún) take about an hour to reach Isla Cozumel (there's also a car ferry most days from Puerto Morelos, as well as flights), docking at the island's only town, formally called San Miguel but generally referred to simply as Cozumel. It's a pleasant trip, especially if you choose a seat on the shaded side of the boat and watch the flying fish. Look out for slender, stiff-looking, silvery items shooting out of the water and then apparently flying just above the higher waves for remarkable distances, staying airborne for up to seven seconds. Actually, icthyologists insist that flying-fish don't really fly, but in fact *taxi* along the surface vibrating their tails in the water; once they build up momentum they use their wing-like fins to *glide* a bit further. But they certainly seem to be flying.

The people of Cozumel are wonderfully helpful, but the famous "blue map" may still show a web of backroads all over the island, most of them in fact blocked since Hurricane Gilbert devastated the island's forests in September 1988. This is a shame, as these roads would if open make perfect roaming grounds for folk like us. Plenty of places rent bikes and mopeds; buses are rare and you may be told that they are for locals only, as tourists are expected to use taxis. If you've become used to living cheaply by camping, renting hammocks and eating lots of tortillas, beans and bananas, Cozumel can be hard on you; it's clear that you're expected to spend money here. There are no formal camping places, and if you do camp wild you'll have to carry all your food and water; it's best to stick to the east and south coasts. One way to escape the hotel zone is to head about 8km (5 miles) north from the pier; take the main highway that follows the beach until it ends abruptly at a turnaround. A dirt road continues north and makes a fine morning walk, through scrubby forest in which endemic Cozumel vireos are rather common. After about 4km more the road passes a smelly sewage plant, then veers left, soon passing through an extensive field of fan palms and then a mangrove swamp, before coming to the beach of a large bay, in the middle of which lies the Isla de Pasión. This is an excellent spot in which to examine mangrove biota, take a dip in the ocean, or simply hang out at the water's edge.

Probably Cozumel's most spectacular offering is its fine **snorkelling** and **scuba diving**. There are plenty of shops offering trips and equipment hire; the best sites are to the southwest of the island and can only be reached by boat. The most famous is the Palancar reef, where coral canyons disappear into the depths (despite visibility of up to 60m) and the 200-plus species of fish disappear into limestone caves. To get here you'll pass the Chankanaab National Park, a lagoon in which you can dive or snorkel with multi-coloured fish and turtles.

San Gervasio

This is the most accessible of Cozumel's thirty-odd Maya ruins. Though fairly modest by mainland standards, it was the island's administrative centre, and is thus its largest site. You can walk down a *sacbe* or "white road" (one of the famous Maya paved causeways; also the name of Mexico's best jazz band!) watching for wildlife; big iguanas are a speciality here, especially a spectacular orange variety, half a metre long, that loves to sun itself on horizontal branches.

San Gervasio is reached by taking the cross-island road for about 6km, to the centre of the island, where a toll-booth stands at the start of the gravel road to the ruins (another 6km, to the left/north). It's not much fun walking from town, through suburbs and then scrub, as unusually for Mexico there's no roadside footpath and the road is dominated by fast-moving taxis. Birders might enjoy an early-morning hike from the toll-booth to the ruins – at least an hour's walk.

South to Tulum

Continuing southwards, you'll pass a variety of resorts – such a variety, in fact, that there should be something for almost everyone. First, at km72 (6km south of Playa del Carmen), is **Xcaret**, an "eco-archaeological park" (ie a theme park); this is big business rather than ecotourism, charging US$20 per day, but it does offer plenty for the money. There's a botanical garden, butterfly pavilion, aquarium, stables, a bat cave, underground river rides, three *cenotes* and a lagoon containing dolphins, turtles, fish and flamingos; all this and the Late Postclassic Maya ruins of Pole. They operate their own lurid buses from Cancún, or you can walk in, either 1km from the highway or 6km along the beach from Playa.

At km92 **Paamul** has a fine beach with good camping and chalets; development is planned, but at the moment it's a pleasant spot for diving; there's a turtle beach nearby. **Puerto Aventuras** (km97) is a big resort, of interest only for the Cedam museum of shipwrecks. At km100 **Cenote Azul** (at the village of Xpu-Há) is a freshwater pool near an excellent beach and an inlet supposedly inhabited by manatís, as well as tiger herons and cormorants in the mangroves. **Akumal** (km103) is a resort owned by the Mexican Scuba-Divers Society, who have an expensive hotel and a diveshop at the north end of the beach; the name means "place of the turtles" but very few green or loggerhead turtles now nest here. A coral reef lies only 100m offshore, within easy reach. **Chemuyil** (km109) is an attractive beach where you'll find Mexicans camping, with good snorkelling, as well as a snack bar. At **Xcacel** (km121) the reef comes right up to the beach, and there's a shipwreck and turtle hatchery on the point to the south; ten minutes south there's a cenote with fine swimming.

Xel-Há, 122km south of Cancún, is touted in the tourist literature as "snorkel heaven". Its coastal lagoons are large enough to allow snorkellers to swim out and more or less feel alone, and you can see nurse sharks and stingrays from the shore when the water is clear. However, the resort is expensive and often crowded. Across the main road to the west are the minor ruins of Xel-Há, unusual in that it was defended by stout walls.

Tulum
Archaeological orientation
As Grijalva's four ships sailed south from Cozumel island in 1518, they took note of "a city so large that Seville would not have seemed more considerable". Actually they were seeing four Maya towns – Tulum, Xel-Há, Soliman and Tancah, clustered so close together that they looked like one city. In those days Tulum was a small port and ceremonial centre with a population of probably no more than six hundred. Despite this awe-inspiring first impression and the huge numbers of visitors today, archaeologists now think of Tulum's ruins as "nice, but not great". The problem is that Tulum blossomed quite late in Maya history, mostly during the degenerate Late Postclassic period (1200 to 1500AD); archaeologists look at Tulum's shoddy workmanship and just shake their heads. Michael Coe refers to the principal temple, the Castillo, as "a miserable structure" and characterises the other buildings as "dwarfish", bemoaning the "strikingly slipshod workmanship" of their upper facades.

Nevertheless, Tulum is "young" enough to have some richly detailed murals with patches of original paint still showing; it's interesting that their style is Mixtec (from Oaxaca), although the content is native Maya. Tulum is one of the few Maya ruins surrounded by a stone wall – a reminder of the strife of Postclassic times, when war gods had supplanted the gods of rain and corn.

At the sea's edge, take a look at that "miserable structure", the Castillo. It's recently been discovered that this temple served as a lighthouse: if lanterns are placed on shelves behind the two windows high in its east wall, a boat at sea that keeps them both in sight at once will find its way through a natural opening in the reef.

Practicalities

The reason why Tulum is the Maya world's most visited ruin is that it lies just 130km (80 miles) south of Cancún on a good road, and its oceanside setting is so spectacular that you don't really mind the site's "dwarfishness". You climb a rise and there before you lie the ruins, shining dazzlingly white in the sunshine, with the blue ocean behind them and sea-breezes whistling through them. You might wonder just what the ancient Greeks – or even the Classic Maya – might have made of a site like this, but you have to admit that it's spectacular enough.

Buses will set you down at a crossroads with a true sufficiency of signs pointing east to the ruins. You'll immediately realise that this park is in fact largely undeveloped, with only a few short trails used by toilet-minded locals and possibly a few die-hard birders. Sadly, 1988's Hurricane Gilbert and a later fire have wreaked havoc on its forest. Follow the paved road for about a kilometre; you'll know you've arrived when confronted with multitudinous tour buses parked everywhere belching black diesel fumes, with the walled ruins clearly visible beyond.

There are all types of hotels in Tulum, 4km south of the ruins; there are also plenty of travellers' hang-outs along the beach between the ruins and the town. There have been robberies and at least one rape here, so take care. Head south from the ruins and after about 500m you'll pass a modern lighthouse, a squarish white building on the ridge to the left. Though some confusing signs may suggest that a campground and cabanas lie towards the lighthouse, this is wrong; just continue past the lighthouse's access road. About another 500m down the road you come to a restaurant called *El Mirador*; here and at similar establishments further along the coast you can rent a hammock or a cabana, or pitch a tent at minimal cost. If you travel far enough down this road you'll find secluded spots where you can frequently see naked humans frolicking in the foam; at one point there's a semi-permanent colony of hippy-types in huts.

On the main highway, a bit south of the main entrance road to the town of Tulum (Tulum Pueblo), there are several less expensive hotels; buses along the highway stop in this area. If you want to catch a bus at the crossroads near the ruins, wait at the yellow concrete *parada* about 50m south; drivers prefer not to stop at the crossroads itself.

Cobá
Archaeological orientation
Cobá is a huge (6,500 mapped structures) Classic period ruin composed not of a single tight cluster of buildings, but rather of several sites linked to a central complex by long, perfectly straight causeways, or *sacbes*. More than 16 *sacbes* have been found here and no one is sure why this site has so many; several run for long distances only to reach what seem to be very insignificant endpoints. *Sacbe* #1 shoots from Cobá all the way to the site of Yaxuná 100km to the west. Michael Coe suggests that the most plausible use of these roads was for ceremonial functions, not commercial ones. Interestingly, several causeways are under water, which supports growing evidence that during Maya times and since the climate has alternated dramatically between hot dry periods and cool wet ones.

Though most of Cobá is in a sorry state of preservation, two major pyramids have been excavated. One of them, Nohoch Mul, is the highest in the entire Mexican Yucatán at 42m (138 feet); from its top you gain an impressive view of the area's lakes and forest. During Cobá's period of greatest influence in the 8th century (mid-Classic period), it was home to about 55,000 people, and served as an important trade centre, especially for Guatemalan jade.

Biological orientation
Cobá is ideal for ecotourism. You can wander for hours on the various paths and *sacbes* linking the three main groups of ruins, and on many minor footpaths, which are simply perfect for looking at birds, trees, low-hanging epiphytes and so on. Spanish moss dangles abundantly from branches, much in contrast to Chichén Itzá, only 90km to the west and not much further north. It's not exactly rainforest, but the much abused word "jungle" seems more appropriate here than in many places. Though Hurricane Gilbert and subsequent fires devastated the forest along the Tulum-Cobá road, here it's in fair shape.

It's possible to spot all three of Mexico's toucans here – the keel-billed toucan, the collared araçari and the emerald toucanet. In addition you may see Aztec parakeets, Yucatán jays, red-eyed vireos and lineated woodpeckers. Anyone interested in spotting marsh birds should walk at dawn or dusk along the gravel road leading on from the ruins' parking lot to a small Yucatec village on the far side of the lake. During the winter (or dry) season two trees are especially conspicuous and easy to identify along Cobá's trails. To your left just past the entrance gate stands a large tree that looks like a tall locust with dangling clusters of yellowish-pink flowers; these are actually conglomerations of winged fruits. In Spanish the tree is called *camarón* (shrimp) because of the fruits' pink colour; in English it's called pinkwing, and scientifically it is *Alvaradoa amorphoides*, a member of the simaruba or quassia family. Also common along the main walkway is a small tree with elm-like leaves and abundant, spherical, very bumpy, green or black fruits; this is pricklenut (*Guazuma ulmifolia*), a tree typically found in regenerating forests, and a member of the cacao (chocolate) family.

After the hot climb up Nohoch Mul, the big pyramid, the lakes will look awfully inviting. To reach one lake take the first right after entering the site, continue past a pyramid (the *Iglesia*, centre of the Cobá group) and over an unreconstructed ruin to eventually descend to the edge of Lake Macanxoc. If you're lucky, here you'll find a large tree trunk growing horizontally above the water's surface; at *siesta* time you can lie on the trunk, caressed by cool breezes, lulled by the sounds of ripples lapping the shore beneath you, occasionally raising your binoculars to watch interesting birds in the canopy above ...

Practicalities
Cobá lies just off a paved road linking Tulum, on the Cancún-Chetumal highway, and Nuevo X-Can, on the Cancún-Mérida highway. In Tulum the junction is at the north end of the town, south of the crossroads by the ruins; from a well-marked turning to the left/west, it's about 3km to the Yucatec village of Cobá, with some rustic restaurants sporting signs (and menus) in English, a couple of general stores and some curio shops. There are three places to sleep; buses (about five a day) stop at the Hotel-Restaurant Bocadito, which costs rather more than the Isabel next door. The elegant option is the Villas Arqueológicas by Lake Cobá; turn right at the far end of the village. You can also camp by the entrance to the ruins (to the left at the end of the village).

Punta Laguna
This tiny Yucatec Maya village lies on the road between Cobá and Nuevo X-Can, served by about five buses a day. Here you can hike, watch spider monkeys (which are protected and sometimes feed right above the huts), get to know some fine folks, and visit some small Maya ruins. In recent years the people of Punta Laguna have suffered from drought and from Hurricane Gilbert, and been offered money for baby monkeys, toucans and exotic flora; so far they've resisted these temptations because they hoped that someday people like us would visit them and pay for ecotouristic services. Lots of people pay lip-service to the idea of ecotourism, but the 50 people of Punta Laguna have put their lives on the line for the concept.

The Punta Laguna Project is still evolving; when a visitor arrives, nothing is assumed about the services being offered. It's all spontaneous: ecotourism as it should be. Obvious options are to follow the trails they've cleared to their nearby ruins and to some good monkey-watching spots. Count yourself lucky if you're guided by Sr Serafio Canul, who discovered the ruins, became their custodian, and knows all about our interest in medicinal plants, poisonous snakes, and chewing *chicozapote* sap.

Sian Ka'an
Orientation
Although perhaps the best-known of Mexico's Biosphere Reserves, Sian Ka'an ("where the sky is born") is not as heavily visited as you might expect; without a permit the only way to get beyond the coastal roads is to take a tour, organised by *Los Amigos de Sian Ka'an* (see below). There are plans to introduce a second tour, but these have been set back by a hurricane which closed minor roads in 1995.

Sian Ka'an covers 528,147ha (that's 1.3m acres), 99% government-owned, which gives a rare degree of autonomy to the park administration. There's a population of under 1,000, all in a couple of coastal villages and 80% of them (organised in five cooperatives) dependent on fishing for spiny lobsters (*Panulirus argus*). It's roughly equal thirds of forest (largely tropical semi-evergreen forest), savannah, and wetland (largely mangroves); there's also some medium semi-deciduous forest and low swamp forest. This includes 120,000ha of water and the Uaymil Protected Area to the south, added in 1994, which is 89,118ha of low swamp forest, medium forest, and mangrove. Around a million migratory songbirds pass through from the USA and Canada each winter, and 345 bird species are seen here in all. These include chacalacas, great blue, little blue, green-backed, boat-billed, tricolored, yellow-crowned and tiger herons, snowy, great and reddish egrets, ospreys, belted kingfishers, jabirú, roseate spoonbills, white ibis, magnificent frigatebirds, pelicans, cormorants, gulls and terns. As for animals, all the Mexican felines, excluding the bobcat, can be found here, plus spider and howler monkeys, white-lipped and collared peccaries, tapir, manatí, white and loggerhead turtles, and three species of crocodiles, including Morelet's crocodile. A lot of research is being done on the invertebrates of Bahía de la Ascensión, with new species (such as *Tetraoptoporpa siankanensis*) being identified and jellyfish never previously seen in the tropical Atlantic found. Offshore the 110km-long *Gran Arrecife Maya* (Great Mayan Reef or GAMA) forms part of the longest barrier reef in the western hemisphere. There are also a couple of dozen Maya ruins in the reserve.

Practicalities
The heart of the reserve is the two bays, Bahía Emiliano Zapata and Bahía Venustiano Carranza (also known as Bahías de la Asención and del Espiritu Santo, respectively), and the marshes and lagoons surrounding them. There are two roads (of sorts) into the reserve, one from the north, from Tulum to Punta Allen, and another from the south, to Punta Herrero. You can drive along these roads, but they are very rough, and seeing the coastal strip is not a key part of the Sian Ka'an experience. The only way to see the heart of the reserve is on a tour run by Xplora Adventours and *Los Amigos de Sian Ka'an*. They are at, respectively, the Westin Regina Resort (km20 in

the Zona Hotelera; tel: 852 612, fax: 853 501), and Av Cobá 5, 3rd floor, offices 48-50, Apdo 770 in Cancún (tel: 849 583, fax: 873 080, email: sian@cancun.rce.com.mx, MCI Mail 7196571); this is right at the rear of the Plaza America complex, at the Av Tulum roundabout. (They put out a bilingual newsletter; in the States, contact the Friends of Mexican Development Foundation.)

Their boat tour starts at Boca Paila, halfway along the Punta Allen road, and takes a 10km natural channel to Laguna Chunyaxche and the Muyil ruins, with time for snorkelling on the return. It leaves at 11.00 daily, with a minibus pick-up at the Cabanas Ana y José (8km down the road from Tulum) at 09.30; for a daytrip from Cancún you'll have to take the 06.30 bus to Tulum and then a taxi, or else a taxi the whole way. The cost is US$40 from Boca Paila or US$50 from the cabanas.

Heading south on the main highway from Tulum, the main town you'll pass through is Felipe Carrillo Puerto, centre of a strongly Maya hinterland; the *Amigos* have an office here (tel: 40813), and there's a UNAM research station just inside the reserve to the northeast, on a dirt road to Vigía Chico, which faces Punta Allen across the bay. Continuing south, at Cafetal (km65, 5km south of the village of Limones where there's a small pyramid just south of the bus-stop), the southern access road heads east to Puerto Bravo. From here one branch runs north into the reserve to Tampalam (where there's a Maya ruin) and Punta Herrero; this is a very rough road and there are no facilities.

To the south, the dry-weather road to Xcalak parallels a beach perfect for primitive camping (no services) and famous for its fishing; buses run from Chetumal to Xcalak at 07.00 daily, and from Chetumal to Punta Herrero at 07.30, and there are also *combis*. Divers might consider hiring a boat in Xcalak to reach the 42km by 16km (26 by 10 miles) coral bank known as Banco Chinchorro, 30km offshore and famous for its 17th to 19th century shipwrecks, which include 18 galleons. The lagoon is an average 5m deep, ringed by islands, the largest being Cayo Centro (5km^2); Cayo Norte is in fact two islets, with two lighthouses, and on Cayo Lobos to the south there are a few fishermen's *palapas*. Below water you'll find delights such as star coral (*Porites asteroides*), brain coral (*Dilporia strigosa*), fire coral (*Millepora complanata*) and black coral (*Antipathes grandis*), with manatí, spiny lobsters, white, hawksbill and loggerhead turtles, barracudas, sharks and much more. Above water, there's red mangrove (*Rhizophora mangle*), and wildlife including hermit crabs, iguanas, marsh crocodiles, magnificent frigatebirds, pelicans, fish eagles, gulls, doves, and, even out here, mosquitoes.

About 40km (25 miles) north of Chetumal, the highway runs along the 56km-long **Laguna de Bacalar**, by which stand several hotels in restful, colourful settings; this is served by *colectivos* from Chetumal (every half-hour from Primo de Verdad and Hidalgo, north of the centre), as well as by buses from the north. The most popular spot is Cenote Azul, an intensely blue flooded sinkhole 200m wide and 80m deep, 34km north of Chetumal and not to be confused with the other Cenote Azul north of Tulum. To the northwest of Bacalar, around Laguna San Felipe, a 1,000ha wildlife reserve protects mammals such as the big five felines, tapir, collared peccary, spider monkeys and white-tail deer, and birds such as the great curassow (*ocofaisán/Crax rubra*), the ocellated turkey (*pavo de monte/Agriocharis ocellata*) and the reintroduced keel-billed toucan (*tucán real/Ramphastos sulfuratus*).

Chetumal

Chetumal, state capital of Quintana Roo, faces Belize across the 160km fault of the Río Honda; because it doesn't stand on the sea Chetumal doesn't possess the kind of beaches that would allow it to become another Cancún, thank goodness. It's simply a pleasant town with a Caribbean flavour, which makes a comfortable base for exploring the surrounding areas. You can take fine evening strolls along the waterfront, shop duty-free on Avenida de los Héroes, and eat seafood while listening to calypso. One fancy local dish is *tikinchic*, grilled fish seasoned with sour orange and spices. Several restaurants offer Lebanese fare, such as kivi balls, made of ground meat and wheat.

Any serious Spanish-speaking buff of archaeology and anthropology would do well to visit the *Instituto Quintanaroense* at the corner of Av Efraín Aquilar and Andres Quintana Roo. Enter from the latter street, beyond some restaurant tables; once inside bear left, looking for the door labelled *Depto. de Promoción*. Here, if you express a more-than-average interest in things Quintana Roo-ish, they may well give you excellent free reading material such as the monthly cultural magazine *Cultura Sur*, a 600-page book entitled *Cultura del Caribe*, and pamphlets such as *Cultivos del Caribe* and *Geografía General del Estado de Quintana Roo*. These folks are proud of their culture and keen to share it, particularly with genuine ecotourists.

The INEGI shop, for maps, is at Av Independencia 229 (at Carmen Ochoa de Merino) and is open Monday-Friday 08.00-15.00, and the new bus station is at Insurgentes and Belice, 2km north of town; there's no city bus route nearby, but *colectivos* and taxis will take you there. Buses now run every hour across the border to Belize.

Southwest of Chetumal, the "road to La Unión", parallel to the Río Honda and the Belize border, leads to several *installaciones rústicas*; especially pleasant are some springs in the town of Alvaro Obregón, just to the west some 50km down the road.

Kohunlich

Archaeological orientation

Kohunlich's structures date from the Late Preclassical period, older than those found further north and to the west. The site is most famous for its Pyramid of the Masks, equipped with steep steps in the style of the Guatemalan Maya temples, flanked by some well-preserved and thoroughly menacing-looking face-masks about 1.2m high. There are also a small ballcourt and more than 200 unexcavated mounds in the forest surrounding the main ruins.

Practicalities

Only second-class buses and *colectivos* from Chetumal towards Nicolás Bravo, Xpujil and Zoh Laguna will set you down at the access road to Kohunlich, about 1km east of the village of Francisco Villa, an hour west of Chetumal. From here the ruins are 9km south, by a well-maintained paved road across a low rolling landscape of hacked-about forests, weedy pastures and abandoned fields. There's precious little traffic, although there's talk of a daily bus from Chetumal. In the hot afternoon sun it's a daunting walk, although on a cool morning it might make for an enjoyable two hours.

Other Information

Conspicuously and significantly, all around the ruins cohune palms (*Orbignya cohune*) grow in abundance, looking like gigantic green feather-dusters. Their presence is significant because Kohunlich's name derived from the English "Cohune Ridge", which the local Spanish speakers couldn't pronounce.

If you're a camper, you'll certainly enjoy Kohunlich's peaceful isolation and the easy access to the surrounding forest. (Watch out for the locals who from time to time come barrelling down the trails on bicycles!) A well maintained grassy area right beside the site's entrance is big enough to accommodate about five motorhomes and maybe 20 tents, although most nights there's absolutely no-one there. As with other Mexican ruins, camping is free, but a *gratificación* to the lonely custodian is appropriate. In fact, the custodian is as entertaining as the ruins themselves. Sr Francisco Ek Gorocica says that his father, Sr Ignacio Ek Dzul, discovered Kohunlich in 1971, and was its caretaker until he, Francisco, took over in the mid-1980s; their family is of a long line of Maya *brujos* and both he and his father are healers. Don Francisco's speciality is "problems of the mind – hysteria, demons, sexual perversions, etc", he says. His methods depend on understanding relationships between planets, wild plants, and parts of the human body. Some nights, he says, looking you straight in the eye, he enters the ruins and there among the ancient temples of his ancestors, he learns the most profound secrets ...

Nearby...

The ruins of **Dzibanché** ("writing on wood") lie an hour north of the highway by the road signposted Morocoy, just before (east of) the Kohunlich turning. They were "discovered" and named by the Briton Dr Thomas Gunn in 1927, but are only really being excavated now; they date, at least in part, from the late 8th century.

The village of **Tres Garantias** has set up an ambitious ecotourism project at the *Campamento La Piramide*; they have 20,000ha of forest, sustainably managed to produce honey, chicle and pimiento as well as timber, and claim over 400 species of birds, as well as crocodiles and large mammals such as tapir, jaguar, ocelot and monkeys. Make enquiries at the *Sociedad de Productores Forestales Ejidales de Quintana Roo*, on Ochoa de Carmen near Hidalgo in Chetumal (tel: 938 25232, fax: 29802).

CAMPECHE

Calakmul

The Calakamul Biosphere Reserve occupies 723,185ha (2,792 square miles) in the southeastern corner of Campeche state; in addition to preserving a huge area of typical Yucatán forest it also contains at least sixty known archaeological sites, most unexcavated. The reserve is home to five of the six species of cat native to Mexico (the jaguar, puma, margay, ocelot and jaguarundi), and also to tapir, deer, anteaters, and spider and howler monkeys. Among the 235 bird species found are the ocellated turkey, great curassow and ornate eagle – all threatened species. About 80% of its area consists of medium semi-evergreen forest (with trees such as *caoba, cedro rojo, guaya* and *guayacán*), as well as high and low semi-evergreen and semi-deciduous forest, savannas, and hydrophytic vegetation; the last is associated with the *akalchés*, or water tanks, that are typical of the area.

This all sounds good, but if you go to any of the ruins outlined below you'll see an astonishing amount of slash-and-burn destruction. The only way for the reserve to survive is for ecotourism to develop. Only when everyone sees more money coming in from this than from traditional development (including illegal logging and tomb-looting) will anything be saved. If you pay for a driver or guide you'll be at the forefront of these efforts.

State and voluntary conservation organisations working here are based in the village of **Zoh Laguna**, 10km north of Xpujil (frequent pickup trucks, and buses from Chetumal at 06.00, 11.30 and 18.00). The village is just to the west of the road to Dzibalchén (see below), and on the right as you enter you'll find a small botanic garden and also some pens where they keep orphaned animals, including a jaguar in 1996. Just beyond here on the left is a "hotel", where I was able to sleep although I never saw the staff at all; there are also two friendly comedors in the village. SEDESOL, the government ministry in charge of rural development and reserves, has a breezeblock garage in Xpujil, two blocks south of the crossroads, and if you ask around here for Don Eliseo Ek he may be able to help you out.

Xpujil
Archaeological orientation
The town of Xpujil, 153km east of Escárcega, is the main settlement in the Calakmul area; what's more, if you want to sample the "Río Bec style" of architecture without hiking all the way out to Río Bec, the Xpujil ruins, about 1km west of town, are the place to go. The steep-sided Late Classic pyramids with steps too narrow to climb, crowned by dummy temples with showy roof combs, exemplify this strange style, so concerned with appearances, and unconcerned with utility, that it amounts to pure fakery. As Michael Coe says, "it is as though the Río Bec architects wished to imitate the great Tikal temples without going to any trouble". Besides false towers, the style is also characterised by lavishly ornamented facades.

Practicalities
Xpujil is the centre of the whole frontier region between Chetumal and Escárcega, so it sees a steady bustle of *campesinos* riding into town on the backs of pickup trucks, selling bags of corn and beans, getting drunk, and leaving with new machetes and hoe handles. All buses stop here; second-classers will drop you at *la ruina de Xpujil* if you ask nicely, but most of these only run from Chetumal to Xpujil town.

On foot, just follow the road west over the hill, and you'll find the entrance on the right; the path straight on at the end of the entry drive leads only to the west end of the airstrip. You can also visit the virtually unknown Xpujil II ruins by taking the first track to the left west of El Mirador Maya and walking south for 600m.

There's not really space to camp outside the entrance, but the custodians will probably allow you to camp for free at the INAH (National Institute of Anthropology and History) *campamento*, where they themselves live. To reach this take the road north from the centre of Xpujil, towards Dzibalchén, and take the first right, a muddy path, after just a few seconds; after about three minutes you'll see some thatched white huts on the slope to the left. These are badly run-down, so it's preferable to sleep in your own tent or camper. If you need to use the toilet, the proper question is "Donde puede irme al monte?", the word *monte* referring to the surrounding woods. Don't forget a *gratificación* for the custodian.

The "touristic epicentre" of Xpujil is *El Mirador Maya*, the thatched restaurant that you'll see on the left at the top of the hill before the ruins. The famous Frenchman Serge Riou (known as Checo), who pioneered ecotourism in this area, has moved to Chetumal, but the owner, Moises Carréon Cabrera, is still keen to help you reach the remotest ruins. Checo was very keen on walking, even where a 4WD road was available, so that a trip to the ruins of Hormiguero and Río Bec took four days; Moises prefers to send you off by car, or 4WD vehicle in the wet season. In Xpujil you can sleep at El Mirador Maya (camping or in a cabana) or in the smaller Hotel Calakmul nearer town.

Río Bec

If you've been itching to hike to one of the more isolated ruins, you probably have your eye on the cluster of ruins south of Xpujil – Río Bec, Hormiguero, Tortuga, La Muñeca, El Palmar and others. Of these, Río Bec is the most accessible.

Archaeological orientation

Río Bec is famous for the architectural style named after it; it's a large, unrestored site spread over a wide forested area, dating mostly from the Late Classical period (600-900AD). The two 15m-high towers have false stairs and a symbolic temple on top, epitomising the Río Bec style.

Practicalities

This site is in Quintana Roo, but it's usually reached from Xpujil; head 13km east on the highway towards Chetumal and then south for 6km to the settlement of 20 de Noviembre and another 7km to the site. This road requires 4WD in the wet, but a car suffices at other times. Halfway down the road to 20 de Noviembre there's a turning to the right/west to the very interesting ruins of Ocolhich, and turning left/east 1km south of the village there's a road (useable by cars all year) to the Ramonal site. In 20 de Noviembre there's a village ecotourism committee, which has put together an exhibition on the local ecology (notably insects), and runs what is claimed to be the first "ecological hotel" in Mexico. Good guides in the village include Victor and Miguel Sosa.

Hormiguero

Typical of the Río Bec style, Hormiguero's claim to fame is a well preserved pyramid on which stands a temple with a richly ornamented monster-mouth door.

Practicalities

To visit Hormiguero, you should either take a guide, or have some experience of navigation and confidence that you can find your way back if you get lost. Disorientation is a risk not because the ruin lies deep in trackless jungle, but because the area is so rapidly being opened to settlement that tracks to new cornfields could be confused with the main road – despite the ruin lying well within the Calakmul Biosphere Reserve. Only in a small area right around the ruin is the road like a tunnel through the jungle, and here you may see monkeys, agouti and deer.

There's no bus service on the dirt road south from Xpujil, so try to find a pickup truck at the crossroads, or walk a couple of kilometres south and hitch from there to avoid local traffic. Hitching is an honoured institution and there's plenty of traffic, at least early and late in the day, so you probably won't have long to wait. You need to go about 12km, to the entrance to the village known both as Ejido Echeverria Castellot and as Carrizal, which lies about 100m to the right/west of the road. Walk through the village and then swing south, and after about an hour turn 90° right to again head west (at 290°) for forty minutes more.

The road is passable by a 4WD vehicle in dry weather, but low-hanging tree limbs can be a problem. A few muddy places can cause trouble even in the dry season; in at least one place it's briefly rather steep and could be very slick when wet, and in these spots there may no longer be any trees large enough to winch from. In addition, parts of the road are buried beneath anthills 4m wide and 0.5m high! These are surely responsible for the site's name, meaning "anthill" in Spanish. Really, you should hike this route – vehicles will only mess up the road for everyone, and they distract from the sensation of eventually coming upon the main pyramid with its monster-mouth door standing majestically "in deep jungle", one of the premium experiences available on the Ruta Maya.

There's no office, parking area or cleared plaza here – just rank forest and ruins. Beneath some trees is an excellent camping spot, where you can visualise yourself lying in your tent at night, dreamily gazing through the insect screen at the moonlit pyramid. However, for the sake of security, bearing in mind that everyone in Ejido Castellot knows where you were heading and that this is the obvious camping spot, you may prefer to find a more secluded spot in the forest.

Becán
Archaeological orientation
Becán, largest of the Río Bec sites, is known for the moat around its main temple area. Originally this was two to four metres deep, three to 24m wide, about 1.9km in circumference and spanned by seven stone causeways. In one of Becán's structures several passageways have been discovered, possibly used in ceremonies involving mysterious divine visitations. Deposits of charred debris and bone material indicate that the site was attacked around 450AD (Early Classic period); it was at its peak between 600 and 1200AD.

Practicalities
Becán lies about 6km west of Xpujil, clearly visible 500m north of the highway. It's easy to find a taxi in Xpujil to ferry you this far, and to Chicanná just 2km further west; it's possible, but not so simple, to get a ride in a

pickup from the crossroads in Xpujil. Second-class buses are much rarer between Xpujil and Escárcega than between Chetumal and Xpujil; the few that do run generally head eastward in the morning, westward in the afternoon.

The ruin is reached by a dirt road, marked with a sign next to a small shop; this ends at the custodian's office, where you'll be allowed to camp once you've paid your entrance fee. Although you enjoy a splendid view of the main pyramid here, the area is too small and exposed to make a good camping site – it's about large enough for two or three tents, or a large camper.

Chicanná
Archaeological orientation
Chicanná is a modest site showing influences of both the Río Bec style and the Chenes style (found in the area of Hochob and Edzna, with lavishly ornamented facades with sky-serpent masks and monster-mouth doors). The site was at its peak in the Late Classical period (600-900AD).

Practicalities
The ruin of Chicanná lies about 1km south of the highway, about 2km west of Becán, and thus 8km west of Xpujil. Though it's small, it's in a more peaceful setting than its two neighbours up the road; a grassy parking lot easily accommodates three large campers.

This is an excellent spot to sit at dusk watching Aztec parakeets cavort in the treetops across the drive, while Yucatán grey squirrels (*Sciurus yucatanensis*) leap from tree to tree among the ruins. Next to the custodian's office grows a tree with egg-shaped, apple-sized slightly scaley fruits; this is the famous anona or custard apple (*Annona reticulata*), with sublimely sweet fruit that melts in the mouth. Though planted in the tropics worldwide, it's native to tropical America.

Calakmul
Archaeological orientation
Here we find a pyramid rising 53m (175ft) from a base that covers two hectares (five acres). This is the centre of an area in which 6,750 structures have so far been mapped; over 2,000 pieces of jade have been discovered, including magnificent masks, and a peak population of 60,000 has been estimated for the site. Though 106 stelae have been found at Calakmul, more than at any other Maya site, there have still been no major excavations. Like El Mirador and Caracol, Calakmul is one of those hidden giants of Maya archaeology that may someday qualify as a destination for average tourist itineraries, but right now it's just too hard to get to for most people.

Practicalities

Calakmul (twin towers) is reached by heading west for 60km from Xpujil and then 60km south; the last 30-odd kilometres are on a dirt road tunnelling through largely undisturbed forest. Trekking there is best attempted in the dry-season months of March and April; in 1981, 4.9 *metres* (16 *feet*) of rain were recorded nearby! Moreover, without proper guiding this trip can be risky because of the area's thriving drug-running and tomb-looting industries. You can get a guide from El Mirador Maya in Xpujil, or it's easy enough to hire a vehicle in Conhuas, 2km west of the junction south to Calakmul, and to get a guide there or at the junction itself; car and guide should each cost about US$30 per day.

There's also a newly opened site at Balamku ("Jaguar Temple"), 2km to the north of the highway 4km west of Conhuas; dating from the Early Classic period (300-500AD), this was found only in 1990. Carvings here are in excellent condition, and the road is likewise in a good state virtually all year.

Escárcega

The small town of Francisco Escárcega is where the highway from Villahermosa splits for Campeche and Chetumal, making it a nodal point in any circular tour of the Yucatán peninsula. There are through buses to most upcountry points, so you're unlikely to have to stop here unless going from Chetumal or Xpujil to Campeche. It's an unassuming typically Mexican town, which comes to life at dusk; there are cheap hotels, and the main drawback is that the first-class bus station, at the main highway junction, is almost 2km west of the town centre and the second-class station.

North from Escárcega

Heading north from Escárcega, Highway 261 crosses low, flat land dominated by cattle pasture and secondary forest, with an occasional banana plantation and a few small villages; you'll be glad to see a vulture, to break the monotony. After 84km it reaches the coast at **Champotón**, a small fishing town with several hotels (three on Calle 30). Lying at the mouth of the Río Champotón, the last river before the arid north, it's usually supposed to have been the site of the town of Chakanputun, from which the Itzá were driven around 1200AD (ending up at Chichén Itzá and Guatemala's Tayasal).

Continuing northwards, there's a new *autopista* to Campeche, but the old road along the coast is more interesting. For the first 5km or so a simple wire fence stands between it and the beach, but then it peters out and plenty of possibilities arise for beachcombing and birding. Among the birds you might spot brown pelicans, olivaceous cormorants, magnificent frigatebirds, laughing gulls, royal terns, white ibises and roseate spoonbills; occasional lagoons and tidal flats are home to mangrove swallows and mangrove warblers. The beach is more muddy than sandy, and then evolves into a rocky one; thus there is little swimming and no campgrounds.

Continuing north, you'll pass through the colourful little fishing village of Seyba Playa, and enter the bustling modern city of **Campeche**. For our purposes, the most interesting places here are the INEGI shop (517, Ah-Kim-Pech shopping area, north of the centre at Alemán and Madero) and the bus terminal, with frequent service for points south and north; however, service is less bounteous towards the ruins to the east and northeast, such as the Chenes and Puuc groups and Uxmal. Almost all traffic to Mérida now takes the direct Highway 180, leaving the road via Uxmal to tourists and local traffic. Your best bet is the *Camioneros de Campeche* company, which has services every two hours or so towards *las ruinas*; on many of them there's standing room only.

Most of these run east to Hopelchén and then turn north towards Ticul, passing near to the Xtacumbilxunan cave and the ruins of Sayil, Labná, Kabáh and Uxmal, which are all very well known and dealt with in other guide books. (Kabáh is surrounded by a State Park of 1,000ha, set up in 1993 to protect typical medium evergreen forest and *acahuales* or secondary woodland; this is the end of a *sacbe* running northwest for 22km to Uxmal and Nohpat.)

However, there is another group of ruins to the south of Hopelchén, reached by a road which eventually ends up in Xpujil, which are better suited to ecotourism. Hopelchén has a few hotels, of which the best is the *Los Arcos*, on the plaza; there's also a Mennonite community nearby, which adds some interest to the comings and goings. From Campeche or Hopelchén you need to take a bus to **Dzibalchén**; there is as yet no formal accommodation here, but Don William Chám provides guiding services and bike hire, and knows some local families willing to put you up in their homes. You won't really need him to visit Hochob, but to reach more hidden places such as Tabasqueño he's certainly worth his pay. To find him, walk across the plaza from the Municipal Palace to its far left corner and on along that street for about 800 metres past a hard left turn to a sign that reads, in English, "TOURIST INFORMATION HERE"; in any case, almost any kid in town can show you where "Don Willem" lives.

The ruins of Nohcacab, near the road from Hopelchén to Dzibalchén, are little more than a pile of stones. Likewise Tahcob is a tiny ruin not much bigger than a gringo camper van, standing in the weeds about five metres off the main road, approximately 2km west of Hopelchén.

The ruins of **Dzibilnocac** are distinguished by their stucco masks; buses run as far as Iturbide, 18km northeast of Dzibalchén. From here it's under a kilometre to the ruins; bear right in the plaza and fork right again after 50m. Again this is a large site but very little has been excavated.

Hochob

Archaeological orientation

Only a small area has been excavated, a small temple complex atop a hill overlooking the surrounding country. Its facade is intricately carved with snake motifs, and it has the standard Chenes-style monster-mouth doorway. Not much is known about it, but because it lies off the beaten track it might become one of your favourite destinations.

Practicalities

The little-used road to Hochob departs from the paved road on the northwestern side of Dzibalchén, just as you enter town from Hopelchén (opposite the cemetery and near the town limits sign), and heads southwest at 210°. It's about 10km to the village of Chenko where you need to take a hard left as you enter the plaza, to leave town past the church. Fork left after 4km more and you'll soon see Hochob on its hilltop. The road should usually be passable to Chincón, but in the wet season it can be a quagmire from there to the ruins.

There are three possible routes from here; the easiest option is to return the way you came. The second is to return to the junction and turn left (ie the right fork if you were to come directly from Chincón); after 15 minutes walking you'll reach a road junction and turn left. Following the tyre marks along the main route for 1½ hours will bring you to a wide path left to Dzibalchén; if you miss this the road will eventually curve around and into the town. This is a fine walk, probably passable with 4WD in the dry season, which passes through a variety of habitats, including some attractive woods where a morning bird-walk should produce an impressive list. A third possibility is to ask the custodian for the path to the ruins of Tabasqueño, from where it seems that there is another path to the Hopelchén-Dzibalchén road.

Tabasqueño

This is a small site but similar in interest to Hochob, but it's not easy to reach without a guide. As mentioned above, there's a path from Hochob, and the locals insist that there's another path to the west from the Hopelchén-Dzibalchén road at km35; unfortunately km35 is unmarked and it's hard to find the path.

YUCATAN STATE

Mérida

Whether you take the direct highway or the Puuc route through Uxmal, you're bound to end up in Mérida, capital of Yucatán state and commercial centre of the whole peninsula. This is well covered by every other guide, but you might need to know that maps can be bought from INEGI's Regional HQ at 378A Calle 60 (Calles 41-39). There's a new museum of contemporary art, and a Museum of the Maya People is planned. About 20km to the north is the Eco-Archaeological Park of Dzibalchaltún ("Writings on Stones"), one of the oldest Maya sites, with traces dating from 1000BC, as well as 8,400 Classic period structures. A causeway leads to the Cenote Xlacah, a sinkhole 44m deep in which you can swim; it also contains an endemic fish. There's an ecological trail through the Park, which protects 539ha of low deciduous forest, inhabited by small mammals such as armadillo, ringtail and rabbit. The site is reached by four buses a day to Dzibalchaltún village, and by more frequent *combis* to Chablekal. About 10km from the Mérida ringroad towards Motul is Colul, where there's the Yax-Nah parrot sanctuary, which can be visited only by reservation (tel: 43 4138); head north from the plaza and left on Calle Cedro.

Ría Celestún

Celestún is a Special Biosphere Reserve protecting 59,130ha of low deciduous tropical forest, mangrove and coastal dunes 90km west of Mérida. Most tourists come here to "see the pink flamingos" (*Phoenicopterus ruber*), but in fact this is considered to be the fourth most important winter migration site for birds in the entire Gulf of Mexico region. From May to September carey and white turtles nest on the beaches; boa constrictors and crocodiles can be spotted among the mangroves, and traces of white-tail deer, collared peccary, raccoons, jaguar and ocelot appear around water holes. But all the locals think of is taking you on boat-trips to see the flamingos; the true ecotourist will not urge the boatmen to inch ever closer to the birds until they take wing. There are clear guidelines, which they should be happy to stick to.

The road (served by hourly buses) crosses a causeway (which has reduced the width of the estuary by two thirds and led to some algal eutrophication) to a spit of land about a kilometre wide and 25km long. Here, in the fishing village of Celestún, three no-star hotels provide rooms, and there's a wonderfully pleasant restaurant by the beach. There are plenty of day-trippers here, but few travellers stay overnight.

Hiking north along the beach or the little-used parallel sand road, you can turn right after about 4km onto another sand road; about 20 minutes walking brings you to several large, shallow ponds where you can see men collecting salt, as they have done since Maya times. Beyond these lie more lagoons where in the winter large flocks of white pelicans gather at dusk, as well as black-bellied plovers, spotted sandpipers, willets, sanderlings, western sandpipers, blue-winged teal, shovellers and herring gulls. The year-round residents of the lagoons include the brown pelican, little blue heron, American egret, reddish egret, magnificent frigatebird, laughing gull and royal tern.

The environmental NGO Pronatura works here; for information call at their Mérida office at 203A Calle 13, Col García Gueres (tel: 251 004).

Ría Lagartos

Similar to Celestún, Ría Lagartos is a Special Biosphere Reserve of 47,840ha which specialises in year-round flamingo watching; as at Celestún, there's far more to see here than big pink birds. This is the only Mexican site listed by the RAMSAR International Wetlands Convention, and its beaches are among the most important nesting grounds of the white and hawksbill turtles (loggerheads and leatherbacks also nest here). Along with both marsh and river crocodiles, white-tail deer, spider monkeys and various felines (including the jaguar), the refuge is home to two endangered species of palm – the kuká (*Pseudophoenix sargentii*) and the chi'it (*Trimax radiata*), and to rare species of cacti. Mangrove swamps here are even more accessible than at Celestún, and include the four main Mexican species of mangrove (red, white, black and button). In the low deciduous forest to the south of the reserve lives the endangered ocellated turkey (*Agriocharis ocelleta*). At least 154 species of birds are seen here (30% of them migratory), including brown pelicans, olivaceous cormorants, herons and ducks; jabirú and peregrine falcons are seasonal visitors.

Practicalities

To reach Ría Lagartos, you'll normally have to go to Tizimín, from where *Autotransportes de Oriente* and *Unión de Camioneros de Yucatán* (around the corner) together offer about eight trips a day to Lagartos, where there's one real hotel, plus various informal lodging places. There's nothing to do in Lagartos itself other than flamingo-watching, but in fact the biggest flamingo colony is beyond Los Colorados, 15km east at the end of a dirt road, where there's another salt works. If you take a boat-trip, remember to observe the same restraint as at Celestún. Responsibly-run tours can be arranged with Ecolomex Tours in Cancún (tel: 843 805/871 776, fax: 843 849). You can actually get a distant view of the birds from the water's edge in Ría Lagartos, looking east through binoculars; in early morning sunlight you may see pinkish birds with long thin necks and legs, and if the pink colour extends up their necks you can be sure that they're flamingos and not roseate spoonbills.

If you leave Lagartos on the Colorados road (past the Pemex filling station), you'll soon see a mangrove swamp to your right, rich in birdlife and other mangrove biota; if the locals would cease to use this as a garbage dump, it could become a prime ecological attraction. About a kilometre from town you'll come to an open area with a *palapa* (thatched shelter) and a swimming hole, which can be busy at weekends; at other times it's a good spot to hang loose or camp.

Other coastal reserves

Heading east from Celestún towards Lagartos (a hypothetical journey, as there is no road following the coast), Sisal was once the main port of Mérida and its hinterland, exporting the product named after it, the fibre locally known as *henequen*; little now happens here other than duck-hunting in winter. From Progreso, nowadays the area's main port, you can take a boat trip to the Arrecife Alacranes (Scorpion Reef), 120km offshore and since 1994 a National Marine Park of 333,768ha. In addition to plentiful fish, divers can also see many old wrecks. From Progreso you can also visit the Huaymitún flamingo colony. To the north of Temax, halfway between Mérida and Tizimín, is the fishing village of Dzilam de Bravo, to the east of which, in the 62,000ha San Felipe State Park, are the Bocas de Dzilam. The *bocas* (mouths) are in fact underwater springs, which support bacteria and algae, and thus a good population of fish, birds, crocodiles and turtles.

Crossing the border back into Quintana Roo state, a road from Nuevo X-can leads north to Chiquilá, from where you can take a boat across Laguna Yalahán ("where the water is born") to Isla Holbox; this is not the tropical island paradise that some claim, but it is peaceful enough. It was blitzed by Hurricane Hugo, but in any case is regularly affected by the *nortes*, which stir up the sand, making the water murky. From Chiquilá you can also visit **El Eden**, a private Ecological Reserve dedicated to research and ecotourism. Habitats include medium semi-deciduous tropical forest (about 15m high, with trees such as chicle (*Manilkara zapota*), chacá (*Bursera simaruba*), tropical cedar (*Cedrela mexicana*) and ramón (the breadnut tree, *Brosimum alicastrum*), festooned with lianas and epiphytes, and inhabited by spider monkeys and jaguars); low deciduous secondary forest (including a new species of Acacia); swamp forest (notably *palo tinto* (logwood, *Haematoxylon campechianum*), *Erythroxylon campechianum* (a relative of the coca tree), and a possible new variant of chicle); other wetlands dominated by cattails (*Typha latifolia*), sawgrass (*Cladium jamaicense*) or waterlilies (*Nymphaea spp*); and grassy savannas. Other wildlife includes the rare marsh crocodile (*Crocodilus moreletti*) in cenotes and elsewhere. The area was densely populated until the Early Classic period, and there are interesting rock alignments up to 700m long, possibly used for controlling water flow and soil erosion. If you want to visit, contact Marco Lazcano-Barrero at Apdo 770, Cancún, 77500 Quintana Roo (tel/fax: 98 805 032, email mlazcano@cancun.rce.com.mx).

114

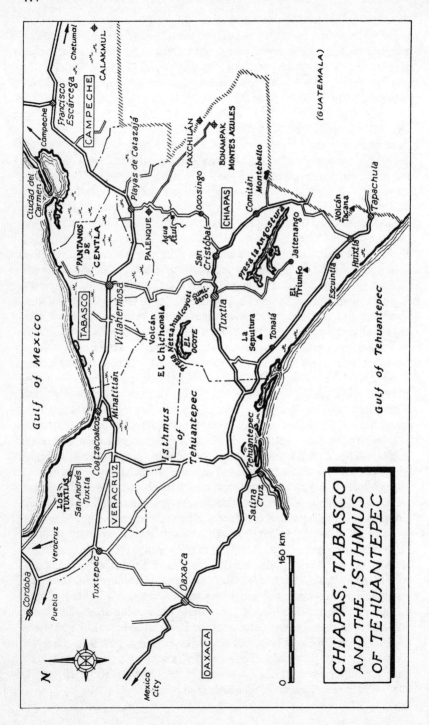

CHIAPAS, TABASCO AND THE ISTHMUS OF TEHUANTEPEC

Chapter Eight

Chiapas and the Southwest

CHIAPAS

Of all the states of Mexico, Chiapas is perhaps the most interesting for the ecotourist; it has the greatest diversity of plants and animals, as well as some of the greatest Maya ruins and a unique mix of indigenous peoples. Biologically and culturally, the state is more closely related to Guatemala than to the rest of Mexico, and it was indeed part of Guatemala for much of the 19th century. The biological similarity is due to the presence of the Isthmus of Tehuantepec immediately to the west of Chiapas: the absence of mountains here means that many montane tropical species can move this far but no further northwards. The forests of the northeast of the state are related to those of the Petén; however, they have suffered far more from logging and other intrusions than those across the Usumacinta River. More than half of the Selva Lacandona (Lacandón Jungle) has been destroyed and settlers continue to flood in, but there are signs that the Biosphere Reserves set up since 1977 may at last begin to be properly protected.

The dominant feature of the state of Chiapas is the Sierra Madre de Chiapas, a range of almost 3,000m altitude running parallel to the Pacific coast; this is covered with much of Mexico's most valuable cloudforest. To its north is the Central Depression of Chiapas (c600m), now largely filled by the Angostura reservoir, and to the north of this is the central tableland (c2,300m), dropping away into the forested lowlands of the Selva Lacandona and Tabasco to the east and north. The Sierra Madre contains the oldest rocks in the state, Archaic (Precambrian) and Paleozoic crystalline rocks (gneiss and schist, then granite, all over 225m years old), with metamorphic intrusions, covered above 2,200m by Mesozoic sediments (225-65m years old); the central depression and the tableland are early Mesozoic limestones too, and the north of the state is formed of Tertiary rocks (under 65m years old). The tableland was lifted, and the depression formed, at the end of the Tertiary period, and the Sierra Madre de Chiapas even more recently, making it a very young range of very old rocks.

There are two active volcanoes in the state: Volcán Tacaná (4,093m) is the northernmost of the chain of volcanoes running through Guatemala, and Volcán Chichón (or El Chichonal, 1,060m), just west of the Tuxtla-Villahermosa road. This latter erupted violently in 1982, destroying six villages, but maps are still based on a 1972 satellite photograph. If you want to hike there it's best to take a guide from the village of Chapultenango, west of Ixtacomitán.

The People

There are almost a million indigenous people in Chiapas. In the highlands most people are of Maya stock, speaking Tzeltal and Tzotzil; in the northern lowlands, around Palenque, you'll hear Chol. A small number of Zapotec live on the Pacific coast, and some Zoque are found in the Grijalva Basin (both are non-Maya peoples found mostly in Oaxaca state). There are still 45,000 Guatemalan-Maya refugees, in camps and villages throughout Chiapas and the Yucatán, and among these folks you may hear anything from Quiché to Kekchi to Cakchiquel. Some Mam people of Guatemalan origin have lived in Chiapas for generations.

The area around San Cristóbal de las Casas is unique in Mexico in the degree that the indigenous people have maintained their culture and dignity in the face of modern *ladino* life. This dignity may seem close to hostility to the camera-laden tourist who comes into their villages, but the *indigenos* simply wish to be left alone to pursue their traditional way of life without their every move being photographed. This indifference to visitors is found less in the remoter villages, and adventurous, sensitive hikers will have a very rewarding time.

Practicalities

The INEGI map shop is at Av 1 Norte Oriente 200a, Tuxtla, at Calle 2 Oriente just east of the zócalo. The state of Chiapas has published a 1:400,000 map of the state which you can see posted at, for instance, the Palenque zócalo and ruins, and a state atlas; both are available from government offices, principally the Department of Geography and Statistics, edificio Plaza San Marcos, 4th floor, Tuxtla (tel: 33936).

Palenque

The highway from the Yucatán Peninsula to the rest of Mexico briefly crosses the northernmost extremity of the state of Chiapas, and at Playas de Catazajá a road turns south to Palenque and San Cristóbal de Las Casas. Only second-class buses will drop you at the junction, but there are direct first-class buses to Palenque from all directions, including Cancún, Mérida, Chetumal and Xpujil.

The town of Palenque (formally known as Santo Domingo) lies 23km south of this junction; its Maya ruins are among the most popular of all, due partly to their own intrinsic value, but also to the fact that they are surrounded, not by the dry scrub of the Yucatán, but by genuine tropical forest which some say offers the best bird-watching in Mexico. Likewise, the town is a welcoming place where travellers often rest up away from the heat of the lowlands, and there are many pleasant hotels, including the Posadas Can Ek and Charito, opposite each other at the top of Av 20 de Noviembre, which offer dormitory-style accommodation in shared rooms.

Biological orientation
To be specific, Palenque is set in a National Park, 1,722ha of high tropical evergreen forest dominated by red cedar, *ceiba, guayacán, chicozapote,* and *ramón*; animals include howler and spider monkeys, anteaters and ocelots. There's a huge array of interesting birds, including all three Mexican toucans (the keel-billed toucan, collared araçari, and emerald toucanet), slaty-tailed, citreoline and violaceous trogons, yellow-winged, crimson-collared, scarlet-rumped, and blue tanagers, red-crowned and red-throated ant-tanagers, dot-winged antwrens, barred antshrikes, red-legged honeycreepers, olive-backed and yellow-throated euphonias, black-headed saltators, grey catbirds, lovely cotingas, masked tityras, crested curassows, white-bellied emerald and rufous-tailed hummingbirds, white hawks, aplomado falcons, tinamou, and various parrots, woodpeckers and vultures. A bird-list is available, published by the NGO *Sierra Madre*.

Archaeological orientation
Palenque is a Classic-period ruin famous for its well-preserved buildings, carved stucco ornamentation, fine bas-reliefs and extensive hieroglyphic texts. The earliest remains (La Picota) date from the Protoclassic period, but the city reached its peak in the 7th century and was then one of the first to be abandoned, the last recorded date being 790AD. It was also one of the first to be rediscovered, a Spanish priest finding the "stone houses" around 1740.

One of Maya archaeology's greatest finds was the tomb of Pacal II the Great (603-683AD), discovered in 1952 by the Mexican archaeologist Alberto Ruz. Before you descend deep into the Temple of the Inscriptions to see the tomb yourself, you may wish to read the riveting accounts of its exploration in Thompson's *The Rise and Fall of Maya Civilization*, Coe's *The Maya* or the December 1975 issue of *National Geographic* magazine. Accompanying Pacal's corpse was a treasure-trove of jade, including a life-size mosaic mask. Pieces of jade were held in each hand and another piece was placed in his mouth – a custom not only of the Yucatec Maya and the Aztec, but also of the ancient Chinese ... Also found were pottery vessels and two sensitively moulded stucco heads. Five young victims had been slaughtered outside the door to serve Pacal in the hereafter. In 1994 the tomb of another nobleman, also buried with his servants, was found in

Temple XIII.

When you enter Pacal's tomb you'll see a great slab of carved limestone that served as the sarcophagus's lid; on this stands a portrait of Pacal himself, apparently descending into the jaws of a monster of the underworld. Note that one of his toes has a nick in it; supposedly this is no slip of the chisel, but rather a real-life portrayal of Pacal's split toe – a congenital defect which may have been caused by repeated inbreeding within the royal family, like the clubfoot shown in two portraits of Pacal. Nevertheless it's believed that he continued the tradition by marrying his sister, Ahpo Hel.

Practicalities

The ruins of Palenque lie about 8km southwest of town; the road is a dead-end, but transport is no problem, with *combis* running to the ruins every ten minutes or so. These pass the infamous Mayabel campsite, known for its mushroom-eating "hippies". This place is a *happening*, man. As you enter, trying to look cool, you may hear bongo drums, and you'll probably see Mary Jo, who's an accountant in LA 335 days of the year, hanging in a hammock, dangling a leg adorned with Maya ankle-bracelets, and blowing way cool smoke rings. You'll start as an outsider, but after a few days of squishing mud between your toes you'll probably find yourself being hugged by someone smelling of wood-smoke, garlic and who knows what else.

The Mayabel also has its share of straight RVers not taking part in any of this. In fact the hippy invasion has provoked the occasional backlash, and police may manifest their authority by being very strict about your having your tourist card on you at all times. Moreover it's good ecotourism, or simply good manners, not to look or behave too weirdly.

Anyway, one delightful thing about the Mayabel is that it's right next to a forest; you can sit on a bank here and spot species typically considered to be denizens of undisturbed rainforest. Sometimes at dawn and dusk howler monkeys roar in the distance.

Continuing up the road, in about 750m more you'll reach the new museum, where you can see a replica of Pacal's tomb cover, and other carved panels. To the left immediately beyond you'll see the start of the "eco-archaeological trail" which leads you past the Cascada Otulum to some beautiful pools of remarkably cool, clear water, and on up to the Grupo Zutz and then the Grupo del Norte of the main ruins; this is the way the early explorers entered the ruins, but you'll need to have a ticket already. Each pool is rimmed with a deposit of travertine, one of the many varieties of calcite ($CaCO_3$); it's rare for such strange and lovely pools not to be in a cave, and one can feel how important they must have been to the ancient Maya.

The road winds up through a couple of hairpin bends to reach the main entrance to the ruins, described in detail in every standard guidebook. An abundance of Maya-related literature is available at the entrance, and fine English-speaking guides will lead you around.

An excellent hike leads to the village of **Naranjo**; the direct path starts outside the ruins (go straight on across the stream as the road turns right to go down to the museum and the town), but it's far more interesting to take the path into the jungle that starts just to the left/east of the Temple of the Inscriptions. You should start by climbing some stone steps, keeping a stream to your left, and after about 50m you'll reach a small temple with a good view of the stream which makes a nice spot to sit and bird-watch. Further up the hill there are other places that give excellent views into the treetops, so it's easy to see birds, and you may be lucky enough to spot some howler monkeys.

If you continue on this path – well worn from centuries of use – you'll cross a sizeable hill and after 6km come to the small settlement of Adolfo López Mateos, on a stream called the Río Chacamás. Ford the stream and you'll soon reach Naranjo, which is big enough to support a store.

The main "problem" for birders on this route is that so many local people pause to talk. They're so friendly that you feel ashamed to remain taciturn and evasive! Besides, they're fun and interesting to talk to. It's surprising that most of them believe that the keel-billed toucan and the collared araçari (both common here) are the male and female of the same species! Both birds are members of the toucan family, but they're in entirely different genera; the toucan sports a rainbow-coloured beak and yellow cheeks, while the araçari's beak is black and white, and its cheeks are black. Likewise some indigenous people believe that frogs and toads are male and female of the same species, and it's a widespread belief that all snakes are poisonous.

From Naranjo you can return by either of these paths, or by a gravel road that winds through pasture for 10km, eventually reaching the main road beside the museum; this gravel road avoids the hills, but it's worth checking whether the streams it crosses are low enough to wade across.

Misol-há and Agua Azul

These are two fine waterfalls south of Palenque which are visited by countless daytrips; they're almost as easy to reach using buses along the Palenque-San Cristóbal road. About 1.5km from the road at about km20 Misol-há is a natural swimming hole formed beneath a 30m cascade on the Río Tulijá. It's still fairly undeveloped, but rooms are available in the ejido San Miguel.

About 40km further south, the cascades of **Agua Azul** are really cascades rather than waterfalls; however, that's one of the nice things about them. They're spectacular enough to be interesting, yet small and friendly enough to play with; however, if it's been raining heavily you should take care. There are a couple of *combis* a day from Palenque which take you all the way to the falls, but the regular buses along the main road will deposit you about 4km short of your destination. The walk is on a paved road, entirely, and steeply, downhill, and thus uphill all the way back. Most visitors only see the falls by the restaurants at the road's end; however, three more spectacular ones lie about 4km below here, by a trail north along the river. This starts as a track past a line of stalls, to the right between the ticket booth and the tourist falls; it runs through farmland and thus can be pretty churned up by horses.

Agua Azul is a Special Biosphere Reserve protecting 2,520ha of high evergreen and semi-deciduous forest of oak, fig, guayacán (*Tabebuia guayacan*), capulín (*Trema macrantha*) and palms, and jaguars, tapirs, macaws, toucans and howler monkeys. It's more developed than Misol-há, and there are now problems due to tourist facilities discharging their waste into the river, affecting the distinctive blue colour that gives the place its name. There are restaurants, cabanas, and places to sling a hammock, and you can camp in a site by the car park or elsewhere; there is a risk of theft. Horses can be rented, but expect to negotiate a fair price.

Ocosingo and Toniná

Ocosingo is the main town between Palenque and San Cristóbal, and the base for the ruins of Toniná. The people in the surrounding villages are mostly Tzeltal, and there is none of the *indigeno*-tourist tension of the Tzotzil highlands. However, this was the heartland of the Zapatista rebellion of 1994, so be prepared for army checkpoints. The town has no pretensions but is friendly and hospitable with a surprising number of no-star lodging places, as well as restaurants and banks. Cheese connoisseurs should try the cheese balls (*quesos de bola*) for which the town is noted.

The Classic-period Maya ruins of **Toniná**, spread over seven terraces, are surprisingly large, although the buildings are not spectacular; most interesting are the carvings and stelae scattered around the site and in the little museum/office at Rancho Toniná. The site is about 14km from the town, taking Calle 1 Oriente towards Guadalupe and Monte Libano; there seem to be no buses as yet, but there are plenty of pickups and *colectivos* in this direction, as well as taxis.

THE SELVA LACANDONA

From just south of Palenque another road heads southeast towards the Guatemalan border – this is the main route into the Selva Lacandona, and you'll see plenty of signs of the runaway colonisation of this supposedly protected area.

The "Lacandón Jungle" is the overall term for all the rainforest from Palenque and Ocosingo east to the Guatemalan border; however, 80% of it (more than half since 1980) has been lost to logging and cattle-grazing, despite official protection. Logging was officially banned back in 1949, but was replaced by a colonisation progamme, whose effects were indistinguishable. The population of the area is still increasing by 7% each year. Meanwhile there are only about 400 Lacandóns left, and even these are not the real, notoriously fierce, Lacandóns, who were wiped out by illness by about 1700, but far more pacific colonists from the Petén and Campeche; 46% of the local population are in fact Tzeltals. Their main settlement is Palestina (officially Nuevo Centro de Población Dr Manuel Velasco Suárez, or just Nuevo Velasco Suárez), established in 1976 to the west of Bonampak. There are 200-plus archaeological sites in the area. There has also been talk for 30 years of damming the Usumacinta for hydroelectricity, with five dams that would flood 106,000km², in Mexico and Guatemala. (Chiapas provides 20% of Mexico's energy, and 55% of its hydroelectricity, yet two-thirds of homes do not have electric power – one more reason for people here to feel exploited.)

The area of 331,200ha between the Río Lacanjá and the Río Lacantún forms the **Montes Azules Biosphere Reserve**, created in 1978; in 1992 an area of 61,873ha to its north became the **Lacantún Biosphere Reserve**, named after Lacan-tún (Big Rock), an island and ruins in Lake Miramar, but the area between the Río Lacantún and the Guatemalan border to the east, known as the Marqués de Comillas (204,000ha), has little protection. Maps show a road through this area, but it doesn't exist much beyond Benemérito; however, you can continue by boat to pick up a bus from Flor de Cacao through Montebello (see below).

Most of the area has a hot humid climate, receiving between 1.5m and 3m of rain per year, mostly from June to October, with an average temperature of 25°C, and 11 vegetational types, mostly on limestone. Medium tropical forest, largely semi-deciduous, covers 70% of the area, with trees up to 25m high, of which about a quarter lose their leaves in the dry season. These include *chacá* or *palo mulato* (*Bursera simaruba*), *matilisguate* (*Tabebuia rosea*) and *Alseis yucatanensis*; in the centre and south of the Montes Azules reserve you'll also find *ramón* or *moju* (*Brosimum alicastrum*), *hule* (*Castilla elastica*), *guanacaste* (*Pithecellobium arboreum*) and *chicle* (*Manilkara zapota*). High (and medium) evergreen forest, up to 30m high, is found more in Lacantún and the Marqués de Comillas area, dense rain forest with lots of vines and epiphytes, and big trees such as *caoba* (*Swietania macrophyla*), *ceiba* (*Ceiba pentandra*), *caishán* (*Terminalia amazonia*), *jobo* (*Spondias mombin*), *guapaque* (*Dialium guianense*), *cedro* (*Cedrela odorata*), *flor de corazón* (*Talauma mexicana*) and *matilisguate*. To the north, at altitudes of about 800m, there's some pine-oak forest (with *Quercus skinneri* and *Q. anglobonduensis*); other habitats include rich riverside gallery forest, *jimbales* or groves largely of bamboo (*Bambusa longifolia*), and savannas. Only 1,000 species have been identified, about 20% of the expected total; these include new species such as *Cybistax millsii*, a 30m tree said to be a type of primrose and probably already extinct, *Yucca lacandonica*, the first known epiphytic yucca, and *Lacandona schismatia*, a member of an unknown family of saprophytes (which feed on dead matter).

Likewise, only 82 of the 124 possible mammals have been recorded; these include jaguars (half the size of those in Amazonia), margays, jaguarundis, tapir, anteaters, armadillos, otters, spider and howler monkeys, collared and white-lipped peccaries, kinkajous, coatis and many bats. Birds (at least 341 species) include everything from harpy eagles and vultures to hummingbirds, via scarlet macaws, guans, curassows, tinamous, toucans, trogons, motmots and scaled antpittas. The 77 reptiles and amphibians include 28 snakes (including boas, bushmasters and the fer de lance), 21 frogs and toads, and the endangered marsh crocodile (*Crocodilus moreletti*) and river turtle (*Dermatemys mawei*). In the rivers and lakes live 71 species of fish, some again new to science; one of the more interesting is the *macabil* (*Brycon guatemalensis*), which feeds on fruit and flowers fallen from trees.

The main research station in the Montes Azules reserve is at Boca de Chajul, at its southern edge on the Río Lacantún; this is reached by boat via Montebello and Flor de Cacao. This was opened in 1984, closed in 1985 due to bad planning, and reopened in 1991 by UNAM and Conservation International under Mexico's first debt-for-nature swap. Among many other things, it boasts 54 species of bat (of 134 in Mexico), making this the most diverse population in the world. To the north, much research is done at Bonampak and Yaxchilán, and at the hamlet of Campo Cedro or Indio Pedro, 15km southeast of Bonampak by a tiny jungle trail (with a population of just 28 Tzeltals).

Bonampak and Yaxchilán

These are the archetypal "ruins lost in the jungle" which those who can afford it visit by light aircraft (from Palenque or Tenosique); however, they are now very easy to reach by public surface transport. A road runs from Palenque to the town of Frontera Corozal (also known as Echeverría), on the Río Usumacinta, and onwards towards the Guatemalan border to the east. It's about 160km (100 miles) from Palenque to the Bonampak turning, taking about four hours by 4WD or six by bus, while Yaxchilán is a short boat-ride from Corozal. There are now plenty of tours organised by the travel agencies in Palenque, and buses and *colectivos* also run along this road, although it's still a pretty rough ride. Buses are run by *Autotransportes Comitán Lagos de Montebello*, on Av Velasco Suárez about three blocks west of Palenque's market. A reasonable-sized group could hire a *combi* for an affordable day-trip.

Bonampak: orientation

The Bonampak Natural Monument lies at about 375m altitude in high evergreen forest, composed of all the classic big rainforest trees such as red cedar, caoba, ceiba, palo de rosa, palo mulato, sombrerete, ramón and guarumbo, draped with orchids, bromeliads, and ferns; inhabitants include jaguar, ocelot, spider and howler monkeys, tapir, harpy eagle, collared araçari and scarlet macaw.

The first reference to Bonampak is dated 402AD, and it reached its peak under Chaan Muan II (Bird Sky Muan), who ruled from 776AD to at least 792AD. It was never a very important city, but it's now famous for its marvellous murals, which narrate the story of a battle, its aftermath, and the victory celebrations. They were painted soon after 800AD and preserved by calcite due to water leaking through limestone walls; early tourists tried to remove this with kerosene, but they were well restored in 1984-88. The Gran Plaza (90m by 110m) is now very much restored; above it stands the Acropolis, eight temples on top of a hill. A 350m *sacbe* leads north across the airstrip to the *Grupo Frey* (named after the site's "discoverer"), three small buildings on a 20m hill, and the third group is the *Grupo Quemado* (Burnt Group), 250m to the northeast, at the west end of the airstrip, where a house and two altars have been excavated.

Practicalities

Buses will drop you at a junction by the San Javier checkpoint, from where it's about 12km to the ruins, turning left onto a path after 4km, just beyond the village of Bethel. If you overshoot you'll come in about ten minutes to a log bridge over a small stream, but as this trip becomes more popular you're less and less likely to miss the turning.

The track to the right leads to the village of Lacanjá Chansayab, a few kilometres away, another friendly village of 250 Lacandóns (half their entire population). You can sleep here or in Bethel, and in both places it's possible to find guides for walks into the jungle; you can also camp at the ruins. From Lacanjá Chansayab you can visit waterfalls, the ruins of Lacanjá (under two hours), or even hike all the way (100-odd km) via Laguna Miramar to Montebello. The best time is between January and April; in the rainy season you'll be calf-deep in mud and might prefer to hire a horse. You can hire a guide in the village of Bethel, where most of the Lacandón people are converts to Seventh Day Adventism; the chief's son, Sr José Mallorca, or Sr Hidalgo González Chankín, will guide you for about US$20 a day; in the hut on the right at the entrance to the village, Sr Antonio Navarro, who is nearly albino, is very helpful, especially if you bring him some vitamin pills!

Yaxchilan

The "Place of the Split Sky" is also a Natural Monument, with 2,621ha of high evergreen forest surrounding the ruins. This was a larger city which dominated Bonampak in the Classic period, and is now one of the prime ecotouristic destinations; the only ways to get here are by air (from Palenque or Tenosique) or boat (from Frontera Corozal), so there's always a feeling of adventure. It was populated from the Late Preclassic period (200BC-200AD) and reached its peak between 629 and 800AD, before collapsing, with no dated carvings after 808. There are over a hundred buildings in five groups (the South Acropolis, the Great Acropolis, the North (or Milpa) Group, the Little Acropolis and the Great Plaza), not yet fully excavated. Some of the most beautifully carved lintels are now displayed in the British Museum's new Mexican Gallery.

A recent theory has it that two piles of stones in the Usumacinta River are in fact the piers of a 200m-long Maya suspension bridge, the only one yet found; certainly from June to January, when the river is in flood, it would have been impossible to cross by boat without a motor.

From Frontera Corozal boats also cross the Usumacinta river to Bethel, or go upstream to Nueva Technica, in Guatemala; from either place you can take a bus to Santa Elena, the base for Tikal, perhaps the most amazing of all Maya ruins. Many tour companies in Palenque offer inclusive packages which will get you there in one long day's travelling (4 hours in a minibus, at least half an hour in a boat, and another four hours on the road). They also offer day-trips to Bonampak, and overnight trips to Bonampak and Yaxchilán.

SAN CRISTÓBAL

The touristic epicentre of Chiapas, though not, since 1892, its official capital, is the beautiful highland city of San Cristóbal de las Casas, at 2,118m, founded in 1528 by Diego de Mazariegos. The cathedral was founded in 1538 (it now has a 17th century facade), and in 1544 the great Bartolomé de las Casas became bishop; he remains revered as a protector of the indigenous population. The tradition was continued by the late Frans and Trudi Bolom, archaeologist and photographer, who did much to save the Lacandón jungle for its inhabitants. Their home, the Casa Na-Bolom ("House of the Jaguar", at Vicente Guerrero 33, at Chiapa de Corzo), is a museum, guest-house, restaurant and study centre – its library is recommended to anyone studying the area. Quite a few of the cheaper guest-houses offer shared rooms at about US$3 a bed – try the Margarita (Real de Guadalupe 34), the Casa de Gladys (Real de Mexicanos 16), or the Casa Blanca (Insurgentes, just south of the zócalo). There are great wholefood restaurants, such as Madre Tierra (Insurgentes 19) and the Casa del Pan (Dr Navarro 10, not Mondays), an excellent bookshop (Chilam Balam, Gen Utrilla 33), plenty of laundries, and all other tourist services – it's a great base! Various places offer ecotouristic or "alternative" trips to nearby villages and reserves; try the Café El Puente (Real de Guadalupe 55), the Café Altura (1 de Marzo 6D, at 20 de Noviembre) or Kanan-Ku (tel: 967 84157, fax: 83723). Los Pinguines (5 de Mayo 10B) offers bike hire and tours; for horse riding, ask at the La Galleria restaurant (Hidalgo 3).

The first-class (Cristóbal Colón) bus terminal is at the junction of Insurgentes with the Pan-American Highway; second-class terminals are nearby, as are the *combis* that run non-stop to Tuxtla, Comitán and other towns. To reach the centre, head up Insurgentes, past hotels and restaurants, to the zócalo, where you'll find the cathedral, tourist information (in the city hall) and the best hotels; continuing north on what is now Gen Utrilla, you'll come to the twin churches of La Caridad and Santo Domingo, with a lively crafts market. The monastery of Santo Domingo houses a crafts cooperative and a regional museum; the city market is beyond this.

La Iglesia del Dulce Nombre

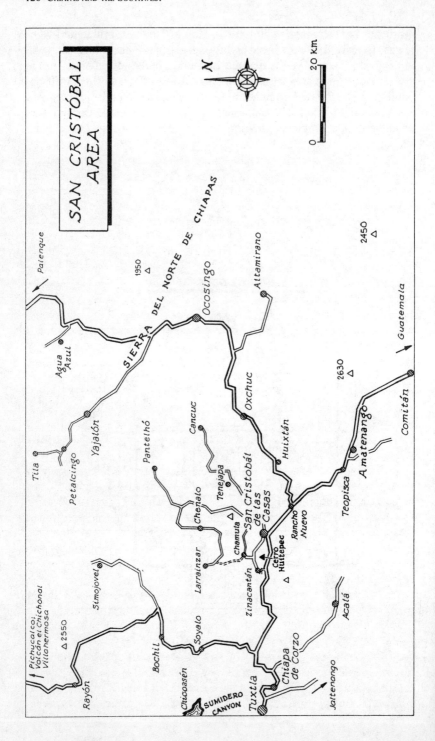

SAN CRISTÓBAL AREA

N

20 km

Palenque

SIERRA DEL NORTE DE CHIAPAS

Agua Azul

1950

Ocosingo

Altamirano

2450

Guatemala

Tila

Petalcingo

Yajalón

Pantelhó

Cancuc

Oxchuc

2630

Chenalo

Tenejapa

Huixtán

San Cristóbal de las Casas

Amatenango

Comitán

Stmojovel

Larrainzar

Chamula

Zinacantán

Cerro Huitepec

Rancho Nuevo

Teopisca

Pichucalco;
Volcán el Chichonal
Villahermosa
△ 2550

Bochil

Soyalo

Acalá

Rayón

Chicoasén

Tuxtla

Chiapa de Corzo

SUMIDERO CANYON

Jaltenango

Around San Cristóbal

Pronatura, Mexico's leading conservation NGO, runs a reserve on Cerro **Huitepec**, at km3.5 on the road to Chamula, west of San Cristóbal. The peak is an extinct volcano known in Tzotzil as Oxyoquet ("Three Peaks"), and this is also the name of the 2km trail through the forest. Officially it's open daily from 09.00 to 18.00, but this doesn't seem to be reliable. Oak trees predominate in the 135ha reserve, and at the top of the hill they are draped with epiphytic bromeliads, ferns and orchids, though perhaps not enough to really justify referring to it as cloudforest. There's a fine assortment of birds here, especially in winter, including trogons, motmots, solitaires and woodpeckers. Most of the mammals are nocturnal (such as opossums, weasels and most of the rodents), but you should see the Chiapas grey squirrel and maybe the Chiapan race of the cottontail rabbit.

Continuing along this road (by *combi*, from just north of the market), it's 12km to **San Juan Chamula**, best-known of the Tzotzil highland villages. These have a certain reputation as being rather hostile to tourists; this is exaggerated, but you should check before you visit, avoid intrusive photography, and in particular be *very* careful around the church – don't go in without a ticket from the village tourist office, and don't even think about taking your camera out. It's only nominally a Christian church; you'll find it full of candles, pine needles and other offerings, notably *posh*, a fearsome home-brewed hooch which you can sample at the village *cantina*. It is a very traditional place, and above all very sexist – women weren't allowed to vote until 1994, even though it's compulsory, and they always walk barefoot and behind their man. Families that have converted to evangelical forms of Christianity have been ostracised, with innocent children excluded from school, and many have been driven from their homes to live in shanty-towns in San Cristóbal.

There's quite a variety of tours, which are recommended if you want to get the most out of a visit and avoid giving offense; the Casa Na-Bolom and the tourist office offer good trips, but perhaps the best are those offered by Mercedes Hernández Gómez – meet in the zócalo of San Cristóbal at 09.00, and look for her trademark umbrella. Many horse trips also come here. From Chamula it's mostly downhill back to San Cristóbal: if you want to walk, you can take the track through the hamlet of Milpoleta, which starts at a cross about 1km south of the plaza. When you reach the *periférico* to the north of San Cristóbal, turn left and after a couple of kilometres right onto Calle Argentina, still a couple of kilometres from the market.

Also about 12km from San Cristóbal, by a good road (with plenty of *combis*) branching left/west before Chamula at km7, is Zinacantán, which has a small museum; you can walk from here to Chamula in a couple of hours. A road also leads 7km south to Nachig; even here, on the highway to Tuxtla (km73), you can see women in their local costume weaving on backstrap looms. Continuing north from Chamula, the road splits at Macuila, with the left branch heading northwest to San Andrés Larrainzar (where the peace talks are currently being held), and the other going to Chenalhó, where there's accommodation.

Heading east on the main road to Comitán (in fact the Pan-American Highway), at km94 (San Cristóbal being at km84½) you'll reach the entrance to an ecological reserve protecting the **grutas de San Cristóbal**, just before the Rancho Nuevo army barracks (scene of almost the only real fighting in the January 1994 uprising) and the junction to Palenque (km96). It used to be possible to camp here, but given the nervy state of the soldiers and local paramilitary vigilantes this is not now a good idea. Even so, it's well worth spending time in the pine forest, which is an ideal place for beginners to try out horse-riding – ask at the ticket-booth, or just hang around, and someone will show up to offer you a horse. The caves have a fine show of stalactites and stalagmites; they've been explored for about 8km, although only 800m is lit and open to tourists; it's suspected that they actually connect with the Gruta de San Felipe, 5km beyond San Cristóbal on the Tuxtla road.

Montebello

The Montebello Lakes are a well-known beauty-spot near the Guatemalan border, reached by a paved road and much visited at weekends. Access is easy, and it's not hard to get away from the crowds. The National Park (established back in 1959) protects 6,022ha of pine, oak, liquidambar (sweetgum) and cloudforest, and anything from 16 to 68 lakes, depending on your definition. At an average altitude of 1,500m, there's a temperate climate (with rain between May and October); in the area of Lakes Montebello and Tziscao there's over 3,000mm of rain per year, with humidity over 80%; to the west in the core tourist area of Bosque Azul there's under 2m of rain and under 40% humidity, and warmer temperatures, an average 18-22°C, while to the east there's 2,000-3,000mm of rain, 60-80% humidity, and 20-22°C temperatures. To the northwest the trees are mainly *Pinus oocarpa*, in the more humid Montebello/Tziscao area there's *P. tenuiflora* and some cypress; to the east (where there's been some deforestation) there's mixed forest of conifers with liquidambar and other deciduous trees, and beyond that (north and east of Lake Tziscao) predominantly deciduous, with sweetgum, oak, *hule* (*Castilla elastica*), treeferns, bromeliads, orchids and mosses. The understorey is made up of shrubs in humid areas, and grass elsewhere. The fauna is largely neotropical, including white-tail and brocket deer, howler and spider monkeys, margay, ringtails, anteaters, armadillos, coatis, tayra, rabbits, weasels, skunks, as well as turtles, iguanas, salamanders and boas. Birds include chacalacas, curassows, quail, azure-naped jays, barred parakeets, blue-crowned chlorophonias, water birds such as white egrets, ducks and roseate spoonbills, and, in a few small areas, quetzals.

These are karstic lakes, of which only the Laguna de Tapancuapan (13km long) is fed by a river (the Río Grande de Comitán), linking to the Lagunas Bosque Azul and San Lorenzo; these three are suffering from some algal eutrophication. Laguna Montebello, to the east, is 2km long, and Laguna Tziscao, at the western end of the park, is 3.6km long. The other sixty-odd lakes are far smaller, and some hold water only in the wet season. The 1:250,000 map of the area is E15-12, *Las Margaritas*.

Practicalities
To reach Montebello, you should take a bus (at least hourly) or *combi* from San Cristóbal to Comitán (km72, 1,650m), and there make your way to the *combi* terminal at Av 2 Poniente Sur between Calles 2 & 3 Sur Poniente, from where there are departures every 15 minutes to Los Lagos de Montebello. If coming from the Guatemalan border, you can pick up the *combi* at the La Trinitaria junction. Comitán claims to be a *zona de rescate ecologico, ciudad limpia* and is a pleasant Maya town, but you're best off basing yourself in San Cristóbal. It's 16km to La Trinitaria, and another 39.7km to the end of the road at Laguna Bosque Azul, 1¼ hours from Comitán; at km31 you'll pass the turning to **Chinkultic** ruins (2km north). This site covers 3km², but relatively little has been excavated so far; the most accessible section is Group A, by the Cenote Azul (a beautiful sinkhole that offers good swimming), where you can climb the pyramid for a wide view over the lakes. Chinkultic was inhabited at least from 650 to 1200AD, but its peak was in the Classic period. At km32 you pass the Hospedaje La Orquidea (universally known as Doña María's), the best place to stay near the lakes, although it takes ecotouristic rusticity to the limit. At km34 there's also the more upmarket Hotel-Restaurant Bosque Bello, at km35 a turning south to Carmen Xhan (on the Guatemalan border – six *combis* a day, but don't attempt to cross the border here), and at km36 you pass the National Park gate (now abandoned). Continuing ahead, the road passes Lagunas Ensueño (to the right) and Encantado (left), and ends at km39.7 at the Restaurant Bosque Azul, where you'll also find food stalls, picnic shelters, rowboat hire and the park administration. At the park gate, there's also a turning to the right to Tziscao (9km east, on the last of the lakes, with an *albergue turistico*); although some maps deny it, this road ends a little further on, at Flor de Café (six *combis* a day), from where you can hike and then take a boat to the Ixcán ruins and Pico de Oro, end of a road from Palenque, which passes Bonampak and Yaxchilán.

Hiking directions
From the roadhead an unpaved road continues for 800m to *las grutas San José el Arco*, where there's not a lot to see. There are plenty of willing guides, and even horses if you fear you might not make it. If you fork left at once you'll cross a bridge known as *el paso del soldado* (and there really was an armed soldier guarding the swimmers when I passed!); you can

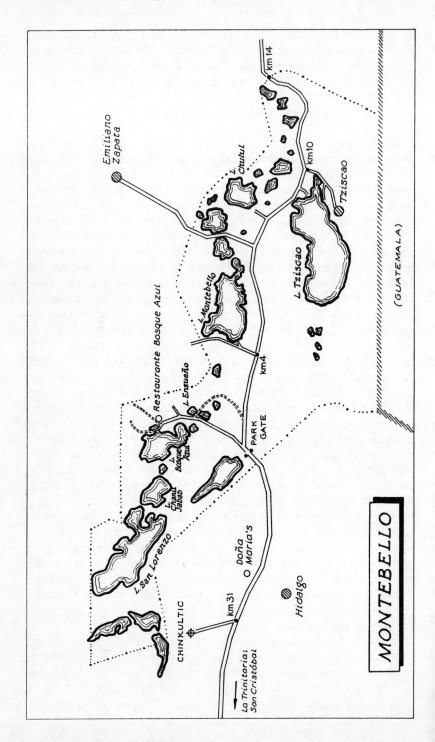

MONTEBELLO

turn right here before crossing and follow a path along the bank all the way to the caves. Continuing over the bridge you'll come in less than ten minutes to a junction; to the left a track drops to a camping area by the lake, while to the right the road passes through a fence to a village. I followed the fence line uphill to the right/east, a steep and rather humid climb of 10-15 minutes. Soon you're in deciduous forest with little in common with the pine around the lake, with lots of mosses and epiphytes. At the top you'll emerge on top of a limestone cliff with a view over a gorge, with one of the caves visible below. You'll almost certainly have to return the way you came.

I was warned not to hike too far to the east, towards Montebello and Tziscao, due to *bandidos*; this is a shame, as the old road to Montebello, a forestry track diverging at km38½ on the present road, would make a very pleasant hike indeed. However, there is a nice short walk which doesn't stray too far from the main roads, allowing you to sample the pine-oak woodland of the area. Exactly 760m along the Tziscao road a path heads left into the trees; after a while it drops through lusher woodland into open pine. About 20 or 30 minutes from the road you should turn left up the valley to a small clearing and then climb quite steeply for ten minutes, with a small lake below to the left. The path emerges onto a forestry track running at about 330° to the left. Almost at once it kinks down to the left, but you should continue straight ahead on a path at 330°; this climbs onto a hill with a view northwest to Laguna Bosque Azul, swings to the right down and across a very small col and up to reach (in five minutes) the edge of a beautiful tree-filled cenote or sinkhole. Turning left along the edge you'll soon turn sharp left onto the forestry track from Montebello, which brings you out onto the Bosque Azul road at km38½, between Lagunas Ensueño and Encantado. There's also a good, safe walk around Lake Tziscao.

West of San Cristóbal

Heading west on the highway to Tuxtla, the road climbs over the south side of Cerro Huitepec; the Pronatura reserve (see above) lies on the north side, and the local office of the Chiapas state Institute of Natural History is on this highway at km76½. The highway runs high along the side of the sierra, with views far to the north, before dropping a long way to Chiapa de Corzo, which it bypasses to the north. This is an historic town in its own right, and also one of the starting points for boat rides through the **Sumidero canyon**. This is visible to the north at various points between Chiapa de Corzo and Tuxtla, a deep gash 12 million years old which is one of the most spectacular geological faults in the Americas. The Chicoasén dam was built on the Río Grijalva in 1980, creating a 32km-long lake in what was a wild river canyon; now 130,000 tourists a year (110,000 of them Mexican) take boat trips of around two hours between Chiapa and Cahuaré. The cliffs tower up to

1,200m above water-level, and you'll also see rock paintings, waterfalls (best in the rainy season), and El Chorreadero, where an underground river emerges.

There are also viewpoints above the canyon; from Tuxtla "km4" *colectivos* leave town by Av 11 Oriente Norte and terminate about 2km short of the first viewpoint, the *mirador La Ceiba*. It probably wouldn't cost a great deal to persuade the driver to take you a bit further.

The area of 21,789ha around the canyon was also made a National Park in 1980, although as there was not enough cash to buy out all the owners, the forest continued to be cleared. There's evergreen forest on the lower slopes, with dry tropical deciduous forest on the rim with cedar, oak, *caoba* (*Swietania macrophylla*), *ramón* (*Brosimum alicastrum*), and *chicozapote* (*Manilkara zapota*). This is a meeting point for the birds of the Pacific and Gulf coasts: these include red-breasted, flammulated and belted flycatchers, as well as great curassows. Other wildlife includes white-tail deer, spider monkeys, anteaters and river crocodiles.

There is a big litter problem, and Mexican tourists light fires and fail to extinguish them; the worst time for fires is from March to May, which is convenient in a way as the tourist peaks are December-January, April, and July-August.

Tuxtla

Tuxtla Gutiérrez, the state capital, is a hot busy city down at 536m that doesn't hold a great deal of interest for tourists, apart from the excellent zoo, which has only species found in Chiapas; it even has a quetzal, although these are traditionally supposed to die in captivity. *Colectivo* 6 runs from Calle 1 Oriente Sur/Av 7 Sur Oriente to the zoo, continues up the hill to the Cerro Hueco prison (making for an interesting mix of passengers!) and returns to town by a different route.

There's also a botanical garden behind the striking modern *Teatro de la Ciudad* and Regional Museum, reached by *colectivos* 3, 7 and 20. The headquarters of the state's Institute of Natural History (for permits and information on reserves) is also here (Calzada de Hombres de la Revolución, Apdo 6, Tuxtla 29000; tel: 23663, fax: 29943, email: ihnreservas@laneta.apc.org).

The Cristóbal Colón (first-class) bus terminal is at Av 2 Norte Poniente/ Calle 2 Poniente Norte, with some cheap hotels opposite; the second-class terminal is at Av 3 Sur Oriente/Calle 7 Oriente Sur, with a cheap hotel at the rear on Av 2 Sur Oriente. The best value is the youth hostel east of the centre at the junction of Blvd Angel Albino Corzo and Calzada Samuel León Brindis (opposite the university and the old state library); *colectivo* 1 runs east-west along Albino Corzo.

EL TRIUNFO

Most of the Sierra Madre de Chiapas is now protected, but the best-established area by far is El Triunfo (a reserve since 1972, and a Biosphere Reserve since 1990), covering most of Mexico's (and thus North America's) genuine cloudforest. It covers an area of 119,550ha, between 450m and 2,750m altitude (an average 1,800m); at least 10,500 people, mostly Tzotzil- and Tzeltal-speakers, live in the buffer zone, while the nuclear zone covers 30,000ha divided into five *poligons*. The largest of these (11,594ha) is the El Triunfo zone, which is the one you are most likely to visit; it has two *campamentos* and the main path across the sierra. The third *campamento* is at El Quetzal, six hours (at most) southeast of Cuxtepec (at about 1,000m, reached by a couple of buses a day from Tuxtla).The reserve does not cover Cerro Paxtal, the highest peak in the range, to the east; it may be extended but more resources are needed first. A power line crosses the range to the south of Cuxtepec. This is a 25m-wide gash through the forest which probably could be hiked but would not be very enjoyable. Another power line is planned to the south of Pablo Galeana, to Huixtla, by the reserve's eastern boundary; it may be possible to build this without forcing a track the whole way through the forest.

If there's just one or two of you, the rangers tell me there's no need to get a permit to visit, but you should do if you are more numerous. See above for the location of the Institute of Natural History; the Biosphere Reserve's postal address is Apdo 391, Tuxtla 29000. They will expect a donation of about US$100 for a group for a week's visit, and also charge US$25/day for a guide, US$15 for an *arriero* and the same for each mule (two per *arriero*), and US$20/day for food. The reserve only had about 250 visitors a year before the EZLN uprising, and there are fewer now; Easter Week is a busy time for Mexican visitors.

Biological orientation

All parts of the sierra receive most of their rain in summer, with precipitation ranging from 800-1,500mm (on the Atlantic slope) to 4,500mm on the summits, and average temperatures from 22°C to just 14-18° on the tops, where it can freeze in winter. The Pacific slope receives 2,000-4,000mm of rain from the southwest between May and October; cloud is often trapped by winds from the north, producing "horizontal precipitation" as well, which sustains a dense population of epiphytes. The drier Atlantic slope has 5-6 months without rain, so there are very few evergreens on this side; here too there are fogs in winter. Elsewhere in Central America and the isthmus of Tehuantepec it's the Atlantic side which is the wetter.

The plateau, above about 1,800m, is covered with dense cloudforest, largely evergreen, of oak (*Quercus oocarpa, Q. sapotifolia* and *Q.*

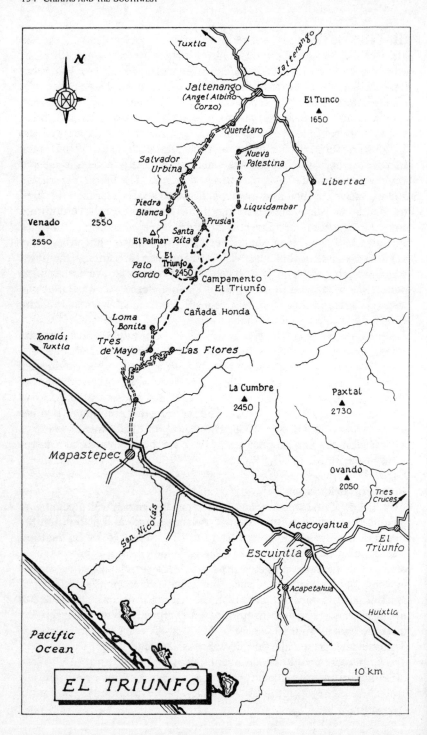

EL TRIUNFO

crispinifolia), *Matudaea trinervia, Dendropanax populifolius*, and the smaller *Hedyosmum mexicanum*, laden with bromeliads, ferns, orchids and other epiphytes (even a cactus, *Nopalxochia ackermannii*), that hold water until they're heavy enough to break branches off. In the understory you'll see *Cyathea* treeferns of 2-4m (some reach 8m), and some palms; there are also ferns in the herb layer. This is the most important vegetational community here, in scientific terms. On the sheltered south side of Cerro El Triunfo trees can reach 40m in height, but generally they're 25-30m, or as little as 10m in exposed places such as the Atlantic escarpment. Most botanical research has been carried out in the Cerro Ovando nuclear zone, at the southeastern end of the reserve, where there are at least 800 species, including the second-tallest trees in Central America, elms (*Ulmus mexicana*) almost 90m in height.

Above 2,300m the trees are smaller and heavily draped in mosses; this is a little-known community known as evergreen cloud scrub, composed mainly of dense shrubs only 2m high, notably *Gaultheria acuminata, Ugni myricoides* and *Vaccinium matudae*. There are patches of *Chusquea* bamboo in open areas, and small trees (*Viburnum* and *Persea spp*) at the edges; from 2,500m there are only conifers (pines, and a few firs and cypress).

The lower parts of the Atlantic slopes are covered by a dry pine-oak forest, with trees only 10m in height, as well as *cafetals* (coffee plantations) up to 1,400m; from around 1,300m to 1,700m you'll move into mixed forest of sweetgum, pine and oak, up to 40m, and quite a diverse range of other trees; in sheltered damper valleys there's less sweetgum and almost no pine, with fig (*Ficus cookii*), elm and *Sterculia mexicana*. There's a dense understorey, including a few cycads (*Ceratozomia matudae*); there are fewer lianas and epiphytes, and more moss and lichen, than on the Pacific side.

The Pacific slope, from about 1,100m to 1,800m, is covered with evergreen and semi-evergreen montane rainforest, with a canopy about 25m high and emergents up to 35m; trees include evergreen oaks such as *Quercus vivens, Q. skinneri* and *Q. salcifolia*, figs (*Ficus cookii*, above 1,100m), and other deciduous trees (shedding leaves in February) such as seagrape (*Coccoloba matudae*) and *Sapium schippii*. With these you'll find ferns (up to 8m tall), epiphytes (fewer than on the plateau), orchids and lianas, which are largely replaced by moss and lichen above 1,600m. There is some illegal harvesting of *Chamaedorea* palm leaves near Cañada Honda and the Palo Gordo-Loma Bonita trail. From about 1,600m to 1,800m there are conifers (*Cupressus benthamii var lindleyi* and *Pinus oocarpa var ochoterenae*), with *Ilex liebmannii*, oaks and alders, and *Erica* shrubs similar to those on the summit of El Triunfo.

Several species of animal endemic to the Sierra Madre de Chiapas are found here; these include green lizards (*dragoncito verde/Abronia matudia, A. smithii*), the dragon-like *turipache de montaña* (*Corytophanes hernandezii*), a salamander (*Dendrotriton xolocaltcae*), the bicoloured fer de lance or pied viper (*nauyaca verde/Bothriechis ornatus*), and above all the very rare azure-rumped tanager (*tangara de alas azules/Tangara cabanisii*), which nests in fig trees between 1,100m and 1,650m, particularly around the Cañada Honda. The horned guan (*pavón/Oreophasis derbianus*) is found only here and across the border in the adjacent mountains of Guatemala. Other wildlife includes the quetzal, solitary and harpy eagles, black guan, great curassow, mountain trogon (*Trogon mexicanus*), macaws, toucans, hummingbirds, flycatchers, forest falcons and manakins, and jaguars, pumas, margay, ocelot, jaguarundi, spider monkeys, tapirs, white-lipped peccary, armadillos and anteaters.

Hiking directions

This traverse of the Sierra Madre de Chiapas begins at the small coffee-trading town of **Jaltenango** (known officially as Angel Albino Corzo); this is reached by buses (12 a day, taking 3½ hours) from the *Cuxtepeques* terminal at Calle 10 Oriente/Av 3 Norte in Tuxtla. The Hotel Liz on 10 Oriente between 1 and 2 Norte is the nearest affordable hotel to the Tuxtla terminal. In Jaltenango buses terminate two blocks east of the plaza; the Hotel-Restaurant Vicky, on the south side of the plaza, is probably the best budget option, while the Esperanza, one block east of the plaza, and the Panalito, at Av 2 Norte 5, three blocks north, are respectively rather better and worse in quality. The Biosphere Reserve office (which can arrange transport) is one block south and one west of the the the plaza (tel: 965 50210).

The dirt road to Prusia starts a bit further to the south and west beyond the RBET office; you should be able to get a ride on a truck a good part of the way, if patient. After 4km the road turns right in Quéretaro; increasingly you'll see lianas, bromeliads and strangler vines, as well as stands of pines. A few kilometres after the hamlet of Salvador Urbina (less than two hours drive from Jaltenango) you should fork left; from here it took me almost 1½ hours to walk on to Prusia (1,075m). This is a coffee finca founded in 1910, and for a long time had the only meteorological station in the Sierra Madre de Chiapas; the average temperature is 21°C, and average rainfall around 2,500mm (most from May to October). At the top end of the finca the road turns left across a bridge to continue as the main muletrack up to El Triunfo; this is definitely the easiest route, but I headed straight on (under a water-pipe), to take what turned out to be a very hard steep path. This begins as a pleasant tree-lined avenue through coffee, which takes 40 minutes to reach the Tzeltzal settlement of Santa Rita, 32km from Jaltenango, and 16km from the El Triunfo clearing.

Here you should take the footbridge (or the ford) to the left and climb steeply past the last kiosk, church and school; after ten minutes you should go straight ahead up a path where the 4WD road turns 90° right and comes to an end. Leave a house to the left and head up into the coffee plantation;

after about three minutes take a staggered junction across a better path and continue up a minor ridge, with zigzags and (at first) a few cutoffs. This is hard going, and not a particularly clear path. After about 15 minutes it passes from coffee into scrub, and after about 20 more into proper forest; the path is very bad at first but soon clears, although I did have a few fallen trees to contend with. After twenty-odd minutes more you should reach the muletrack, and turn right breathing a huge sigh of relief. This is a very good route, easily graded and with well-made zigzags. After 45 minutes it passes around Cerro El Triunfo and after five minutes more reaches the El Talisman stream, the first water since Santa Rita. There are two smaller streams just beyond; after twenty fairly easy minutes (three hours from Prusia) you'll reach a gate opening into the clearing of **El Triunfo**, at 1,850m. This was cleared for grazing, and cattle were brought up here until 1983; this is still the traditional route for *indigenos* coming from the coast to work on the fincas, with at least 1,500 passing through between November and February. Nowadays it's alive with birdsong at dawn and dusk. The first building is the rangers' house, then beyond the footbridge you'll come to the excellent bunkhouse and beyond this the kitchen. To the right of this last is the start of the path to Palo Gordo ("Fat Tree"), where there's another ranger station, usually unoccupied; there's primary forest from the first stream crossing onwards, and between the second and third crossings (about 1km from El Triunfo) there's often a quetzal – one of the rangers will probably take you here and imitate their call.

The 25km route down to Tres de Mayo, on the Pacific side, begins at the south end of the clearing, beyond the rangers' hut; there is a sign where it enters the forest. The path crosses a stream and winds uphill, in a cutting up to 2m deep, and crosses the watershed after almost 25 minutes. The descent starts with easy zigzags, but then rises to the left to reach the Deslave viewpoint after another 12 minutes. The path continues down to the left; after 25 minutes you can ignore the small path down to the right to a cypress grove on a small ridge, as the main route ends up here anyway. It continues with a zig down to the left; you'll pass a sign reading *Cipresal* after five minutes and can soon hear the Arroyo Sicilar way below you. It takes another fifteen minutes to get to the water, at a small waterfall and a shallow pool. After crossing the stream, the path rises for a couple of minutes, and soon emerges into the open, with a view across a valley. It then drops to cross a creek after twenty minutes; the Cañada Honda campsite is just below the path on the far side, but there's nothing there beyond a fireplace (with tripod) and level sites. Remember this is the best place to look for the azure-rumped tanager.

The path soon continues, dropping gently to the left, and crossing two streams after forty and fifty minutes; after about 35 minutes more the path runs along a ridge through open forest. It rises briefly, then follows a ridge down, entering coffee after another 35 minutes. After *another* 35 minutes (beyond a ruined hut) you'll reach a river by a *rancho*; the track crosses to the left bank, rises for three minutes and then drops for ten minutes to reach the dirt road to Loma Bonita.

In the other direction the turning is easy to find, a path rising to the right immediately before a house where the road turns left to ford the river. There's a pedestrian suspension bridge here, although three sets of planks are missing. Following the dirt road downstream you'll come to 3 de Mayo, where there's a kiosk; I was warned not to hike down here due to the risk of robbery; you'll want a vehicle to cover the 25km to Mapastepec in any case.

The last pickup heads down the valley from Loma Bonita at about 15.00, taking about 1¼ hours to reach Mapastepec (known as Mapa') on the coast highway. This is served by hourly buses between Tuxtla and Huixtla, which stop on the old main road, a couple of kilometres before the town. You'll find the *Hotel Diana* by the bus station; there are also the *Hospedaje economico El Paso* by the footbridge on the new bypass, and the *Hotel Ramdich* at the western end of the bypass.

The rest of the Sierra Madre de Chiapas
The Sierra Madre is in theory protected throughout, but the **La Frailescana** reserve, immediately to the northwest of El Triunfo, has existed on paper alone for around twenty years. However, in 1995 the **La Sepultura Biosphere Reserve** was established to protect 167,309ha of montane rain and cloudforest, low deciduous forest (almost the last left in Chiapas) and cloud scrub, stretching from La Frailescana to the Oaxaca border, straddling the main highway from Tuxtla to Tehuantepec. There are plenty of endemics here too, including cycads which are grown in a nursery, half for export. Animal life includes jaguars, spider monkeys, tapirs, quetzals, the rose-bellied bunting (*Passerina rositae*) and the black solitary eagle (*Harpyhaliaetus solitarius*).

To the north of La Sepultura, on the south side of the Presa Netzahualcoyotl (or Malpaso) reservoir is **El Ocote** (or Selva del Ocote), a Special Biosphere Reserve set up in 1982 to protect 48,140ha of high evergreen tropical forest, as well as cloudforest, deciduous forest and savanna. This is the northern limit of the harpy eagle (*Harpia harpyja*), the world's most powerful bird of prey, which can take small monkeys. It's reached by boat from Apic-Pac, at the east end of the reservoir, to the north of Ocozocuautla; you'll need to get permission and book this with IHN in Tuxtla. Trips are run by the Café El Puente in San Cristóbal. The reserve is known for its caves, almost lost in the jungle and barely explored. The Santa Marta and Los Grifos caves show signs of habitation from 7400-3500BC and 1100-900BC.

The Río La Venta (nothing to do with the La Venta archaeological site in

Tabasco) flows north into the El Ocote reserve; from km48 on the Tuxtla-Tehuantepec highway a gravel track leads north for 2km to the **Cascadero El Aguacero** ("The Downpour" waterfall). Almost 800 steps lead down from the car park (where camping is possible) to the foot of the waterfall. From here it's a 70km raft trip down the **Cañón de la Venta** to La Junta, where the La Venta meets the Río Negro at the edge of the El Ocote reserve, just south of the Netzahualcoyotl reservoir.

There are waterfalls and caves such as, 28km downstream, the Tapesco El Diablo, 35m above the right bank; in 1993 cavers found the entrance blocked by a horizontal wooden screen and a Late Classical Maya burial inside. The narrowest section of the canyon is El Encajonado, 3m wide and about 100m long, with another waterfall on the left bank. One of the most interesting caves for speleologists is Los Ojos del Tigre (1,840m long and 171m deep), on the Río Negro 2.5km above its confluence with the Río Venta.

La Encrucijada

Heading southeast along the highway from Mapastepec, the first major town is Escuintla, from where you can reach the **La Encrucijada Biosphere Reserve**, one of the largest and most important areas of mangroves and other wetlands on Mexico's Pacific coast (144,868ha, protected since 1972). There's a paved road as far as Acapetahua, where you'll cross the railway, and then 18km on dirt (drivable all year) to Las Garzas, from where you can take a boat to the IHN *campamento* at La Concepción, or to the fishing village of Las Palmas.

The area of Lago Chantuto and Las Salinas, at the northwestern end of the reserve, is disturbed by human activities, notably shrimp fishing, but the area around Lago Panzacola and La Concepción is wilder and well worth visiting. You must get permission to visit from the IHN in Tuxtla or Escuintla.

A long spit, the Barra San Juan, separates the sea from the *Canal Principal* or el Huetate estuary; the coastal dune vegetation is composed of *Graminea* grasses, *Acacia farnesiana*, and other salt-resistant species. Behind this is a large expanse of mangrove swamp, with five species of mangrove; on islets there is sub-evergreen forest (cedar, fig, *guanacaste, chicozapote*), as well as palms (*Sabal mexicana*), and *canacoitales* of *Bravaisia integerrima* (*canacoite*). The climate is hot and humid, with abundant summer rain from May to November, with a *canicula* or dry spell in July/August, and occasional rain in February/March, a total of 2,500-3,000mm precipitation per year.

There's a surprising range of mammal species, including jaguar, ocelot, margay, jaguarundi, collared peccary, agouti, grey squirrels (*Sciurus aerogaster*), raccoons, anteaters, otters, white-tail and brocket deer, and spider monkeys. Reptiles include *Crocodilus chiapensis* and *C. acutus*, two iguanas (*Iguana iguana* and *Ctenosaura similis*), boas and other snakes, four marine turtles (leatherback, green, hawksbill and ridley turtles) and at least four freshwater turtles. Resident birds include ospreys, parrots, wood storks, jacanas, anhingas, white ibis, neotropical cormorants, roseate spoonbills, brown pelicans, Muscovy ducks, and black-bellied tree-ducks (*Dendrocygna autumnalis*), whose local name *pijiji* is presumably reflected in the name of the next town along the highway northwest from Mapastepec, Pijijiapan. Migrants include white pelicans, magnificent frigatebirds, avocets, gulls, and other ducks (such as the blue-winged and cinnamon teals, *Anas discors* and *A. cyanoptera*).

Fish include bass (*Centropomus nigrescens*), striped mullet (*Mugil cephalus*), perch (*Cichlasoma spp*), and a "living fossil" known as *peje lagarto* or *pez armado* (*Lepisosteus tropicus*), which is gastronomically esteemed.

Volcan Tacaná

The highest peak in southern Mexico is usually seen, in terms of fauna and flora, as an extension of the Sierra Madre de Chiapas, but geologically it is an extension of the volcanic chain that runs through Guatemala. It lies on the border, and indeed Mexican and Guatemalan mountaineers meet on the summit on Good Friday. The volcano erupted in 1885 and is now extinct, but the area is affected by up to 90 earthquakes a year. About 25km to the northwest El Boquerón (about 2,550m) is a volcanic cone, about 300m high. This is now a coffee-growing area, populated by Mam people who moved here to avoid military conscription in Guatemala. There's cloudforest high on the volcano, with humid tropical forest below; a reserve is proposed, to create a wildlife corridor between Guatemala and the El Triunfo Biosphere Reserve.

From Tapachula, the main town near the southern border crossings, you should head towards the Puente Talismán border crossing, passing (after 10km) the Izapa ruins, which are now seen as a transitional phase between the Olmec and Maya cultures. From here you can continue by bus northwards through Cacaohatán to Unión Juárez, centre of an area known as the Switzerland of Chiapas, due to its climate and vernacular architecture. It is however a centre for coffee growing; there are two hotels here and a few other services. You can ask for a guide at the Restaurante La Montaña, on the north side of the plaza.

A dirt road continues north for about 3km to Talquián, from where you can hike up Tacaná; an alternative route turns left to Chiquihuites, from where a path leads up the volcano. It's a two- or three-day trip and you should be prepared to camp, although there are some refuges. The Plan de la Ardilla (Squirrel's Plain, 3,400m) is a good place to camp before climbing to the summit. Old craters lie at 3,510m, 3,720m and about 3,870m; the summit is at 4,110m (or 4,093m).

TABASCO

The state of Tabasco is similar to Chiapas and Oaxaca in its semi-feudal social structure, due to which illegal logging and other eco-crimes are rampant and unrestrained by any form of law. Most of the loggable timber has gone, leaving only a large area of swamp to the east of the capital, Villahermosa. The state had no protected areas at all until 1992, when 302,706ha of this swamp was declared the **Centla Biosphere Reserve**. This protects mangrove and other swamps, low and medium semi-evergreen forest, providing a refuge for crocodiles, manatí, green turtles, jaguars, ocelots, howler monkeys, and many endangered birds, including wood storks and falcons. Access is via highway 18, heading north from Villahermosa to Frontera.

Most visitors are more likely to visit the **Yumká Nature Interpretation Centre**, a sort of safari park 14km east of Villahermosa, which opened in 1992. This boasts three ecosystems, only one of which is actually authentic; this is *la selva*, where a 650m-long path leads through 31ha of "jungle", including ceiba (*Ceiba pentandra*), caoba (*Swietania macrophylla*), ramón (*Brosimum alicastrum*), palms and heliconias. There are howler monkeys, macaws and toucans here, as well as great curassows, which are not native to Tabasco; there's also 24ha of supposedly African savanna, stocked with emus, antelopes, gaur, elephants, rhinos and giraffes, and an artificial lake, in, on and around which you can see spider monkeys, caimans, herons, white egrets, snail kites, kingfishers, vultures, ducks and gulls.

There's a more authentically ecotouristic project in the Huimanguillo hills, up the Grijalva valley; this is known as **Agua Selva** (Water Jungle), and is centred on the village of Malpasito, in the southeasternmost corner of the state. You can get here by a daily bus from Huimanguillo, south of Cárdenas, and can stay in an *albergue ecológico* and hike to waterfalls and ruins, or just relax in the forest and the river gorge.

A Botanical Garden or Ecological Park is proposed at km21 of the main highway west from Cárdenas, which would save one of the last relics of medium *canacoite* forest (*Bravaisa integerrima*), 90% of which has been lost in the last thirty years.

In Villahermosa, the INEGI shop is at Av Madero 909.

OAXACA

Oaxaca shares the feudal tradition of Chiapas and Tabasco, with a large and oppressed indigenous community, and environmental degradation at the hands of rich and cynical men who are above the law. Nevertheless, in 1991 a state Ecological Conservation Law was passed and a Basic Ecological Programme prepared for 1994-98. Action is essential, as Oaxaca, with a very wide range of habitats, from high evergreen forest to drought-resistant scrub, has more endemic vertebrates and butterflies than any other Mexican state or Central American nation, and only Chiapas has more plant species. It boasts 264 species and subspecies of mammals (44% of all those in Mexico), 701 birds (47%), 467 reptiles (66%), 1,100 butterflies (75%), and 8,000 vascular plants (50%), of which 600 are endemic or quasi-endemic to Oaxaca and/or Guerrero (including 60 oaks and pines). There are 690 species of ferns, 70% of all those in Mexico. *Pereskias* (a genus of primitive cacti) are plentiful in the Isthmus of Tehuantepec, and there's a unique forest of Oreomunna (*Engelhardtia mexicana*) in the Sierra Norte. Nevertheless the state has lost 50% of its forest in the last 22 years, cleared largely for cattle, whose numbers have doubled since 1960.

The indigenous population numbers some 600,000, mostly Zapotec (40%), Mixtec (23.7%) and Mazatec (12.4%), with 13 others, of which the Ixcateco (0.01%) and Tacuate (1%) seem doomed to disappear.

Very little of the state's area is protected; there are no Biosphere Reserves and only two National Parks. However the **La Joya Biosphere Reserve** is proposed in the Sierra de Juárez, off the Oaxaca-Tuxtepec road; this will protect 8,600ha of relict high evergreen forest, 200m-high waterfalls and karst formations. There's access to the former sawmill of Valea de las Flores at 2,980m. This is not to be confused with the **Benito Juárez National Park**, which covers 2,737ha in the Sierra de San Felipe, just north of Oaxaca city. This is of importance as an escape from the city rather than for any great ecological value. It comprises pine, oak, and low deciduous forest, with raccoons, armadillos, foxes, squirrels, rabbits, ringtails, peccary and deer in residence.

The **Lagunas de Chacahua National Park** lies on the coast west of Puerto Escondido, with 14,187ha of low and medium evergreen forest, coastal dunes and mangroves surrounding the Pastoría, Chacahua and Salinas lakes. Here you may see white-tail deer, anteaters, collared peccary, coatí, raccoons, armadillos, foxes, bats, rabbits, ospreys, white herons, black and green iguanas, boas, rattlesnakes and crocodiles; however, great curassows, jaguars, margays, brocket deer, and tapir have all vanished. Thanks largely to road-building in the 1970s, the human population has increased from 50 in 1936 to 1,500 in the 1980s. Six species of turtle nest on 28km of beaches here; to the east, before Puerto Escondido, the **National Turtle Centre** has recently been established at Mazunte, on the Playa de Escobilla, which stretches 15km from the Río Cozoaltepec to the Río Tonameca.

There are ecotourism possibilities here, and also in the hills above Huatulco, where coffee is grown organically as the understorey of the forest;contact Alberto Perez Mariscal, Union Estatal de Productores de Café, Posada la Casa de la Tia, Cinco de Mayo 108, Centro Oaxaca 68000, Oaxaca. **Huatulco** itself is being developed as a new megaresort, with roads now reaching eight of the nine bays; it is being designed for an environmentally-conscious clientele (75% of its area is to be kept green), but with developments such as the largest Club Med in the western hemisphere it's hard to believe it really will be a destination for ecotourists. Ultimately there should be 30,000 rooms here, accommodating two million people a year, as many as Cancún.

To the east of the Isthmus of Tehuantepec is the Sierra Atravesada (2,250m), an extension of the Sierra Madre de Chiapas; at its western end are the villages of San Miguel Chimalapa and Santa María Chimalapa Selva, centres of an area of 594,000ha of high evergreen forest that was bought from the Spanish crown by the Zoque people in 1687. This sale was confirmed 30 years ago (and in 1993 and 1995) by Presidential decree; nevertheless invasions have been happening, with official support, for 40 years. Now the state government is building a track into the forest of Las **Chimalapas**, supposedly to help agriculture. Those who illegally clear the forest for lumber and cattle-grazing are never imprisoned, while local indigenous leaders who protest are locked up for long periods. CIPAMEX (part of the International Council for Bird Preservation) is interested in ecotourism here, to help save some of the most important rainforest in Mexico, but much more pressure is needed to bring about changes in the corrupt way the state is run.

144

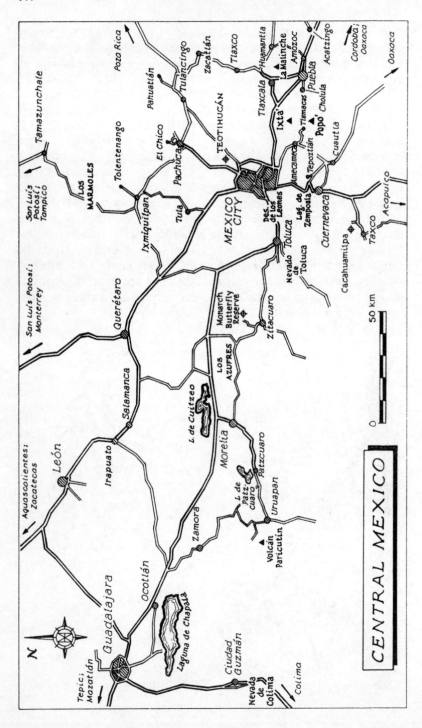

Chapter Nine

Central Mexico
– the Volcanoes,
Puebla and Veracruz

The Transversal Volcanic Axis (or Trans-Mexico Volcanic Belt) dominates
the area immediately south of the capital, running east-west for 930km
with an average width of 120km. Its western part consists largely of isolated
peaks, but the eastern end is a plateau with an average altitude of 1,500-
2,500m. The Sierra Nevada is a spur that runs north, immediately to the
east of Mexico City, from Popocatépetl through Iztaccíhuatl, Teyotl (4,570m,
the sixth highest in Mexico), El Papayo and Telapón, ending with Tláloc.
On a Mesozoic base (over 65m years old), the volcanoes developed recently
in the Tertiary and Quaternary periods, with uplifting since the Miocene
epoch (in the last 23m years). The Axis' climate is mostly temperate with
a mild dry winter (with cool evenings) and a wet summer; average
temperatures are in the 12-18°C range. Above 2,600m the climate is semi-
cold humid (4-12°C), and of course it's colder above 4,000m.

There are wide swathes of fir (*oyamel/Abies religiosa*) between 2,700m
and 3,300m; then there's pine to about 4,000m, higher than anywhere else
in the world. Above this to the crests is open subalpine grassland known as
zacatonale. The volcano rabbit (*Romerolagus diazi*, variously known as
teporingo, teporito or *zacatuche*) is the best-known endemic mammal in
this area, a small featureless creature with tiny ears and tail, found only
above 3,000m.

JALISCO

The Transversal Volcanic Axis has its western end in the state of Jalisco,
which contains two major Biosphere Reserves. On the coast the **Chamela-
Cuixmala Biosphere Reserve** protects a wide range of habitats, 13,142ha
in all: important turtle beaches, coastal dunes, the Cuixmala estuary, lagoons,
mangroves, drought-resistant scrub, low deciduous forest and medium sub-
evergreen forest. UNAM has a research station here, 2km from the Pacific,
described by Lott et al in *Biotropica* 19: 228-235; average precipitation is
707mm (80% of it from mid-June to September). All five of Mexico's

felines other than the bobcat are found here, as well as otters, pocket mice, ospreys, roseate spoonbills, green macaws, green iguanas and crocodiles.

In addition to the three turtle beaches in the Chamela-Cuixmala reserve (Teopa, Cuitzamala and El Tecuán, each about 6km long), there's also the 69-km long Playa Mismaloya, stretching from Ipala to Roca Negra.

The **Sierra de Manantlán Biosphere Reserve** is very important to Mexicans because this is where the primitive form of maize called *teosintle* (*Zea diploperennis*) was found, growing in abandoned corn fields. It is resistant to many diseases that affect the contemporary species, so there are high hopes that this resistance can be introduced to commercial varieties; it also grows in a cool, damp environment, so it could boost world production by 10%. The University of Guadalajara has a field station at Las Joyas, working on this and also on sustainable development projects with local communities, which have a long history of conflict over resources. There's a high level of biodiversity, with at least 2,070 species of vascular plants, 336 birds and 108 mammals. Habitats include cloudforest, pine and pine-oak, fir, low deciduous forest, medium semi-deciduous forest, riverside gallery forest and savanna, so 139,577ha of the sierra have now been protected. Wildlife includes jaguar, puma, margay, bobcat, armadillo, coati, white-tail deer, peccary, green macaw, iguana, and rattlesnakes.

The Sierra de Manantlán lies to the east of Highway 80 (Guadalajara-Barra de Navidad), to the southeast of Autlán de Navarro; take the road east towards Ciudad Guzmán and then turn south before El Grullo to reach Manantlán.

Nevado de Colima

Just west of the *autopista* south from Guadalajara to Colima, you'll see the twin peaks of Nevado de Colima and Volcán de Colima (or Fuego), immediately east of the Sierra de Manantlán. Nevado ("Snowy"), to the north, is an extinct volcano, the ninth highest peak in Mexico at 4,240m, while Volcán de Colima (3,825m) is still active (having erupted in 1991). They have been covered since 1936 by the 22,200ha Nevado de Colima National Park, a fairly dry area of pine, fir, oak, alpine pasture and spiny scrub, although some of the low-lying gullies harbour lusher forests. Wildlife includes puma, fox, white-tail deer, armadillo, skunk, rabbit, coati, falcon, raven, jays, quail and partridge.

Rough dirt roads approach fairly close to both peaks, but traffic is so infrequent that you shouldn't depend on being able to hitch a ride. It is very dry and dusty, and there are no springs on either mountain, so you'll need to carry a lot of water.

The nearest town is **Ciudad Guzmán** (1,520m), reached by direct buses from Mexico City, Guadalajara and Colima. Formerly known as Zapotlán el Grande or Zapotlán de Orozco, this was the birthplace in 1883 of the painter José Clemente Orozco; now it's a pleasant town, with an excellent little museum (Tuesday-Sunday, 10.00-16.45) on Calle Dr Angel González, just off Reforma, the main road from the highway and the bus station to the centre. To the north of town is the Laguna Zapotlán, and beyond that Laguna Sayula, which is largely dry in summer but provides an important stopover for migrating ducks and geese from Canada and the USA.

Hiking directions
There are several routes up Nevado, but only one real way up Volcán de Colima to the south. For **Nevado de Colima** you should take any bus from Ciudad Guzmán towards El Jazmín, Zapotitlán de Vadillo, Tolimán, Tonaya or Autlán just as far as El Fresnito; after a long straight stretch, about 12km from town, a dirt road forks half-left into the village just before the main road swings right. Get off either here or a couple of hundred metres further on (to the right), where a sign to the *Parque Nacional Nevado de Colima* points up a track along a row of conifers to the left. This rough, dust-ridden track leads in about six hours (on foot) to a hut at La Joya (3,500m), from where it takes about 3½ hours to reach the summit (the last 30 minutes being spent scrambling up loose scree). This trail is easy to find and passes through stunted forest often covered in mist. An uncomfortable night's sleep is possible at La Joya for those with no tent, but you should not rely on finding water here. The track continues to a saddle at 3,800m and swings left around the west side of the mountain to a microwave station at about 3,900m, from where it's an easier two-hour hike to the summit. Returning downhill, you may be tempted to take one of the numerous trails, hoping that it's a shortcut; Shauna Picard tried this and spent the best part of a day lost before finding her way back to La Joya.

For a better route with more chance of getting a lift, take the dirt road (shown as a main road on the INEGI map) through the upper (southwestern) end of El Fresnito (at about 1,775m); it takes five minutes to reach a kiosk, and another 35 minutes on the level to the start of a track signposted up to the right. This is immediately after a dirt road to the east down through Las Canoas to the main road. This road up the mountain, through Los Mazos, is the one used by Telmex vehicles, but it's a more roundabout route. If you ask around in El Fresnito, it's possible to rent a vehicle to take you up to La Joya.

To reach **Volcán de Colima**, you should take one of the five daily second-class buses between Ciudad Guzmán and Colima (there's no shortage of first-class buses, but they all take the new *autopista*). (You could take the hourly Tuxpan (*via corta*) or Tecalitlán buses, which set you down at a junction a few kilometres the wrong side of Atenquique.) You need to pass through the small town of Atenquique (just below 1,000m), where a paper mill fills a narrow valley, and climb up some steep hairpin bends. Get off the bus at km56, 3km south of town at about 1,200m, where a dirt road forks to the right, signposted *MicroOndas Cerro Alto*.

Again, it's a very dusty track, and you'll dehydrate fast. It rises gently at first; soon you'll see some isolated pines, but some thorny bushes in brown fields could be out of Africa. It takes 40 minutes to reach Loma de la Cruz, and another ten minutes to the last farm, after which the track begins to zig more steeply uphill; fifty minutes more brings you to a junction where you'll see the first sign to the national park, to the right. It's another fifty minutes to the junction to the microwave towers, another 1½km to the right at 2,000m. You're about 11km from the main road here; the track climbs steadily for another 15km (at least four hours net) to the 3,200m col between Nevado and Volcán de Colima; it continues a little bit further to two abandoned sawmills. To reach the summit of Volcán de Colima, just scramble up the pumice slope to the south/left. It's also possible to head right to Nevado or to the microwave station on its west side.

MICHOACÁN AND MÉXICO STATES

Lakes Pátzcuaro and Chapala

The **Lago de Pátzcuaro** lies at 2,110m not far east of Uruapán, at the centre of the Tarascan (or Purépecha) Indian country; there's a population of almost 50,000 *indigenos*, whose language is related to that of the Quechua of Peru. The town of Pátzcuaro is very picturesque, with a wealth of buildings dating from the 16th century when the bishopric was based here. It's a bit of a walk to the lake (buses and *combis* run from Plaza Bocanegra); from the *embarcadero* you can take boat trips around the lake and to various islands. The best-known of these is Isla Janitzio, also picturesque but crowded with souvenir shops, but Isla Yunuén is also developing a communal tourism project. Cabins on several islands can be booked through the INI (National Institute of Indigenous Peoples) in Pátzcuaro. Fish are the local speciality, above all the endemic *pescado blanco* (*Chirostoma estor*), which is said to taste rather bland and is in any case threatened by four introduced species and by pollution and over-fishing. It's probably best avoided in restaurants. The Tarascans use a trademark butterfly net from their canoes, but these days they're used more for posing for photos than for fishing.

The **Laguna de Chapala** lies at 1,524m 50km south of Guadalajara; it's the largest lake in Mexico, about 113km by 30km, and is well developed for tourism, with plenty of hotels, and boats for hire. A large community of retired Americans and Canadians lives permanently there, many of them (particularly in Ajijic, back in Jalisco state) pretending to be artists or writers. The University of Guadalajara and Baylor University (Texas) share a field station on the lake, partly to study endemic fish species such as *Xenotoca variata, Chirostoma chapalae, Amenurus dugesi* and *Girardinichthys viviparus*.

Volcán Paricutín

Volcán Paricutín grew from a hole in the ground to be the 17th highest peak in Mexico (c2,774m) in just nine years, from 1943 to 1952. It spewed forth around a billion tonnes of lava, which now cover an area of 20km² and form a 300m-high cone; it was usually vulcanian (building up pressure and then exploding) but unusually shifted occasionally to the strombolian mode (with steady release of steam and pasty lumps of lava). The two villages of San Salvador Paricutín and San Juan Parangaricutiro were buried by the lava (with no loss of life); the church tower of San Juan, now called San Juan Quemado (Burnt) lies on the tourist route to the volcano, while Nuevo San Juan Parangaricutaro lies just to the west of Uruapán. A painting by Gerardo Murillo (Dr Atl) in the *Museo Nacional de Arte* shows the volcano in 1947.

It's a big tourist sight, so the road is now asphalted; head north from Uruapán for 18km, then turn left for 20km to Angahuán, served by hourly buses to Los Reyes (de Salgado). This is a Tarascan community which, having lost its land to the volcano, is now doing very well out of tourism, while also raising avocados and maguey. The bus will drop you on the main road, from where you should walk in to the plaza, and keep left to the new *albergue* or hostel, about half an hour in all; bear left to follow the power lines where the road forks by a large wooden house with fancy carvings. You can stay the night and park a car at the *albergue*; there's a view of the volcano and the one remaining church tower of San Juan Quemado. The trail to the church is clear and there's no need at all for a guide to go this far; the area of the church is swamped with hawkers and litter, and you'll be pestered to hire a guide and a horse here and everywhere else. To continue south to the summit you might wish to hire a guide; although the volcano is perfectly evident in front of you, the rough sharp lava can shred your footwear if you're not careful. It takes about four hours to the volcano from San Juan, with an easy climb to a secondary crater and then a good path to the top.

By horse (or 4WD) you'll probably follow a dirt road around to the far side of the volcano, then cross the lava for an hour (less by horse) and climb to the top in another hour at most, on another good path. You'll pass various fumaroles and hot patches of rock; the craters themselves are now vegetated and seem tranquil enough.

Nevado de Toluca

The Nevado de Toluca (or Xinantécatl, "naked man"), in México state, is the easiest of all Mexico's volcanoes to visit, as there is a road all the way to the crater. It's hard to pin down its altitude accurately; it's somewhere between 4,558m and 4,704m, which means it's probably the fourth highest peak in Mexico. Humboldt made it to the top in 1803, and nowadays the runner Germán Silva, winner of the 1994 and 1995 New York marathons and sixth in the 1996 Olympics, runs up once a week to train and spend the night at altitude before running down; he claims to be only two minutes slower per kilometre than at sea level.

The volcano is inactive, but it's known for sudden thunderstorms, so you shouldn't take it totally for granted. It's been a National Park since 1936, covering 51,000ha of fir, pine and (above 4,000m) *zacatonal*; only 48.5% of the Park's area in a good state, and 29.7% is greatly altered. Wildlife includes bobcats, coyote, white-tail deer, opossums, volcano rabbits, falcons, woodpeckers and rattlesnakes.

Heading southwest out of Toluca on the highway to Zihuatanejo, turn left after 21km, and then left again after about 7km, just after the village of Raíces. Buses (every two hours, from Toluca to Sultepec) will drop you at this point, from where you may be able to get a ride with weekend visitors or traffic to the radio station. The road loops right around to the east side of the mountain to enter the crater, where there are two lakes, named after the Sun and Moon, about 27km from the road. Traces of ritual offerings by the Matlalzinca people have been found in these lakes. There's an *albergue* here, where you can eat or sleep. The highest peak, Pico del Fraile (the Friar's Peak) is to the south, about 500m above, with the lower Pico de la Aguila (the Eagle's Peak) to the north; the easiest route up is along the rim of the crater.

The Monarch Butterfly Reserve

Every year millions of monarch butterflies (*Danaus plexippus*) arrive to spend the winter in the mountains of Michoacán and México states. They are several generations removed from those that spent the previous winter in Mexico, but amazingly they have no problem finding their way from Canada and the northern USA. They totally blanket the firs and pines, turning them bright orange, but cold weather can cause them to fall to the ground. A cold spell in the winter of 1995/96 produced huge piles of inert butterflies, and it was thought that half the population had been lost, causing great concern in Canada, if not in Mexico; in fact only 7% died, the rest reviving with warmer weather.

There are several reserves, but only one is open to visitors, and that only from November to late March; it's usually known simply as the *Reserva Mariposa Monarca*. There's been an explosion in visitor numbers from just 9,000 in 1984/85 to over 70,000 now, and there are strict rules banning smoking, noise and touching butterflies, (seemingly) dead or alive; you can only visit with a guide.

From Zitácuaro, on the old highway from Toluca to Morelia (through traffic now uses the Mexico City-Guadalajara *autopista*), you should take the hourly bus north to Ocampo, and another (much less frequent) from there east to the village of El Rosario, from where you'll have a half-hour walk if the bus doesn't continue to the reserve. There's accommodation in

Angangueo (not to be confused with Angahuán), an old silver-mining town further up the road north of Ocampo (and reached by the same buses); there's a direct track from here, starting as Calle Matamoros, to the reserve. This covers 1,888ha of the Sierra el Campanario, mostly with a semi-cold sub-humid climate (14-16°C and 2,500-3,000mm precipitation, most of it in summer). Up to about 3,000m there's a mixed forest of pine-oak (largely *Pinus pseudostrobus*, with five other pine species, two oak species, two species of *Arbutus*, and *Cupressus lindleyi*); above this there's dense fir (*Abies religiosa*). Other than the butterflies, there's not a lot of interesting wildlife – coyotes, weasels, foxes, white-tail deer, rabbits and many birds.

The scientific research centre is in the Sierra Chincua, to the northwest of Angangueo, where there's a larger reserve of 2,695ha, and the third main reserve (2,014ha) is in the Cerros Chivati-Huacal, to the southwest of El Rosario. In all of these reserves deforestation is a major problem, and there's little sign that environmental education or ecotourism are changing attitudes yet. It's thought that many butterflies are being knocked to the ground by rain and snow through gaps in the canopy caused by illegal logging.

MORELOS

The northern part of this small state just south of the capital is covered by the Ajusco-Chichinautzín Biological Corridor, which protects 37,302ha on the south side of the Transversal Volcanic Axis, linking it to the Balsas Valley at about 2,100m. Thus it covers a continuous range from low tropical jungle to high mountain grassland, with a predominance of boreal species (at their southern limit) above and neotropical species below. There are 89 species of wild mammals, of which 40 are bats; others include bobcats, white-tail deer, volcano rabbits, armadillos, skunks, squirrels, raccoons, ringtails and coati. There are also axolotls, salamanders, turtles and over 200 birds including ospreys, 17 hummingbirds and seven falcons. The corridor includes the Lagunas de Zempoala and El Tepozteco National Parks, on either side of the roads and railway from Mexico City to Cuernavaca.

The **El Tepozteco National Park**, northeast of Cuernavaca, protects the area around the town of Tepoztlán, a small Nahuatl community which was immortalised by Oscar Lewis' classic anthropological study *Life in a Mexican Village*. The Tepozteco pyramid is at 2,100m altitude, 2km from the town along a well-signposted path (which it seems can take tourists up to an hour); it's dedicated to Tepoztécatl, god of *pulque*, represented by rabbits, of all things! There are great views of the surrounding volcanoes.

The park, set up in 1937, protects 24,000ha (200ha in the Federal District), rising to the 3,450m peak of the Volcán de Chichinautzín. It's composed of low deciduous forest, oak, pine, fir, and even, supposedly, cloudforest,

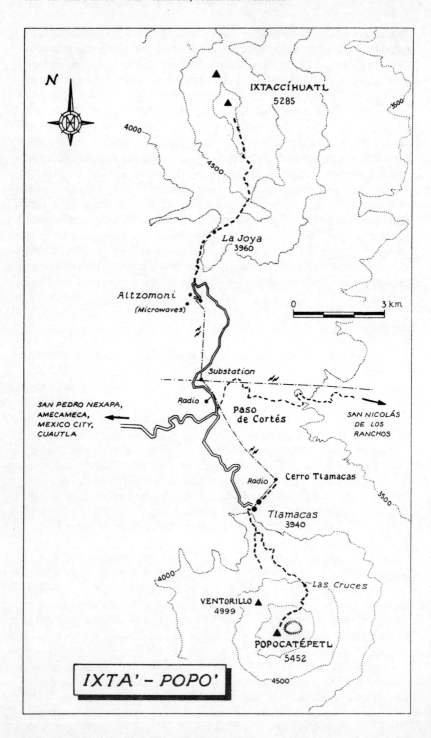

N

IXTACCÍHUATL
5285

4000

4500

3500

La Joya
3960

Altzomoni
(Microwaves)

0   3 km

Substation

Radio

Paso
de Cortés

SAN PEDRO NEXAPA,
AMECAMECA,
MEXICO CITY,
CUAUTLA

SAN NICOLÁS
DE LOS
RANCHOS

Radio   Cerro Tlamacas

3500

Tlamacas
3940

4000   Las Cruces

VENTORILLO ▲
4999

POPOCATÉPETL
5452

4500

IXTA' - POPO'

with at least 714 plant species, 81 fungi and 236 animals. The richest areas are those most threatened by the Mexico-Cuernavaca motorway, railway and powerlines. A US$350m plan for a golf course was abandoned in 1996 after protests which led to the shooting by police of a demonstrator, and the arrest of 60 police officers.

The **Laguna de Zempoala National Park** lies to the west of the main road, on the border with Mexico state. There are six lakes (Quila, Prieta, Hueyapan, Tonatihua, Compila and Zempoala) set in alder, willow, pine and fir. It's a popular area for camping, horse-riding and fishing (permit needed). Turn off the main road at Tres Marías/Santa María and head west through Huitzilac.

IXTA-POPO NATIONAL PARK

This is more or less the official name of the park that includes the second and third highest peaks in Mexico. Popocatépetl is the classic Mexican volcano, but it has been erupting since 1994. However, the lower Ixtaccíhuatl is in any case a far more enjoyable expedition. Because the park is only 70km from Mexico City it's very busy, especially at weekends, but neither mountain should be tackled without proper equipment and due preparation; roughly five people die every year, largely due to faulty equipment. As this is a guide for backpackers rather than serious mountaineers, we concentrate on the most straightforward routes. Even so, we can't stress enough the importance of gradual acclimatisation; travellers who come up from Mexico City to Tlamacas in the evening and then attempt to reach the top of Popo' next morning usually fail and beat a hasty retreat suffering from nausea, headaches and double vision.

The best time to climb the mountains is from mid-September to the end of December, when visibility is good and the snow is firm, although it is chilly; from January to March the winds are stronger and the snow may reach below Tlamacas, with a minimum temperature of -10°C. The climbing season ends at the end of March, although ice-climbing continues into May. It's dry from mid-March to early May, with a minimum of -5°C; the summer is the rainy season, with lots of soft damp snow on the mountain, and you may be hit by *aguaceros* (downpours) even in the shelter of the forest.

Getting there

To visit either mountain, you need to get first to **Amecameca** (usually known as Ameca'), which is reached by buses every 15 minutes from the TAPO terminal in Mexico City (metro San Lázaro) and *colectivos* from the Candelaria metro stop. Although the *autopista* to Oaxaca via Puebla is now open, some buses still run through Ameca', giving access from the south. If you're coming from Puebla you can change buses on the outskirts of Mexico City at Cárcel de Mujeres/Acatitla. Ameca' (at 2,315m) is a lovely town, with great views of the volcanoes looming behind the church on the plaza. On the other side of town, to the west, is the 90m hill of Sacromonte, on top of which is the second holiest shrine in Mexico (after Guadalupe, in the north of Mexico City); it's a National Park, but has no ecological importance, being largely planted with eucalyptus. There are several hotels, on the plaza and (better value) a block north, and the *Loncheria Flecha Roja* on the plaza, which is open not just for lunch but for dinner too. Tlalmanalco, on the main road to the north of Ameca', is worth a visit, with the church of San Luís Obispo (1533), a 16th century open chapel with striking indigenous sculptures, and the hacienda de Zavaleta.

Buses run from Ameca' to San Pedro Nexapa, 6km up the road to the volcanoes (which start by the Pemex station at the south end of town); you can ignore "Popo Park", which is a resort further south on the main road. When Popo' is not erupting, there'll be *colectivos* all the way to the Tlamecas hut at weekends, but they weren't running in 1996. You can either hike/ hitch from San Pedro or take a taxi, from Ameca' or San Pedro. It's about 24km to the Paso de Cortés, at 3,670m on the col between the two volcanoes, where there's a refuge and one of Mexico's few roundabouts! A rough track follows powerlines down towards Chamula to the east; you can catch a bus in San Mateo Ozolco or San Nicolás de los Ranchos. A couple of kilometres down this track is the Buenavista tourist villa, base for hiking and riding on the lower slopes. At the Paso de Cortés you're just leaving the boreal forest (2,900m-3,600m), mainly of *Pinus montezumae*, with volcano rabbits, coyotes, white-tail deer, foxes, ringtails, bobcats, weasels, and rattlesnakes. Above 4,000m there's nothing but sub-alpine grassland, and then bare rock and ice; field mice can be found up to 4,200m, and lizards to 4,250m.

INEGI's 1:50,000 map E14B41 *Huejotzingo* covers the peaks of Popo' and Ixta', but virtually nothing to the west. There's also a 1:20,000 map E14B42-D, which is too detailed for most uses, and a *Rutas de Popocatépetl* map by Alfredo Careaga, which is available from the *Club de Exploraciones en Mexico*. There's also a photocopied guide to Popo' by José Manuel Casanova Becerra, who teaches *montanismo* at UNAM.

Popocatépetl

Popocatépetl (or Popocatzin, "Smoking Mountain", 5,452m) is not, as some assume, the highest mountain in Mexico (Pico de Orizaba is higher), but it is the best-known, with its classic cone shape and easy access from the capital. The volcano began to develop in the Miocene epoch, 5-23mya (million years ago), creating a base 25km in diameter and maybe 2km deep, then 10mya when the subsidiary cone of Nexpayantla, now known as Ventorillo, formed, and then 2.5mya, when the main cone formed.

The first European to climb Popo' was supposedly Diego de Ordaz in

1519, two years before the conquest, but there is doubt about how far he got, as the mountain was then erupting; in 1521 Francisco Montaño definitely made it to the crater to collect 140kg of sulphur for gunpowder; this remained an altitude record for Europeans until the 19th century. In 1927 an eruption was accidentally initiated by dynamiting the crater to mine sulphur; activity increased from 1991, and Popo' has been erupting since 1994.

Turning right at the Paso de Cortés, it's about 4km up the road (closed while Popo' is erupting) to Tlamacas (3,940m), where you'll find two large refuges and the mountain rescue service (*Socorro Alpino*, open at weekends; at other times phone 674 3670 to report your plans). You can rent crampons and ice-axes here, and get meals at busy times. The fine *Albergue Vicente Guerrero*, with 98 beds, was built in the 1970s, and there are also 76 beds in the 1952 hut; in normal conditions up to 15,000 a year stay here (11,000 of them Mexican), with perhaps 500 cars coming up at busy winter weekends. They like you to reserve beds, especially out of season: tel: 553 6286 or 553 5896. This volume of tourists means that, before the current eruption, there was litter all the way to the summit, and the stream below Tlamacas is polluted for at least 5km. There's a camping area along the road from the Paso de Cortés to Tlamacas. The road continues northeast to the radio towers on Cerro Tlamacas, from where there may be views to the peaks of Malinche, Orizaba and Cofre de Perote. If, as suggested, you spend a day at Tlamacas to acclimatise, there's little to do other than the easy stroll here.

Hiking directions
The main route to the top of Popo' is the Las Cruces route, which starts along the ash trail rising gently to the left (east of south) to the Las Cruces hut (4,400m); this is a broad track and is easy to follow if, as is usual, you set off before dawn, to get up and down while the snow is firm and frost binds the ash slope. It takes two to three hours to Las Cruces, where only the foundations of the hut remain, with memorial crosses to dead climbers. From here you head straight up the 30° scree slope, just west of south; you'll soon be on snow, and it takes about three hours to reach the rim of the volcano at 5,100m (where there's another ruined hut). It's a much easier hour's hike to the right to the summit, above the west end of the crater. The crater is about 850m by 700m, or 2,300m in circumference and 300m deep. There used to be a smaller crater in the bottom, created by the 1920-29 eruption, with a lake in it, but who knows what will be there after the current eruption.

There's a slightly shorter but more difficult route passing the former Texcalco refuge (originally El Canario), 100m above the path at 4,300m, about an hour from Tlamacas. Other routes require more experience and equipment: the Queretano route starts by turning right off the Las Cruces route at about 4,100m and passing the Queretano hut set on a cliff at 4,650m. Stay high to reach the Teopixcalco hut at 4,930m on the saddle between Popo' and Ventorillo, from where it's an easy scramble up Ventorillo (4,999m), or a 40° climb (rope required) up to the summit of Popo', seven to eight hours from Tlamacas. This is the route used by the conquistadores. The Coyotes route loops around to the right from Teopixcalco to pass below the snowcap and reach the summit from the southwest, where there's the least snow to cross.

Naturally there is less snow and ice on the south side; you can approach from Ecatzingo or Tetcla del Volcán, to the south, but you'll need map E14B52 as well. El Pico del Fraile (The Friar's Peak, 5,249m) is a rocky crag on the south side, which is usually snowfree. In Ecatzingo the El Tepeylhuitl Mountain Festival is held on October 24, reflecting ancient indigenous beliefs about the powers of the mountains; there's also a meeting of mountaineers every third year on the weekend nearest October 12, when the flags of all the world's countries are taken to the summit.

Ixtaccíhuatl

Ixtaccíhuatl, also known as Iztatepetl or Cihuatepetl ("White Lady", 5,285m) is the third highest peak in Mexico, and one of the most satisfying and challenging climbs in the country. Like Popo' it was originally formed 10mya, with the current cone dating back 2.5m years; there's plenty of evidence of glaciation above 4,000m, and where glaciers flow below that level. Traces of idol worship have been found on the summit. The first European got there in 1889, or possibly in 1772. TrekMex run a two-day trip to Ixta' for US$167-plus, and Grey Line (tel: 208 1163) do the same for US$200; when Popo' is safe these and several other companies will again run trips there, but these tend not to allow any leeway for acclimatisation.

Hiking directions

Ixta' is seen as a sleeping maiden, and various features are known as *Las Rodillas* (the Knees), *La Barriga* (the Belly), *El Pecho* (the Breast), *El Cuello* (the Neck), *La Oreja* (the Ear), *La Cabeza* (the Head) and *La Caballera* (the Hair). The summit is the Breast or Chest, and the standard route up (also known as *La Arista del Sol*, the ridge of the sun) is via the Knees. From the Paso de Cortés the left/north turning leads past the Altzomoni microwave station to La Joya (3,960m), about 12km away. There's car-parking here, and sometimes a food stall; theft from cars has been known. The path leads straight up the hill from the carpark, then swings left to reach a ridge (*el primer portillo*) by the memorial to a dead climber, after forty minutes. From here the path heads to the right, down then up to the *secundo portillo* (with another memorial cross) in 25 minutes. The path climbs easily, reaching a pass (with rock windbreaks) in 25 minutes more, and continues easily up before climbing steeply to the left where white arrows are painted on the rock. It crosses two ridges, drops briefly past a ruined hut and reaches the Republica de Chile hut (4,750m), 30 minutes from the windbreaks. A larger new hut was completed alongside this in 1996, but you should not take it for granted that there'll be space as long as Popo' is out of bounds.

It's well worth just coming this far if your level of acclimatisation doesn't permit you to go higher; the views are fantastic, with stupendous rock walls jutting from the mountain's flanks like the arms of a giant starfish. Huge hanging valleys are draped between them, filled with untold tonnes of volcanic scree. A hauntingly desolate landscape, and very different to Popo'.

The Esperanza (de Lopéz Mateos) hut is visible above, on a ridge at 4,850m, just below the prominent rockband of the Knees. Further on is the Luís Menendez hut, at 5,000m, an igloo also just visible from Republica de Chile. You need to scale the cliff by climbing on the snow to the left, or if there is no snow go over the scree then climb the class 2-3 rocks to the right. The route to the summit now traverses across snowfields and false summits (the Knees and the Belly); it's usually clear enough, but it's easy to get disoriented if there's fresh snow covering the footprints. The summit is a plateau about 500m long, with the highest point at the far, northern, end.

Other routes are definitely for mountaineers; the Nexcoalanco hut (3,600m) can be reached by 6km of dirt road from Tlamanalco (north of Ameca') to San Rafael and another 6km hiking. From here you can go to the Chalchoapan hut (4,650m), and then either by La Cabeza (5,108m) and El Cuello (5,000m) to the summit, or by the *Directa al Pecho*, which requires ice-climbing. From the Ayoloco hut, to the south of Chalchoapan, routes go up the *Glaciar de Ayoloco* to the Belly, or the *Glaciar de las Rodillas* to the Knees. To the north a route leads from the Laminas hut via *La Oreja Derecha* to the Head, and from the northeast another leads via the *Glaciares Orientales* hut to the Head.

PUEBLA

Puebla, between the Sierra Nevada and Veracruz, is one of the most attractive of Mexico's states, with a wide range of ecosystems including plenty of fresh, cool, high-altitude scenery. It's easily accessible and the city of Puebla is one of the friendliest and most attractive in the country (its former airfield, on Av 24 Sur, is being converted into an Ecological Park, with a modern aviary).

Coming from Mexico City, the *autopista* crosses the Sierra Nevada north of Ixtaccíhuatl, cutting through the **Zoquiapan National Park**, protecting 19,418ha of forest and sub-alpine pasture. To begin with you'll see cypress

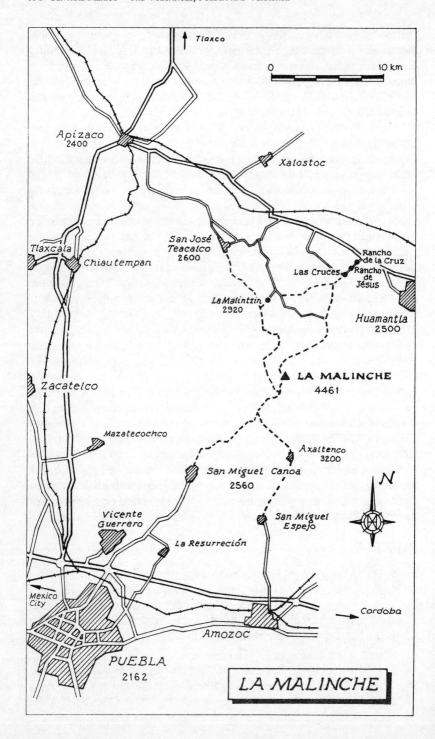

↑ Tlaxco

0   10 km

Apizaco
2400

Xalostoc

Tlaxcala

Chiautempan

San José
Teacalco
2600

Rancho
de la Cruz
Las Cruces
Rancho
de
Jésus

La Malintzin
2920

Huamantla
2500

▲ LA MALINCHE
4461

Zacatelco

Mazatecochco

Axaltenco
3200

San Miguel Canoa
2560

N

Vicente
Guerrero

San Miguel
Espejo

La Resurreción

Mexico
City

Cordoba

Amozoc

PUEBLA
2162

LA MALINCHE

(*Cupressus lindleyii*) and oaks (*Quercus rugosa* and *Q. mexicana*), then pine (*Pinus montezumae, P. hartwegii*), fir (*Abies religiosa*) and alder (*Alnus firmifolia*); the pass is at km 64, at about 3,250m, from which you soon descend into scrappy farmland. Even in the national park repeated burning is leading to soil loss, and trees weakened so that they are susceptible to parasitism by dwarf mistletoe (*muérdago enano/Arceuthobium spp*).

La Malinche

Malinche (named after Cortés' translator and lover, and also known as Matlalcuéyetl) rises to 4,461m to the northeast of Puebla city (which is at 2,162m). From Puebla it can be climbed as a day-trip, but it makes more sense to spread it over two days; you'll need to carry water as well as a tent. It's the oldest volcano in the area, and now is very eroded; even so it's the seventh highest in the country.

It's been a national park since 1938, covering 45,700ha of pine-oak, fir and sub-alpine *zacatonal*; it's much less affected by tourism than Popo' and Ixta', but equally it is affected by deforestation and reforestation. Wildlife includes coyotes, volcano rabbits, white-tail deer, bobcats, foxes, falcons, woodpeckers and hummingbirds.

Maps are a problem, as the peak lies close to the junction of four 1:50,000 sheets. The summit and all the southern and western slopes are shown by E14B43 *Puebla*, which also shows Puebla and Cholula; E14B44 *Huamantla* covers most of the route described here, and E14B33 *Tlaxcala* shows the area to the north.

Hiking directions

There are various routes up; the easiest route is via the small town of Huamantla, on the far side of the volcano at just below 2,500m. It's reached by buses every ten minutes from Puebla's CAPU bus station, one of the biggest and busiest in the country, which take about 1½ hours. There's a hotel here, the *Centenario* at Juárez Norte 209, and a new museum of puppetry (*Títere*), of all things, on the zócalo. Take Av Hidalgo, the road between the museum and the church, and turn left after ten minutes at the PEMEX fuel station. You need the right-hand of the two roads in front of you, past Win's New Disco. Here you can pick up a Rancho de Jésus *combi*, which passes through the suburb of Rancho de la Cruz and terminates at the end of the built-up strip (c2,640m); from here it's 40 minutes walk on up the asphalt road to the hamlet of Las Cruces (or Altamira), where you'll find a shop and two small radio towers. Five minutes further on the road bends right and you should turn left on a dirt track into the conifers. It took me 15 minutes to reach a Malinche National Park sign ("kill no rabbits, graze no goats, leave no litter, light no fires"), at which I turned right. The way is unclear at first but soon a good small path develops through pine and tussocks of bunchgrass; after ten minutes you'll join a better path from the right. After a couple of minutes turn left onto a cart-track and then right off it, and climb steadily on up, as the shrub and grass layers get shorter. After 15 minutes turn left (ie west) onto a cart-track which winds uphill (with a couple of shortcuts to the left); after 15 minutes more you'll pass a path to the right which would ultimately bring you to the La Malintzi holiday centre. The track fades out after 15 minutes more, where you have to turn right with a cliff to the left dropping into the Barranca Axaltzintle – don't even think about shortcuts for the next 15-odd minutes, even though you'll be aware that the peak is over to the left.

Before long you'll be able to make your way more directly up to the left, still on a good clear path, and still among fir trees – my kind of mountain! It took me another 40 or so minutes to reach the treeline, from where you can slog up through the tussocky grass to the southwest towards the summit; it's in fact easier to head to the right to pick up the ridge from the crag of Tlachichihuatzi. There's a path up the ridge, while beyond it is bare scree. Depending on the state of your lungs and legs, it's another hour or so to the summit, perhaps 3½ hours from Las Cruces.

If you head over the top or around to the right, you can descend by one of the other routes; directly to the north of the peak is the La Malintzi holiday centre, reached by a path to the right/west of the Barranca Zoquiaque. There are microwave towers at 2,915m, from where you may be able to get a ride for the 15km down to the Huamantla-Apizaco road; there should also be occasional buses to and from Apizaco, and *colectivos* to and from San José Teacalco, the village below the microwaves.

To the southwest you can descend more or less directly towards Puebla; however, picking the goat-track which will turn into a proper path down the mountain is a matter of some luck as well as skill, so you should not come this way unless you have plenty of time or are prepared to spend a night on the mountain. You need to keep to the left/southeast of the very large and obvious Barranca Hueyziatl, and if possible follow the tongue of high land between the Barranca La Trinidad and the Barranca Atitlanbuyero. If you get this right your path will eventually develop into a track which passes a shrine and two radio towers, and after 3½-4 hours brings you into San Miguel Canoa. Buses run to the school at the top of the village; if going up by this route you should keep to the right when you reach the school's archway. In the evening plenty of buses from Puebla terminate here, but none of them return to the city; you need to get down to the plaza, about a kilometre further down, to catch a *Flecha Blanca* bus to the *Unión* municipal market at Blvd Norte 1506 in Puebla. Again, if you're going up by this route it's easier to take *colectivo* 72 from the centre, running north on Héroes del 5 de Mayo (not to be confused with 5 de Mayo *tout court*) to Calzada Ignacio Zaragoza, where you can pick up the Canoa bus.

Pico de Orizaba

Pico de Orizaba (also known as Citlaltépetl or Star Mountain) is the highest mountain in Mexico. It's a dormant mid-Pliocene volcano on the continental divide where Veracruz and Puebla states meet, rising in classic volcano shape to an altitude of about 5,747m. It was first climbed in 1847-48 by US soldiers (then occupying Veracruz) led by Lt WF Reynolds; now it's a pretty straightforward climb, with crampons and ice-axes generally advisable. TrekMexico operate a three-day trip, from US$348.

The 19,750ha around the volcano have been a national park since 1937; this has a cold semi-humid climate with average temperatures of -10°C to 20°C, and the vegetation comprises pine (particularly *Pinus hartwegii*), fir, oak, and high altitude *paramó* or *zacatonal*, sheltering rabbits, coyotes, squirrels, foxes, white-tail deer, raccoons, weasels, rattlesnakes, lizards, ravens and hawks. The relevant INEGI 1:50,000 map is E14B56 *Orizaba*.

Hiking directions

The best season for climbing to the summit is from November to March; there's lots of good hiking on the lower slopes, which should be enjoyable at most seasons. The nearest town is Ciudad Serdán (reached by at least six buses an hour from Puebla), but it's best to approach via Tlachichuca (2,750m). Coming from Mexico City and Puebla on the main road towards Xalapa, you'll find the Hotel Imperial at the junction to Ciudad Serdán in San Salvador El Seco (km36). There's nothing at the Tlachichuca turning (km43), but there's no need to stop here, as there's an ACOSA bus every half-hour from Puebla. From Tlachichuca a dirt road leads 15km through San Miguel Zoapan to the village of Hidalgo; after crossing a bridge (about 3.5km further) you should turn left, then after 2km turn right and right again, and right again after 1.3km to reach the Piedra Grande hut in another kilometre or so (8km from Hidalgo, at 4,260m). It takes about four hours to hike up from Hidalgo, or US$70 for a 4WD from Tlachichuca. There is water here, but you'll need to bring a stove and sleeping bag. From here the standard route is the *Ruta Norte*, which passes to the right of a gully and cliffs and reaches the Jamapa glacier at about 4,900m. Avoiding the crevasses, the general route is obvious to the main crater; about 200m below the rim you should traverse to the right, then follow the rim to the summit, reached in between six and nine hours from the hut.

An alternative route is via Atzitzintla, to the south of the mountain, just off the Mexico City-Veracruz *autopista* at the Ciudad Serdán junction; from here a dirt road continues to Texmalaquilla, and then a path to the Fausto González hut (the "red hut", at 4,800m, about eight hours), from where it's another four or five hours to the summit. From Texmalaquilla another path leads to Volcán Atlitzin (also known as Sierra Negra or Sierra Nuestra Señora de la Agüita), which has a huge collapsed caldera reaching down to the treeline to the south. This is often considered a subsidiary peak of Pico de Orizaba, but it is in fact older (dating from the late Miocene) and geologically separate, making it the fifth highest peak in Mexico at 4,583m.

Northern Puebla

To the north of the Transversal Volcanic Axis lies a very rugged area, little visited by outsiders, which is inhabited by indigenous groups, notably the Otomie, who were not subdued by the Spanish until the 1690s. There's a set of seven volcanic lakes in the Llanos de Puebla (the Llanos de San Juan and de San Andrés), which are known for their endemicisms and for the way in which they "sicken", for largely unknown reasons. They lie at about 2,350m, in a dry temperate climate with only 400-800mm of precipitation per year; the water levels are dropping, due largely to over-extraction for irrigation. Lago Aljojuca turned orange in 1989, probably due to hydrogen sulphide emissions from residual volcanic activty, and Lago Atexac turned from blue to red in 1988 and 1989, a flowering of *Nodularia* algae due perhaps to thermal variations. These processes are not understood, risking the survival of the endemic fish species. These are all derived from a common marine ancestor; the most common is *Poblana letholepsis* in Lago La Preciosa and Lago Las Minas, with other species of *Poblana* in the Lago de Alchichica, Lago de Quechulac, Lago de Almoloya, and in the Río Tula system.

The Valley of Tehuacán

In the far south of Puebla state, the Valley of Tehuacán constitutes one of the 17 floristic provinces of Mexico, where perhaps 30% of plant species are endemic; it's proposed as a Biosphere Reserve. In particular there's a rich crop of cacti, such as *Fouquieria purpusii, Pringleochloa stolonifera* and *Chaptalia texana*, as well as *Hechtiae, Salviae* and *Compositae*. The scenery is dominated by a giant branched cactus (similar to *saguaro* and *cardón*) called *teteche* (*Neobuxbaumia tetezo*), and by a simple unbranched column up to 12m tall called *órgano* (*Cephalocereus hoppenstedtii*). Other succulents include 19 species of agave, 16 of which are in bloom from June to November.

It's an isolated patch of desert in the rainshadow of the Sierra Madre Oriental, with just 380mm of precipitation per year and *very* rare frosts. The town of Tehuacán is the main stop on the old main road from Mexico City and Puebla to Oaxaca, but it has now been bypassed by the new *autopista* to the west of town. This passes close to Zapotitlán, on the Tehuacán-Huajuapan de León road. There's a botanical garden 1km east of Zapotitlán (25km from Tehuacán).

VERACRUZ

Veracruz is known mainly for its dense Gulf-coast rainforest, particularly on the volcanic hills of Las Tuxtlas, but the state does also boast Mexico's highest peak, the volcano Pico de Orizaba (on the border with Puebla), and some marvellous rafting possibilities. The state capital is not Veracruz, the country's main port, but Xalapa (or Jalapa), pleasantly located in the hills.

There is significantly more rain along the Gulf coast south of Tampico than to the north, brought by cool winds from the north between September and February. The natural vegetation of the coast is tropical evergreen forest (with deciduous forest and savanna around Veracruz and north of Los Tuxtlas); inland there is oak-conifer forest, ending up as sub-alpine forest on the slopes of Pico de Orizaba and Cofre de Perote. The coastline is followed by migrating birds, notably raptors such as the peregrine falcon.

The road from Puebla

Heading east from Puebla state into Veracruz on the *autopista*, you'll soon pass through the Cumbres de Maltrata and enter the **Cañón del Río Blanco National Park**, established back in 1938 to protect 55,690ha of medium evergreen forest and cloudforest. It is proposed to link this, the Pico de Orizaba National Park, and the adjacent Barranca de Metlac conservation area, which collectively form one of the most ecologically important sites in the region, with a range from 800m to 5,747m within 25km. Ecosystems include riverside gallery forest, medium evergreen forest, deciduous forest, pine, fir, lion's claw grasslands, high altitude pine forest, and finally *paramó*, with a rich mix of nearctic and neotropic species.

Also just to the east of Pico de Orizaba and Córdoba, the Sierra de Atoyac is proposed as a reserve, a karst area with a hot humid climate and medium semi-evergreen forest, as well as the Quauhtochco pyramid on the north bank of the Río Atoyac. To the south of the city of Orizaba a road leads into the Sierra Fria (or Sierra de Zongolica), a wild, remote, cold, damp area inhabited by poor Nahuatl people. They are known for their *sarapes*, coloured with natural dyes from, among others, oak (orange and rose), Spanish moss (brown), squaw root (purple), blackberry (purple), alder and dodder.

Cofre de Perote

Cofre de Perote is so called because of an an immense rock in the shape of a chest on its peak. It's Mexico's eighth highest summit (4,274m or 4,282m), a limestone peak at the southern end of the Sierra Madre Oriental, and not part of the Transversal Volcanic Belt as you might expect. It towers over the town of Perote (2,465m), km101 on the Mexico City-Xalapa highway (in fact 278km from the capital); there are several hotels here, including the Esperanza opposite the AU bus station. At km120 you should follow a dirt road south for 6km to a microwave station; from here the north road is better, leading in 14km to huts at the western false summit. From here you should head northeast to reach the summit (scrambling up a class 3 chimney).

The Ecological Park of Cofre, by the highway to the east of Perote, is home to a bizarre selection of animals, such as reindeer, llamas, elk, bison and bighorn sheep. Leaving aside such surreal stuff, you can also hire horses or mountain bikes to explore the flanks of Cofre de Perote, including some lovely little lakes.

Xalapa

Xalapa is the oldest city in Mexico and is now the capital of Veracruz state and home to its university. From 1925 it was home to the *Estridentistas*, a group of poets led by Manuel Maples Arce (1900-81) who had some similarities to the Italian Futurists, focusing on modern urban life and indigenous peoples. It lies at 1,427m and has a pleasantly temperate climate with an average temperature of 8°C and rain all year – almost every second day on average, although it's usually *chipi-chipi*, a fine mist, which means that average precipitation is only 1,485mm per year. The vegetation is a transition phase between savanna and sub-alpine forest, but the area is best known for the riotous sub-tropical vegetation that fills the nearby *barrancas* or steep narrow valleys. This includes sweetgum, oak, willow, araucaria, cedar, coffee and banana trees. Immediately south is Coatepec, less than 200m below Xalapa at 1,250m, but much warmer, with an average temperature of 19°C. To the west, 3km from the village of Xico, an old iron bridge crosses a gorge, giving a view of the spectacular Texolo waterfalls.

The old road to Coatepec passes (2.5km south of Xalapa) the Francisco Clavijero Botanical Garden, which also contains the *Instituto de Ecología* (as opposed to the *Instituto Nacional de Ecología* in the capital), the country's leading research body in the fields of ecology and conservation. Buses to Coatepec (via Briones) run from the *terminal* at the western end of Ursulo Galván. Xalapa also boasts the second-best Museum of Anthropology (ie archaeology) in the country – after the one in Chapultepec Park, of course. It's on Av Xalapa well north of the centre; take any *Xalapa* minibus. Just east of the museum is Cerro Macuiltepec (1,590m), which now calls itself an Ecological Park.

Rafting the barrancas

Xalapa is the chief centre for white-water rafting in Mexico. The leading local operator is *Veraventuras* (Santos Degollado 81, Int 8, 91000 Xalapa, Veracruz; tel: 28 189 579/779, fax:189 680, Mexico City 663 0971). Others working here are *Expediciones México Verde* (José María Vigil 2406, Col Italia Providencia, Guadalajara, 44640 Jalisco; tel: 800 36288, 641 1005, fax: 641 5598), *Río y Montaña*, Prado Norte 450-T, Lomas de Chapultepec,

11000 México DF; tel: 520 2041, fax: 540 7870) and *Ecogrupos de México* (Av Insurgentes Sur 1971-251, Col Guadalupe Inn, 01020 México DF; tel: 661 9121, fax: 662 7354). Most tour companies in the capital, such as Trek Mexico, also operate raft trips here.

The best rafting in the area is on the Río Antigua, which can be divided into three parts, the Barranca Grande (32km of Class IV-V, navigable from November to May, the Pescados (21km with 30 Class III-IV+ rapids, all year) below Jalcomulco, and the Antigua (Class III-IV, June to October) from Paso Limón to El Carrizal and Puente Nacional. Río y Montaña and México Verde have bases in Jalcomulco, at 400m in the sub-tropical forest of the *tierra caliente* (lowlands). Veraventuras have their base 28km further downstream, at the hot springs (40°C) of Aguas Termales del Carrizal, where there's a hotel, campsite and trailer park, with swimming pool and waterslide, and basketball and volleyball facilities. It's at 347m, 45km from Xalapa; turn south at La Cumbre, 35km down the highway towards Veracruz.

Just north of Xalapa is the Río Actopán, 11km of Class II-III rapids from the 7m waterfall of El Descabezadero ("the guillotine") to the village of Actopán; this is navigable from November to May, and is a popular easy day trip from Xalapa.

The Río FiloBobos is a relatively easy run (from June to October), but in addition to floating through sub-tropical forests it also offers a unique chance to visit El Cuajilote and Vega de la Peña, a couple of archaeological ruins which can effectively only be visited by water. These are Totonac sites, dating from 200AD to 900AD, with ballcourts, pyramids and massive basalt carvings. The river rises on Cofre de Perote and flows north, passing close to Tlapacoyan and reaching the sea at Nautla. The Alto Filo is Class IV-V, through a limestone canyon, the second stage past the ruins is 25km of Class II-III to the El Encanto canyon and waterfall, from where it's half a day to the take-out at Palmilla.

It's also possible to make your way down the Río San Marcos, starting from the village of Pahuatlán (2,300m) at the western edge of Veracruz state, which is reached by turning north from the highway from Tulancingo (Hidalgo) to the oil town of Poza Rica. After an exciting start the river largely parallels this highway to Poza Rica.

Los Tuxtlas

The **Sierra de Tuxtla** is like a cork at the northern end of the Isthmus of Tehuantepec; it's essentially a pair of Late Cenozoic volcanoes (composed of andesitic and basaltic alkaline lavas) covered in rainforest. The area is very important for migratory birds and medicinal plants; there's a high diversity of species here but a low level of endemicity, especially among the birds (with only three endemic subspecies: the common bush tanager *Chlorospingus opthalmicus wetmorei*, the chestnut-capped brush-finch

Atlapetes brunneinucha apertus, and Lawrence's quail-dove *Geotrygon lawrenceii carrikeri*).

The more northerly peak, Volcán San Martín (1,748m, and still active), is protected by a Special Biosphere Reserve of 1,500ha, and the southern one, Volcán Santa Marta (1,878m), by another of 20,000ha, which covers coastal dunes, mangroves and medium semi-deciduous forest, as well as the high evergreen forest. There are two research stations, one belonging to UNAM (the National University) near Volcán San Martín, and another belonging to the University of Veracruz at Pijiapan near Volcán Santa Martha. Between the two mountains, at about 500m, lies the Laguna de Catemaco, where the University of Veracruz manages a wildlife refuge, protecting 230ha of evergreen tropical forest; this is notable for the 500-plus species of butterflies and moths found here. All the protected forests of the area are suffering from the depradations of the pet trade, affecting toucans in particular, and from slash-and-burn agriculture, used primarily to claim ownership before putting cattle in.

Practicalities

There are hotels in the small resort town of Catemaco, where you can take boat trips on the lake or visit a small waterfall; the more impressive *Salto de Eyipantla* can be reached from Sihuapan, 5km west of Catemaco. The main town in the area is San Andrés Tuxtla, 15km west of Catemaco, where you can visit a volcanic lake, *La Laguna Encantada*, 2km from town. It's also possible to stay at the UNAM research station, booked through the Instituto de Biología, UNAM, Ciudad Universitaria, Deleg. Coyoacán, 04510 México DF (tel: 616 1558, fax: 616 2326) at least ten days in advance (US$25/day for a room and meals). There are also cheap hotels in Monte Pio, 6km away on the coast. UNAM is due to publish a large book on the natural history of the Los Tuxtlas region in the summer of 1996.

Offshore

The **Sistema Arrecifal Veracruzano Parque Marino Nacional** protects 23 coral reefs just off the port of Veracruz, which can be visited by boat. There are islands with salt-loving vegetation, coconut palms and marine grasses, and lizards, geckos, green turtles, brown pelicans and magnificent frigatebirds.

Chapter Ten

The Sierra Madre Oriental

The Eastern Sierra Madre is not a high range, only 20% of it being over 2,000m in altitude, and it's generally less than spectacular, particularly in comparison with its western *compadre*. However it does have its moments, although many of them are underground – beautiful caves and immense sinkholes called *sótanos* (literally basements). It's formed of Paleozoic and Mesozoic marine sediments, with some more recent (Cenozoic) rhyolitic volcanic rocks; the range was formed in the Laramidian orogeny in the early Tertiary and folded in the Upper Eocene (around 50mya). On the eastern slopes there's a temperate climate and no defined dry season, with typically a semi-hot humid climate between 1,200m and 1,500m, with 2,000-4,000mm of precipitation per year and an average temperature of 18°C; above 2,000m the climate is temperate, with 1,500-2,500mm of precipitation and an average temperature of 16°C. On the western slope there's less rain, with a dry winter season.

Immediately to the north of Mexico City you'll find pine-oak forest, but most of the Sierra Madre Oriental is covered with a scrub (*matorral*) of mezquite and grass. There is an intrusion of tropical deciduous forest (rainforest) from the Gulf coast to the area of El Cielo, which marks the northern limit of neotropical species. To the southwest of Monterrey there's some alpine vegetation, above 3,600m.

North from Mexico City

The Pan-American Highway leaves Mexico City northbound as a dual carriageway (divided highway) to Pachuca, which is served by no less than 14 buses an hour from Mexico's *Terminal del Norte*. Pachuca is an old silver-mining town, but there's no reason to stop there unless you want to visit the **El Chico National Park** to the north of town. This is 2,739ha of weird rock formations (highest point 2,900m) amid forests of pine, fir, oak and alder, inhabited by bobcats, coyote, foxes, white-tail deer, falcons, woodpeckers and rattlesnakes. It's a popular weekend resort for camping and climbing in particular. To get here, take highway 105 towards Tampico

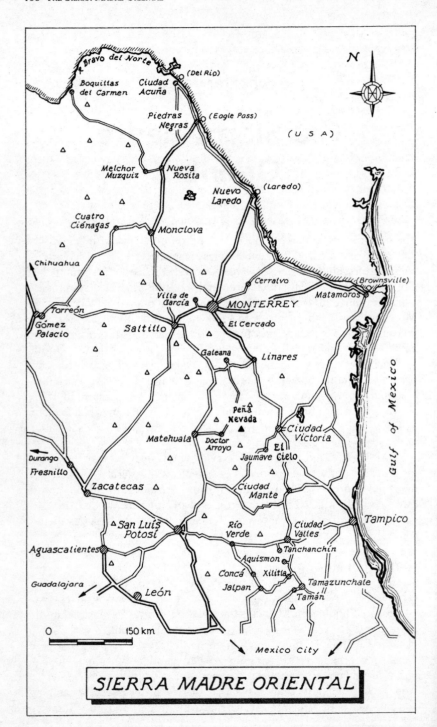

N

R. Bravo del Norte

(Del Río)
Boquillas del Carmen
Ciudad Acuña

Piedras Negras   (Eagle Pass)

(U S A)

Melchor Muzquiz
Nueva Rosita
Nuevo Laredo   (Laredo)

Chihuahua
Cuatro Ciénagas
Monclova

Cerralvo   (Brownsville)
Villa de García
MONTERREY   Matamoros
Torreón
Gómez Palacio
Saltillo   El Cercado

Galeana   Linares

Peña Nevada

Durango
Fresnillo
Matehuala   Doctor Arroyo   Ciudad Victoria
El Cielo
Jaumave

Zacatecas   Ciudad Mante

San Luis Potosí   Río Verde   Ciudad Valles   Tampico
Aguascalientes   Tanchanchín
Guadalajara   Aquismon
Concá   Xilitla
Jalpan   Tamazunchale
León   Tamán

Gulf of Mexico

0   150 km

Mexico City

SIERRA MADRE ORIENTAL

and turn left at km9; Real del Monte (or Mineral del Chico) is a picturesque mining town at 2,750m, which is served by *colectivos* from Pachuca.

Continuing to the northwest, the Pan-American Highway (no longer the main route towards the USA) heads for Actopan, Ixmiquilpan and Zimapán; to the right you'll see the parallel Sierra de la Navajas, which would seem to offer some good climbing. The highest peak, at 3,250m, is Cerro de los Ingleses or "Englishmen's Peak"; you'll find plenty of obsidian here, in pine-oak and fir forests. The **Barranca de Tolentenango** is a gorge several hundred metres deep, with a waterfall, thermal spring, and caves; it's also known as a centre of endemism. It lies in the *ejido* of San Cristobal Tolentenango, about 40km northeast of Ixmiquilpan; you can take a bus to an unmarked junction about 3km before the village of Cardonal.

To the southwest of Zimapán, the Cañón de Zimapán or Infiernillo, where the San Juan and Tula rivers meet to form the Río Moctezuma, is a snaking limestone canyon, 10km long and 400m deep, with some good climbing possibilities. Not far north of Zimapán the main highway passes right through the **Los Marmoles National Park**; from around km133 it rises into conifers and cloud, and at about km146 you'll pass the Barranca de los Marmoles, rising to the right. This park covers 23,150ha of pine-oak, fir, drought-resistant scrub and arbutus, with white-tail deer, skunks, armadillos, bobcats, rabbits, hares and falcons.

SAN LUÍS POTOSÍ

The hike described below, near Tamazunchale, is in the southeasternmost corner of San Luís Potosí, which is one of the larger states, stretching north over the *altiplano* almost all the way to Monterrey. Most of the state is *matorral* and desert, but the Tamazunchale area is more tropical.

Frankly there's not much else of ecological interest in the state: only two national parks and one virtually unknown Biosphere Reserve. The El Gogorrón National Park covers 25,000ha just south of the city of San Luís Potosí, with thermal pools, camping and a Vacation Centre; there's pine (and some oak) above *matorral*, with coyotes, foxes, ringtails, coati, hares, deer, flying squirrels, roadrunners, falcons and rattlesnakes. To get here, head south on highway 57, now the main route from Monterrey and Texas, for 25km, then right for 22km towards Villa de Reyes and San Felipe. The El Potosí National Park lies just north of Río Verde; it's only 2,000ha, and 45% of it is actually farmed. The rest is a *matorral* of mezquite and *cardón* cactus, with pine, oak, walnut, poplar, and coyote, white-tail deer, skunks and falcons. The Sierra del Abra-Tanchipa Biosphere Reserve lies to the east of Ciudad Valles; created in 1994 it protects 21,464ha of low and medium evergreen and semi-evergreen forest, low deciduous forest, oaks and secondary palms. There are about 50 species of mammals, 80 birds, and 30 herps (reptiles and amphibians).

The INEGI map outlet is at Av Venustiano Carranza 1138, 78250 San Luís Potosí.

Tamán to Xilitla

This trip, which has a good deal of sustained but not drastically steep climbing in it, can easily be done in two days. A peaceful camping area lies by the beautiful, isolated Río Tanquilín, midway along the walk. Even during the rainy season the Tanquilín is only knee-deep and can be crossed without great difficulty, except immediately after very heavy rains, when you should allow at least a couple of days for the waters to subside. In winter the ford is only about ankle-deep. After rains this trail can be miserably muddy; keep in mind that limestone, the region's dominant rock, is treacherously slick when wet and muddy.

This hike is different from most because it passes through "heartland Mexico" – it's not inside a national park or across an isolated mountain chain, nor does it lead to an archaeological ruin or any major touristic destination. This walk through the humid hills facing the Gulf of Mexico uses "Indian trails" and rudimentary roads that carry you into villages hardly ever visited by any outsiders, let alone gringos. You'll meet farmers on their way to their much-eroded hillside cornfields, and regular people walking across country, to save the cost of a bus ticket. Most of them speak Nahuatl at home, and they told Jim Conrad that their trails have been in use since before Moctezuma II (the Aztec king when the conquistadors arrived), which may well be true. Nahuatl is very closely related to Aztec, which Moctezuma spoke.

By the way, Jim has written a nature-and-Indian-oriented book about this area; if you want to get a feel for it before you go, get hold of *On the Road to Tetlama* (Walker, New York, 1991). Briefly, it's an area of karstic limestone, where you'll see typical rainforest trees such as ceiba, *cacuite* (*Gliricidia sepum*), *Bursera simaruba*, strangler fig, bromeliads, as well as nopal cactus and fruit trees such as guava, papaya, mango, citrus, banana, and coffee. Above Xilitla there's oak, pine and sweetgum.

Practicalities

To get an early start you'll really have to spend the night in a hotel, and the only place for this is **Tamazunchale**, a small but bustling town in the extreme southern corner of San Luís Potosí state; it's at 200m at the very foot of the Gulf Slope, about 300km (185 miles, or six hours by bus) northeast of Mexico City. Although the Pan-American Highway is no longer the main route up to the USA, there are still plenty of buses along this road. The main bus line serving the area is *Flecha Roja*, which has departures every half-hour from the *Terminal Norte* in the capital. *Omnibus de Mexico* and *Estrella Blanca* also have services (mostly overnight) to Ciudad Valles via Tamazunchale, but these won't set you down at Tamán.

In Tamazunchale, there are several standard but noisy hotels along the main drag; for a cheap place that's as colourful as it's seedy take the first through street north from the park and look for the *Casa de Huespedes*; the most pleasant place in town is the *Quinta Chilla*, about 500m south of town. You can only buy biscuits, drinks and cowboy hats in Tamán, so buy your supplies before getting there. There are plenty of *colectivo* minibuses from Tamazunchale to **Tamán**, 13km back towards Mexico City at km261. Coming from the capital it's easily missed, little more than a bridge on the main road, with the village to the left/north; it's two blocks to the *MiniTodo*, a small general store under a fig tree (an American fig with elliptic leaves, not the Old World fig with three-lobed leaves) the base of which is surrounded by a concrete wall about 0.5m high. This is the place to find a pickup truck for the next stage of this journey, to Agua Zarca, a village virtually on the ridge; *colectivos* from Tamazunchale turn left here to terminate in Plaza Juárez. The Agua Zarca trucks take the road to the right but then swing left to cross a bridge just 100m (on foot) from the plaza. It takes about 1¼ hours to reach Agua Zarca by truck, or perhaps six to eight hours on foot; it's mostly uphill, usually hot and dry, and the lower part of the route is weedy scrub rather than anything interesting or attractive. One possibility is to ride halfway, say to the El Coyol turning, from where you can walk on in more pleasant surroundings; but make sure you will have time to reach the Río Tanquilín camping spot without problems.

Hiking directions
The centre of Agua Zarca, where your pickup will leave you, is a basketball court; walk straight on through the village (at 320°), and in five minutes you'll reach the ridge. Continue down the main fork to the right, bearing north; in five minutes more the 4WD track ends but the path on is obvious, dropping north-northwestwards to reach a dry stream in another ten minutes. There's an obvious junction here, with earth steps to the right and stone steps to the left, which is the way you want to go (unless you want to end up back in Tamazunchale). You'll know you've taken the correct path if within about 10m you see a path, forming the third side of a triangle, coming in from the right.

The path to the left (which heads west-northwest at about 300°) heads into coffee plantations (some freshly cleared, but with shade trees left in place) and pasture. It climbs easily, to reach a ridge in five minutes, continues to another rise after ten minutes and then drops into more coffee. Jim has hiked this route three times and each time ended up guessing which way to go at the junctions, but nevertheless arrived each time at precisely the right spot to cross the river; this may indicate that all the trail's forks in fact converge on the same crossing point. In 1996 the main route always seemed obvious to me, but even so you should keep your wits about you. It takes about 35 minutes from the last ridge to the river, without allowing time for anything else; that's 70 minutes from Agua Zarca, so allow at least 1½ hours.

If you've arrived at the correct spot on the Río Tanquilín, the following details should be true. The river should be flowing towards the west-northwest (300°) and then curving hard to the right. Across the river, at a bearing of 220°, you should see a white limestone boulder about 2m in diameter. At least when the water is low, you should see a bar of cobblestones in front of the boulder. Camping on this bar gives you a nice view and a breeze; if you prefer more shade and a softer, more regular substrate, probably the best place is on the river's Agua Zarca side. Return inside the forest and walk downstream for a few metres; you may even be lucky enough to spot some stones that are part of a prehispanic ruin, as well as some primitive fishtraps just downstream.

To continue, ford the river where you first met it, heading more or less towards the boulder; the path to Xilitla begins on its left side (by a fence and two trees) and goes to the right at about 325°. This soon climbs steeply, and after ten minutes swings left around the ridge and enters coffee again. The path rises through a field to reach the ridge (a good place for a break) in 20 minutes. The first houses and power lines are already visible just ahead, and there's a clear path through the settlement of Poxtla, leading in 15 minutes to a stream where a 4WD track comes in from the right and continues straight ahead. In under 20 minutes this reaches a better road also coming in from the right; from here it's 11km to Xilitla, much of it rising easily enough. It takes just over an hour to reach two bars on top of a ridge, from where the road drops steeply to cross a stream after half an hour and then climbs for half an hour more to reach Highway 120 five minutes east of the centre of Xilitla, at about 1,000m. You may very well have to walk the whole way as there's virtually no traffic on this road, although an early start from the river might allow you to catch a pickup in Poxtla.

Xilitla

You'll find food stalls on the highway next to the *Vencedor* bus office; the town centre, with restaurants and shops, is up the steps to the right. The town holds its Coffee Fair in the first week of November; Las Pozas, the home of the eccentric Briton Sir Edward James, lies about 3km north and is now a popular tourist sight. This is a caving area – there's a big opening in the cliff above the highway 2km east, which you'll have seen across the valley south of Xilitla, and there's another well-known one about 7km west on the highway and to the left on a dirt road; see also p.77 for other caves, and p.79 for a river trip just to the north. The *Flecha Amarilla* bus office is just a bit further up the hill from the *Vencedor* office, with services at least hourly in each direction; the junction with the Tamazunchale-Cuidad Valles road is 13km to the east.

TAMAULIPAS

Mexico's northeasternmost state has almost nothing left of ecotouristic interest, thanks to agro-industrial development. The one interesting site is El Cielo Biosphere Reserve, which is of great interest to researchers as the northernmost extremity of the Neotropical sphere. However it's relatively little known, being managed by the state alone and not part of the national system of protected areas (SINAP).

The state's most typical natural plant cover is *matorral tamaulipeco*, a thorny scrub of mezquite (*Prosopis juliflora*), acacia and mimosa; however, 90% of this has been lost in the 20th century. Oak is widespread between 400m and 2,320m (although it prefers temperate, rather than semi-hot humid, climates), with pine-oak forest between 1,400m and 1,700m in the centre and northwest of the state; this includes *palmitos* (*Brahea spp*) and *manzanita* (*Arctostaphyllus spp*). There are 844 vascular species in all, plus 154 fungi; 14 are endemic, eight of them in El Cielo, together with some cacti and one cycad in the Jaumave valley, immediately west on the Ciudad Victoria-San Luís Potosí road. In addition to the mammals listed below for El Cielo, black bears can be found in the Peña Nevada area northwest of Miquihuana; there are 60 reptiles, such as indigo snakes, western diamondback rattlers and Texan tortoises. Birds include scaled quail, green jays, chacalacas, great curassow, turkeys, and roadrunners.

Maps can be bought from INEGI, Calle 22 Carrera Torres 601, Col A Gómez, 87000 Ciudad Victoria, Tamaulipas.

El Cielo

The El Cielo Biosphere Reserve covers quite a large area (144,531ha) southwest of the state capital of Ciudad Victoria, but the main nuclear zone (28,695ha) is in the Sierra de Guatemala, at its southern end, in the municipality of Gómez Farías (one of many places of that name, in honour of Valentín Gómez Farías, vice-president in the 1830s and founder of the Mexican Society of Geography and Statistics). It's an area of folded Lower Cretaceous limestone, with some intrusions of lava and basalt. The rainy season is, as usual, from mid-May or June to September, and above c1,200m it can freeze in December and January.

Its claim to fame is the northernmost *bosque mesófilo de montaña* or montane cloudforest in the Americas; this lies between 700m and 1,400m, in the most humid zone, and is composed of sweetgum (*Liquidambar styraciflua*), maple (*Acer skutchii*), beech (*Fagus mexicana*) and oak (*Quercus germana*), between 15m and 25m high. There's an annual average 2,520mm of precipitation here, and an average temperature of 14°C. Above 1,400m on the eastern slopes is pine-oak forest, largely composed of *Pinus patula, P. pseudostrobus, Quercus laurina, Q. laeta, Q. affinis*, magnolia (*Magnolia schiedeana*), lime (*Tilia mexicana*), holly (*Ilex pringlei*), yew

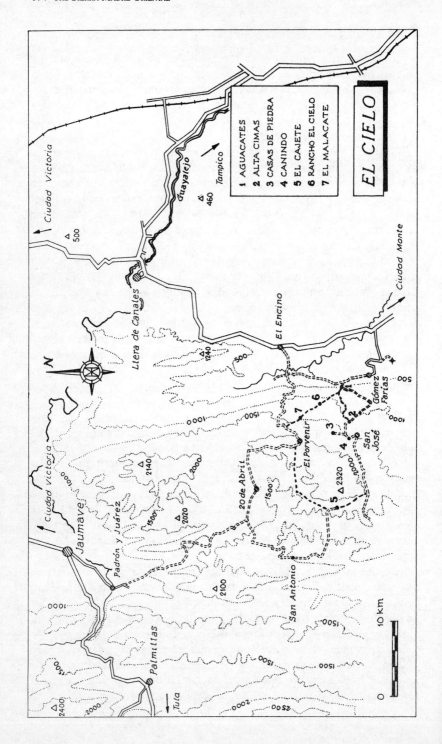

(*Taxus globosa*), dogwood (*Cornus excelsa*) and shrubby *Clethra pringlei*. By streams there are treeferns (*Cyathea mexicana*), elm (*Ulmus mexicana*), hornbeam (*Carpinus caroliniana*), palms (*Chamaedorea spp*), and heliconias. Mammals include jaguar, ocelot, margay, coyote, raccoon, skunk, peccary, coati and white-tail and brocket deer. There are no less than 40 species of bats (including Mexican free-tailed bats), 23 rodents, and three types of squirrel (including the threatened Allen's squirrel *Sciurus alleni*). There are 255 resident bird species and 175 migratory ones; they include warbling vireos, amethyst-throated hummingbirds and least pygmy-owls.

The area was logged until the 1960s, and most of the ten settlements still in the reserve are former sawmill sites, settled in the 1930s and 1940s by immigrants from Michoacán and Hidalgo. Forestry is still largely uncontrolled, as is grazing, but the authorities are working hard on environmental education projects, and installing solar panels to reduce the need for fuelwood.

Occasional tours are operated by the Texas Parks & Wildlife Service (tel: 512 389 4901, fax: 389 8029). To stay at the Canindo research station, you should contact the state's *Dirección de Ecología*, Torre de Gobierno, piso 8, Ciudad Victoria (tel: 24252) – the government tower is very visible to the south of the bus station.

Practicalities
From Ciudad Mante there are six buses a day to Gómez Farías, 11km west of Highway 85 from the junction 39km north (at km130½ from Cuidad Victoria). There's no hotel in Gómez Farías, so you may have to base yourself in Mante. The bus will drop you in the plaza, from where you should walk straight on along the asphalt; this ends in about 2km, after which the road, running north with the sierra parallel to the west, swings left and crosses the valley towards it. There's a junction at Aguacates, at the foot of the sierra, with a new road taking off to the left, and the old road to the right signposted as a hiking route. Both climb to the escarpment and then dip slightly to meet at the village of Alta Cimas, at about 1,200m in the transition zone between medium tropical mixed forest and cloudforest. The new road is steep and pretty rough going, so I hate to think what the old one is like! The escarpment of the Sierra de Guatemala rises from 300m to 2,100 in under 7km; its summit is at 2,320m.

In Alta Cimas you'll pass the last shop (in fact an *ecotienda*, where the village women's co-op sells home-made jams and books about the reserve), go through a gate out of the village and in a couple of hundred metres reach the Hotel El Pino, which boasts a few rudimentary cabins and also offers guides for ecotourism. The road continues, but a genuinely experienced 4WD driver is needed, so many people leave their vehicles in Alta Cimas. Entering the nuclear zone, the road soon climbs steeply into a remarkably dry form of cloudforest, and after about 1¼ hours reaches a junction where a little-used track heads right/north to the settlement of Casas de Piedra. Continuing to the left, it's about 20 minutes, more downhill than up, through a large clearing to the Canindo research station, in a pine-oak zone; the village of San José lies less than a kilometre further on (under ten minutes' walk), at just under 1,400m.

It's best to base yourself either here or in Alta Cimas and then make day trips into the forest; from San José the road continues west to La Gloria and El Elefante, and then north to El Indio and El Cajete. The other main route into the Reserve heads right/north from Aguacates to the Rancho El Cielo research station (of the University of Texas at Brownsville, formerly Texas Southernmost College); this is in cloudforest (at 1,280m) but is not open to tourists. This road continues northwards to El Malacate, in the smaller Nuclear Zone I, and then westwards to the villages of El Porvenir and 20 (Veinte) de April (also known as Joya de Salas); tracks continue towards Jaumave and the Mante-Victoria road south of Llera de Canales.

NUEVO LEÓN

Monterrey and around

Monterrey, capital of Nuevo León state, is the third largest city in Mexico, and a bustling industrial metropolis; tourist information staff have been known to imply that this is a "modern" place, and why would you want to know about countryside? In fact one of the largest and most popular national parks in Mexico lies immediately to the west of the city. The **Cumbres de Monterrey** cover 246,500ha of pine-oak, submontane scrub, tropical deciduous vegetation and desert *matorral*, inhabited by a wide range of animals such as puma, bobcats, coyotes, white-tail deer, opossums, collared peccary, ringtails, armadillos, skunks, hares, rabbits, raccoons, coati, and some black bear, as well as hawks, falcons, owls, quail, chacalacas, dwarf macaws, crimson-collared grosbeak, and many reptiles and amphibians. It's known as a venue for camping, climbing, riding and caving. The most popular excursion is to the Grutas de García, which are near Villa de García, on the main highway from Monterrey to Saltillo; from here you can take a funicular or walk, climbing 800m. Alternatively, at weekends there are a few buses from Monterrey directly to the caves. Illumination covers 2.5km and 16 chambers, housing spectacular stalactites and stalagmites, as well as an underground lake. There are many waterfalls, particularly to the south of the city; take a bus down highway 85 (towards Ciudad Victoria), through the Huajuco gorge, to (Villa de) Santiago or El Cercado, from where *colectivos* will take you 2km west to the falls. The best-known is the Cascada Cola de Caballo (Horsetail Falls), where there are full tourist facilities, especially horses for hire for trips into the mountains. You can hike on to the Cascada de Chipitín, which falls 75m to the Charco Grande pool and another 15m from this into the Río Ramos. To get here hike up to Puerto Genonvevo, at the watershed of the Sierra Mauricio (with a fine view of the Cañón de las Adjuntas), and then take the lower fork to Potrero Redondo. Finally the Mesa Chipinque (1,280m) offers views over the city, and more horse rides.

North of Monterrey
To the northeast of Monterrey the Sierra de Picachos is the first trace of hilly land met by people, and birds, coming this way from the USA. It rises to just 1,500m, with pine-oak forest above about 1,000m and dryland *matorral* below. There's a remarkable degree of biodiversity, with black-headed orioles, white-tipped doves, ferruginous pygmy owls, black-chinned hummingbirds, peregrine falcons, Montezuma quail, acorn woodpeckers, yellow-green vireos, trogons, black bears, ocelot, pumas and ringtails all found here. It's all private land with no public access, so you should visit only by arrangement with the landowners.

South of Monterrey
Turning west at Linares, 132km down the Monterrey-Victoria highway and home to the University of Nuevo León's botanical garden, it's 64km to Galeana, a picturesque town in the mountains. From here it's about 35km west to **Cerro Potosí** (3,720m), not to be confused with that in San Luís Potosí state. This was long thought to be the only place where *Pinus culminicola* (*piñonero enano*) existed; it's now been found on three other peaks (the Sierras La Marta, San Antonio de la Alazanas, and La Viga) just across the border in Coahuila. This Pleistocene relict, the only shrubby pine in Mexico, forms virtually impenetrable thickets up to 5m high on the eastern, southern and western sides of the peak; between 2,800 and 3,450m is a transition to *Pinus hartwegii*, which covers the northern side to 3,700m. An area of 106ha in 1960 was reduced by fire to 70ha in 1970, since when there has been only limited regeneration. In all there are 81 species of vascular plants here, 13 exclusively here, 16 at their southern limit, and two at their northern limit. A road serves radio towers on the summit. Also near Galeana, a reserve is proposed for the Mexican prairie dog (*perro de las praderas/Cynomys mexicanus*), now reduced to just 800km² of its natural *altiplano* habitat.

Peña Nevada
The peak of Peña Nevada rises to something between 3,635m and 4,054m on the border of Nuevo León and Tamaulipas; however, it is reached from the town of Matehuala, just over the border in San Luís Potosí. A hike there has two main attractions: firstly, you'll pass through some very interesting traditional Mexican towns seldom visited by foreigners, as well as some fine desert scenery, and secondly Peña Nevada is isolated enough not to be totally deforested as yet.

Though the Spanish word *nevada* means "snowed-on", Peña Nevada is usually snow-free. In fact, I've also seen it spelt Peña Lavada ("washed"). Nonetheless, when Jim Conrad came here in February it did indeed snow and he was unable to make it to the top; however, readers have sent us more information. Looking at Peña Nevada from the western side, exposed to bright afternoon sunshine, it's hard to know if there's any snow on top; but drifts can linger for days beneath the tall pines on the northern and eastern slopes. The trail is easy to follow and there's little chance of your losing your way.

When locals hear that you're planning to visit Peña Nevada they nearly always open their eyes wide and say "*Y los osos?*" – "And the bears?". Everyone talks about the bears, and some are genuinely terrified of them, but for the most part this is just good-natured kidding. If you really seem to be worried, they'll usually laugh and admit that the bears will almost always run away from a human. *Almost* always ...

In all there are 91 species of mammals here, mostly in the semi-deciduous tropical forest and only 18 in the pine-oak forest that covers the higher parts; there are three endemic rodent subspecies and three endangered subspecies of felines (*Felis onca veracrucis, F. wiedii oaxacensis* and *F. yaguaroundi cacomitli*).

Getting there
The closest town to Peña Nevada regularly served by buses bears the odd name of Doctor Arroyo; it lies about 50km east of Matehuala, which is on the Saltillo-San Luís Potosí highway. Matehuala's new bus terminal is too far from *el centro* to be worth walking in, and there's no need, with connections almost every hour to Doctor Arroyo (mostly with the *Transportes Tamaulipas* bus line). Doctor Arroyo is more attractive; it's about as sun-baked and somnolent as a town on a main road can be and the people couldn't be friendlier. The bus station is next to a pleasant park, some small general stores and a fruit store.

Parked in the shade by this park you should spot some pickup trucks or *colectivos*; you want to find one for San Antonio Peña Nevada – it may actually say "Peña Nevada" on the windshield, but the vehicle will only take you to San Antonio, about an hour to the east, dropping into a huge trough along the western flank of the Sierra Madre Oriental. (The time depends on how many deliveries the driver has to make along the way and how many deep conversations he needs to engage people in.) If you liked Doctor Arroyo's sunburnt, dusty and friendly feel, you'll love San Antonio. This is your last chance to buy any food other than crackers and *refrescos*; there are no hotels, but there's plenty of desert to camp in.

Hiking directions
As you set out to continue along the gravel road towards the peak you immediately begin climbing. However, it's a gradual climb, passing through

spectacular desert – above all Joshua-tree yuccas, but also large barrel cacti, prickly-pear cacti, leg-stabbing lechuguilla and medicinal-smelling creosote bushes. It's 6km to the small village of Santa Lucía, which you'll see at the very base of the range. You'll see the gravel road climbing to a high gap maybe 5km to the left/north of the highest peak, which is Peña Nevada, and various forestry trails, any of which will apparently lead you to the peak.

From Santa Lucía it's about 14km on the gravel road to the high gap, known as El Puerto; there are more direct routes, but don't be embarrassed about sticking to the road, as it sees only two or three vehicles a day, and the scenery is very pleasant. The road forks at El Puerto, and you should take the right branch, towards the hamlet of La Siberia, and then the only turning to the right between El Puerto and La Siberia. This is a new logging road which is closed by a locked gate and runs almost all the way to the peak. If you can drive to this turning, you can have a splendid day-hike to the summit; otherwise you will have to camp. This new road does, of course, presage the destruction of the forest, so you may wish to enquire in the villages before hiking up.

It's also possible to take a bus from Matehuala to Zaragoza (not the Zaragoza on the main road northwest), where there are a couple of hotels; you can camp at the El Salto bathing resort/trout hatchery, with a waterfall, which is busy with trippers at weekends. From here a long gravel road (with only three or four vehicles a day) leads to La Siberia via La Encantada, both cool, damp, green spots at about 2,500m.

COAHUILA

On the far side of the Sierra Madre Oriental, Coahuila state lies for the most part on the *altiplano*, with desert and steppe habitats on marine sediments. It is in fact of interest to fossil-hunters, with huge ammonites found in the north of the state, and the first dinosaurs found in Mexico (*Kritosaurus*, 70m years old) discovered at Parras. There are two areas of interest to ecotourists, neither yet prepared for visitors.

Cuatro Ciénagas

Cuatro Ciénagas ("Four Basins") is the site of the only gypsum dunes in Mexico, and a major centre of endemism. In a generally dry area there are lagoons here in which unique ecosystems have developed, with 60 species found nowhere else. The area has been inhabited for 10,000 years, but it was the Spanish who introduced *burros* and horses, now living wild in the desert scrub, and dug the first canals in the 17th century; the water is too mineral for drinking, but can be diluted for irrigation. The dunes are virtually 100% pure gypsum, and have been heavily mined (for wallboard and fertiliser), so that they are now about 6m high instead of an average 15m.

Pressure from scientists, largely from the USA (so conveniently close), led to Cuatro Ciénagas being declared a Biosphere Reserve in 1994 and mining being limited to specific areas. However, jobs are badly needed in the area, and ecotourism is not yet an adequate alternative – even scientists, who should know better, bring their own food rather than use the local shops and restaurants. The water table continues to sink, due to extraction for cattle and irrigation, and some of the lagoons are drying out, with endemic fish threatened with extinction.

Total average precipitation is under 200mm a year (September is the wettest month), with frost on up to 20 days a year. Thus the vegetation is largely drought-resistant *matorral* and salt-loving plants, with cattails surrounding the pools; to the north the valley is overlooked by the high limestone Sierra de la Madera (3,023m), covered in pine and pine-oak forest. The easiest lagoons to reach are the Laguna de los Burros (on a minor road southeast of the town of Cuatro Ciénagas de Carranza) and the Pozo de la Becerra (on Highway 30 to the southwest); see the National Geographic magazine of October 1995 for a map. The Laguna de los Burros is home to the Coahuilan box turtle; eight of the sixteen fish found in the pools are also endemics, in addition to water snails, scorpions and cacti. You'll also see resident ducks and other, migratory, waterbirds.

The Sierra Maderas del Carmen

The other area of interest lies across the Río Bravo del Norte (the Río Grande) from Texas' Big Bend National Park. There's been talk for a long time of creating an international reserve here, and in 1994 the **Sierra Maderas del Carmen** became a Protected Area for Fauna and Flora, protecting 208,381ha of drought-resistant *matorral* and pine-oak forest, similar to the Sierra Madre Oriental, with pasture and samandoca palm. With snow (often heavy) in winter, and thunderstorms in late summer, there's water all year, although you should purify it.

Highway 53 ends on the Río Bravo at Boquillas del Carmen, a small town in an impressive limestone gorge. The town's electricity comes from the Texas side, but there's no bridge; you can however cross by boat. Nearby in Terlingua you can find Marcos Paredes, who acts as an outfitter and will find you horses and a guide, if required. About 20km back down the graded dirt highway, at Muzquiz, turn east into the Sierra Fronteriza (2,718m), the heart of the park. Black bears (*Ursus americanus eremicus*) are relatively common here, and when it's particularly dry or there's a lot of burning they can cross into Big Bend. The shrew *Sorex milleri* is endemic to higher elevations in the Sierra Maderas del Carmen and the northern Sierra Madre Oriental.

On the far side of the Big Bend, in Chihuahua state, the Cañón Santa Elena was also created a protected area in 1994, comprising 277,209ha of desert scrub, pine-oak and pasture.

Chapter Eleven

The Sierra Madre Occidental

To the north of Mexico City and Guadalajara, the Western Sierra Madre divides the high *altiplano* from the Pacific coastal plains. It's a far more rugged and impressive range than the Sierra Madre Oriental, with canyons that provide some of the most impressive scenery and best hiking in the country.

It's one of the largest areas of volcanic rocks in the world. These were extruded in the early Tertiary, then lifted and formed during the Laramide orogeny, then eroded during the mid-Miocene (around 13mya), faulted and broken, with intrusions of fresh volcanic rock. The lower, older, volcanic rocks are andesitic, the upper ones rhyolitic (silicic ignimbrite), with up to 400 calderas, up to 40km across. The climate is generally classified as temperate humid, with no dry season in the upper regions, a dry winter (particularly so to the north) and a warm wet summer below, and a tropical climate near the coast to the south.

Over half of the area of the sierra is over 2,200m altitude, and this is dominated by pine-oak forest, consisting of cypress (*pinabete* or *cedro/ Cupressus benthami*), pines (*pino real/Pinus pseudostrobus, pino prieto/P. ayachuite, pino triste/P. patula*), juniper (*táscate/Juniperus virginiana, J. deppeana*), oak (*encino colorado/Quercus virens*), arbutus (*madroño/ Arbutus varians*), and *manzanilla (Arctostaphyllus pungens)*. There are a few black bears in remoter corners of the massif, but no wolves other than a captive pair at La Michilía; white-tail deer are common and there are plenty of rodent species. Birds include parrots, wild turkeys (*guajalote silvestre/Meleagris gallopavo*), woodpeckers, warblers, vireos and flycatchers.

The deep valleys on the western side of the sierra, known as the *quebradas*, have an almost tropical vegetation related to that of the Pacific coast, with big trees such as *Ceiba grandiflora, Chlorophora tincteria, Pithecellobium dulce, Caesalpinia spp, Guazuma ulmifolia, Tabebuia palmeri* and *Casimiroa edulis*, animals such as puma, jaguar, peccary, otter, coati, armadillo, white-tail deer, and birds such as chacalacas, parrots and solitaires. On the eastern

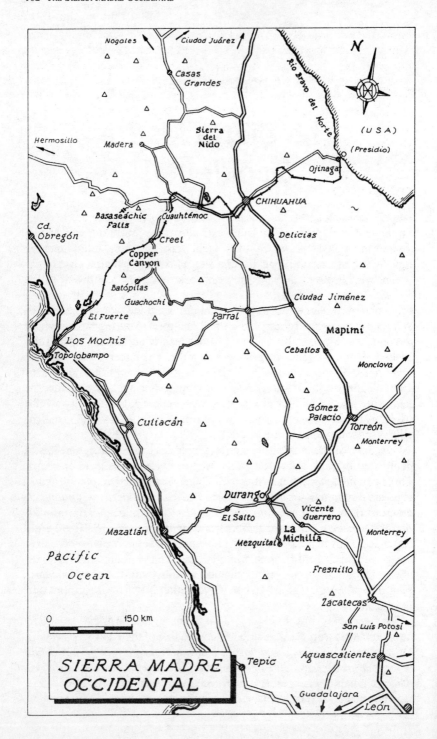

SIERRA MADRE
OCCIDENTAL

flanks, the valleys (1,800-2,000m) are less dramatic and form a drier habitat, with grass, oak, pino de piñón (*Pinus cembroides*), mezquite (*Prosopis juliflora*), acacia (*huizache/Acacia tortuosa*), elm (*sabino/Taxodium mucronatum*), poplar (*alamo/Populus monilifera*), willow *(saúz/Salix boplanidiana)*, alder (*aliso/Alnus glabrata*), ash (*fresno/Fraxinus viridis*), Durango nopal (*nopal duraznillo/Opuntia leucotricha*), and animals such as coyotes, hares, rabbits, pronghorn, hawks, eagles, owls, ravens and doves. Durango is known for its highly venomous scorpions, which you may see set in glass paperweights.

DURANGO

All the hikes and other areas described in the Sierra Madre are in either Durango or Chihuahua state; Durango has two very well-known reserves, which introduced the concept of Biosphere Reserves to Mexico in 1978 and are as well managed and documented as any in Mexico.

The city of (Ciudad Victoria de) **Durango** is a good base for this area, with few major sites but all services and good-value accommodation. There are plenty of fine colonial buildings, but because they are largely single-storey, except on the plazas, the overall effect is not as impressive as for example in Zacatecas. You'll usually arrive at the *Central camionera* at the junction of the Torreón and Zacatecas roads to the east of town; from the layby outside white minibuses 1 and 2 take you into the centre via the INEGI offices (at the Guadalupe Victoria roundabout, also served by any bus to the *Tecnologico*) and the rail station (at the north end of Calle Martinez). There are cheap hotels (and two vegetarian restaurants) in the centre but by far the best value is the youth hostel, in the sports centre within easy walking distance of the bus station on the main road into the centre (Av Heróico Colegio Militar). This looks like the middle of nowhere, but if you go a few blocks northwest you'll find supermarkets, pizza and Chinese restaurants, and the best *torta/licuado* joint in town. Other than colonial plazas and churches, the two main sights are the university's regional museum (*El Aguacate*, built in 1896) at Serdan and Victoria, and the Museum of Popular Culture at Juárez 302 (opposite the Templo Santa Ana); be sure to visit the *Banamex* premises in the Casa del Conde Súchil at 5 de Febrero and Madero as well. Musicians (more *norteño* than *mariachi* here) wait for business on Plazuela Baca Ortiz, south of the centre, which is also the meeting point of the city's bus routes.

The Abandoned Rail Route West of El Salto

Once upon a time (in about 1898) it was obvious that a rail route was needed from the *altiplano* to the Pacific, and a route from Durango to Mazatlán was chosen. From the beginning, everyone knew it'd be a monumental task because of the precipitous drop from the Sierra Madre to

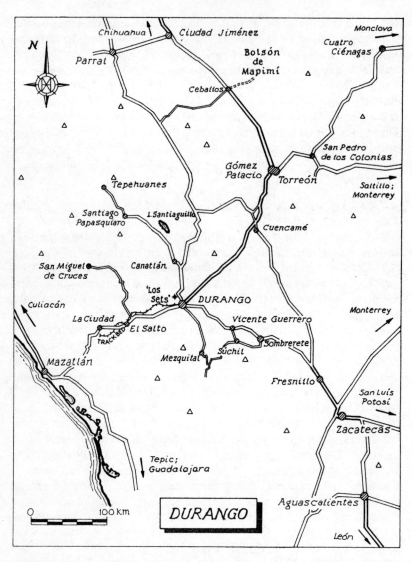

the coast. The builders met their first deep canyons west of El Salto – slab-sided gorges reminiscent of the abysses of the Copper Canyon area to the north. At first they managed to find a way by winding back and forth atop a west-jutting tongue of the plateau; however, near La Ciudad, at about 2,600m, they finally had to dive towards the lowlands. Just beyond the lovely waterfall known as Mexiquillo they began blasting a roadbed for the track along the north wall of the canyon; on the right rose a near-vertical rock wall; on the left opened stomach-churning emptiness.

Nine tunnels were completed before the project had to be abandoned, in about 1925. Landslides were carrying away too much of the work and too many workers were being killed. No track was ever laid on the westernmost part of the trackbed and today it's good only for walking. (A rail route was finally completed in 1961, from Chihuahua to Los Mochis – see the Copper Canyon section below.) There's a fine start out of El Salto, following the rim of a canyon; then you have 35km hiking through pine and oak-pine forests, pastures and the odd village. Finally there's the truly spectacular stretch of the hike, along the canyon side, which can be done on its own if you prefer. I got through every tunnel without a torch (flashlight) but for one in particular you really should have one; however, there's a way around every tunnel.

Getting there
The railway is still, more or less, operational as far as El Salto, with mixed trains leaving Durango at 07.30 on Wednesdays, Fridays, Saturdays and Sundays, returning at 16.00; but if you just want to get there in a reasonably efficient way you should take the bus. There are first-class services from Durango to Mazatlán, but if you want to go from Durango to El Salto you'll probably be sold a ticket for a second-class bus (at least a dozen a day, plus eight as far as La Ciudad); from Mazatlán there are only first-class buses. Second-class buses run from the *Central camionera* and pick up at the *Farmacia Santa Fe* (by the level/grade crossing west of the rail station) and just west of the *Instituto de Ecología*. The road crosses the Río Chico at km30½; you might wish to get off the bus at Las Metates (km26½) and walk down the canyon to the right to pick up a later bus at the bridge. At km57 there's the El Tecuan National Park; there used to be a deer-breeding programme here, but now it's just a quiet resort, with cabanas. There are also cabanas at km85, the *Paraiso de la Sierra*. From km90 a dirt road runs north for 115km to San Miguel de Cruces, which would make an excellent excursion into a scenic backwoods area that never sees tourists. It's another 10km to **El Salto** (2,358m), now a bustling town of 15,000, with a true frontier atmosphere. Its hotels are very overpriced; the Olimpico (next to a decent supermarket, on the road south to the centre from the plaza where buses stop) is the cheapest, if they'll let you stay the night; the best restaurant is Bambino's Pizza, one block west.

The train crosses the Río Chico on a spectacular 120m-long viaduct at km54.2; summits are at km44, km77, and km127, and after 5½ hours you'll reach El Salto, only 467m above Durango and 134.8km away. There's also a branch south to Regocijo, which sees a mixed train from Durango at 06.30 on Mondays; this would be an interesting trip into a roadless area of logging settlements. Likewise there are trains north from Durango to Tepehuanes at 11.20 on Mondays, Wednesdays and Fridays; but again it's easier to go by bus. Just to the east halfway to Tepehuanes is the Laguna de Santiaguillo (between Campo Verde and Castillo del Valle), below the Sierra del Promontorio, another important area for migratory birds.

Incidentally, at km128, just before El Salto, is a halt called Los Negros (and an army base); at one time there was talk of the Parque Nacional Puerto de Los Ángeles y Barranca de Los Negros, covering a vast hunk of land immediately to the south, but this seems to have been forgotten now.

Hiking directions

From the plaza where the buses drop you (by a new footbridge) you should head west across a bridge over a filthy stream and then drop down to the right to the railway tracks, at this point largely buried by a dirt road through a shanty town. Walking to the right along the line, you'll be out of town in under ten minutes and hiking along the trackbed with a canyon opening to the right. There's a lot of rubbish dumped along here, and everyone believes that you'll be robbed if you camp here – so don't. After 20 minutes you'll pass through a limestone cutting; it's partly blocked by fallen trees, but there's a path to the left. Then the route passes through pastures; at rainy times this can be awfully soggy, and as the culverts are missing you may have to get your feet wet. After 15 minutes you'll enter the logging settlement of 1010 ("Mildiez" – certainly not referring to its altitude); there's nothing much here other than a sawmill, one shop and some cola kiosks, but it still takes 15 minutes to walk through. If you wanted to avoid the shanty town at the start of this hike, there's a track to 1010 from km101½, at the western entry to El Salto.

The trackbed swings left, with a rather more attractive stream to the right; if you're into birds you'll find it far more interesting to walk along the bank, but if not the trackbed offers an easier route. The *extremo via* (limit of track) was, I think, somewhere along here at km140.229 precisely. About 20 minutes from 1010 you'll reach a girder bridge across to the left bank of the stream. In this direction you'll have to cross the stream over the rocks below, perfectly straightforward in the dry season but perhaps impossible in the wet. In the other direction you may be able to use the bridge; the problem is at this end where the abutment has washed away from the pier, so that it should be possible to drop down but not to climb up. The main span of the bridge itself is perfectly solid and worth looking at once you get to the other side.

Continuing with the stream to your left, the trackbed is soon a dirt road passing houses and pasture; after 30 minutes this swings right to the sawmill of San Juan. If you carry on along the trackbed you'll have to climb three barbed-wire fences (no problem); after 30 minutes you'll pass two good springs at the trackside and some camping spots by the stream, and also some good scrambling cliffs to the right. The route swings right under three powerlines and then goes dead straight through conifers; after 15 minutes the road comes back in from San Juan, and after about 20 minutes more you'll pass through the tiny settlement of Lechería ("dairy", not "lechery"), with the highway just to the left. Again there's a long straight stretch, used as a road and rather dusty; after 45 minutes (at km115 on the highway) you'll pass some weird wind-eroded rock mushrooms. Passing through a small sawmill, you'll cross to the south side of the highway in 15 minutes.

If you want to start the hike here, this is just east of Las Adjuntas (km117½), a scattered village with no real facilities. Bus crews probably won't know anything about *el ferrocarril antiguo*, but you should spot it.

The first cutting is boggy and fenced off, but you can avoid this by taking the highway west for five minutes and then a dirt road left to the second cutting. The trackbed runs through pasture and straight towards a rock pinnacle on a ridge; however, instead of plunging into a tunnel it swings right to pass behind some graziers' huts and through a cutting. Almost an hour from the highway it crosses a forestry track and soon reaches the first tunnel; a small stream flows out of this and there's a pool at the east end, but you can get through using concrete barriers at either side of the tunnel. Like all the tunnels on this route it's bigger and higher than it seems (built for filthy steam trains); you can see straight through to the far end, but in fact it's about 300m away. There's a rockfall at the far end, but a track passes around to the left.

It's 15 minutes to the next tunnel, also about 300m long and no problem, from where the trackbed begins to drop steadily, with a pine-filled valley to the left. After 15 minutes more the trackbed crosses a side-valley on a high embankment, with a dirt road heading down the valley via a tunnel through the base of the embankment. In another 15 minutes forestry tracks head off to the left and right, and the trackbed shows no sign of being driven on; this is partly because the highway is near (shattering any delusions of tranquillity) and partly because of a washout and fallen trees. *Another* 15 minutes on a big new dirt road comes in from the right; you should follow this for about 50m and then again pick up the trackbed above to the right. This is the road to Chavarría Nuevo, served by the occasional bus from El Salto. Yet another dirt road crosses ten minutes later, and 35 minutes further on the second of a pair of cuttings is blocked by a rockfall with a track around it to the left.

Now you have almost an hour and a half of uninterrupted coniferous nature until you pass a cabin and a corral to the left, from where there are signs again of the trackbed being used by vehicles. In another 25 minutes (five hours from the highway) you'll reach a good stream to the right, the first permanent water since the springs at least 30km back, before Lechería. In 20 minutes you'll pass over a river on a high embankment, and then another 20 minutes on enter a cutting with a very rough floor. There's plenty of picnic-type litter around here, and in ten minutes you'll emerge right in front of the Mexiquillo falls.

These are distinctly unimpressive in the dry season, but in the wet they attract lots of visitors who arrive via La Ciudad, another logging town on the highway about 5km north. The Hotel-Restaurant Lupita is opposite the bus office; it looks very basic but is probably alright; some maps show tourist facilities near the falls, but there's still nothing there. The turning is signposted at about km145½, forking left after a minute or so; it's under 1km to a sawmill, which you should walk around to the right (during working hours you can cut through, but given the risk of robbery in this area it's unwise to draw attention to yourself, especially if it's obvious you'll be camping). When you reach the exit from the mill take the left-hand fork, which brings you in about 2km to an area of "fairy toadstools", bizarre rock pillars formed by soft rocks being eroded under hard caps. It's another kilometre to the trackbed, at the start of the rough-floored cutting; go through the cutting to reach the foot of the falls, or stay on its uphill side to reach the top of the falls. There's also an easy rock-scramble up on the far side.

Continuing westwards, the route becomes much more interesting in 30 minutes, when you start to get cliff-edge views and the first cacti along this route. In ten minutes there's a poor spring, soon followed by a better one. The cuttings are blocked to vehicles by rockfalls, but a well-used muletrack continues. Tunnel 3 is just after the second spring; it curves right but is in excellent shape and only takes a couple of minutes to get through. Tunnel 4 is 100m further and only about 100m long; its west end is flooded, but again you can get by on the concrete barriers, or go around on a path to the left. In five minutes (under 200m) there's a steep drop to tunnel 5, which has a very uneven floor and took me 25 minutes without a torch – far easier to take the path to the left, were it not for my professional duty. It's dead straight, so it's never *totally* dark. A track up from the valley hairpins down over the west end of this tunnel, making an obvious route out if you've had enough (you should emerge at the sawmill). There's a washout immediately west, with a path around to the right and (more importantly) a stream and all-year pool, with cascades above. Tunnel 6 is five minutes further, very short and in perfect condition, with a concrete floor! Tunnel 7 is another five minutes on and is almost as good. There's a very steep incline out, indicating that the trackbed here was just a sketchy indication of the final version. Ten minutes on there's a cascade with no engineering work at all; the path is well used but might be impassable in the wet.

You'll notice the forest is changing, with fewer conifers (but those that are here have huge cones and 30cm/12 inch needles) and more epiphytes and cacti. After ten minutes a path goes down to the left to a hut and field you'll have noticed on the shoulder of a side-ridge; keep right and a couple of minutes further on you'll have a good view of the rest of this hike, with the trackbed winding along the cliff-edge. There are some rock towers and caves above the track, which gradually becomes more overgrown although there's always a path. After 30 minutes it crosses a stream (another good cascade in the wet), and turns around the head of a side valley, likewise impressive in the wet season. Keep to the right in ten minutes from the stream, and pass another waterfall in 15 minutes; the route curves tightly and ducks up and down, but just when you're beginning to wonder if it really is the rail trackbed, you come to tunnel 8. This is about 200m and wet inside; you emerge into a waterfall where the route is totally washed out. It's possible to get down by turning sharp left, but it's easier to take the path to the left avoiding the whole tunnel. It's just a couple of minutes to tunnel 9, shorter and quite straightforward, followed by a steepish climb.

The cliff gradually changes to a hillside, with more oak trees, and after 35 minutes a dirt road comes in from the right, crossing a stream and bypassing a boggy cutting after ten minutes more. A path heads right up to the village of Los Bancos, which you'll have seen across the valley; but if you continue for twenty minutes the dirt road also turns right and zigzags up the hill through the village – a surprising distance, taking half an hour to emerge at the highway (km162.4). If you continue along the trackbed, it finally comes to an end in about 400m, where the hill gets steeper again.

You're 62.4km from El Salto by road, and rather further if you've hiked the whole way. Good going! You'll need to camp if you hike the whole route; this is no problem as long as you have water and are discreet, bearing in mind the warning about camping at Mexiquillo. If you're continuing to the coast, the lagoons south of Mazatlán (around Teacapan) are known for the variety and quantity of birds stopping during their migrations; many other species follow the mountains, passing in the vicinity of El Salto, so the area is an ornithologist's dream, in season. About 5km west of Los Bancos is El Espinazo del Diablo, a well-known viewpoint where the road crosses a narrow spine between two massifs.

La Michilía

The La Michilía Biosphere Reserve lies just east of the highest part of the Sierra Madre Occidental, so conditions are slightly drier than in the El Salto area; as in many other reserves there are overlapping elements of Nearctic and Neotropical fauna and flora here. Since the Pleistocene epoch the Sierra Madre Occidental has been the main corridor for Nearctic fauna (especially montane insect species) moving south. The reserve covers 35,000ha, of which 7,000ha form a nuclear zone around Cerro Blanco (2,860m); the plateau is at about 2,250-2,500m here, and the highest point is in fact Cerro del Purgatorio (2,970m; also known as Cerro las Iglesias) to the east in the Sierra de Urica (or Urique). Rocks are mostly extrusive rhyolites and basalts, with some conglomerates in the high part of Cerro Blanco and the lower part of the western slope of the Sierra de Urica, and alluvia. Above 2,350m the climate is temperate semi-dry to sub-humid, with average temperatures of 17-20°C, and precipitation of 525-610mm, mostly from June to September, with occasional winter snow. In the dry

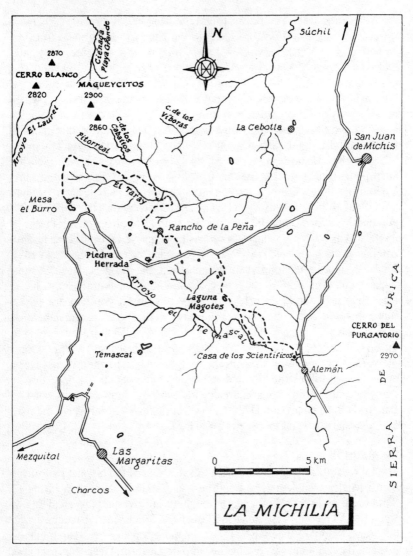

season the only water is found in the arroyo de Laurel and the *ciénagas* of La Taza, Pitorreal, los Caballos, Taray and Las Víboras.

Above 2,000m there's a temperate forest of pine and oak, typical of the Sierra Madre Occidental. This is very well researched and documented: in all there are nine species of oak (mainly *Quercus sideroxyla, chihuahuensis* and *rugosa*) and seven of pine (*mainly Pinus engelmanni, arizonica, chihuahuana, ayachuite var. brachyptera* and *lumholtzii*), but I'll spare you full details of their habitats and Spanish and English names. *Pinus teocote, P. cooperi* and *Quercus microphylla* are here found only in a small area to the east of Rancho de la Peña. The shrub layer features *Arctostaphylus pungens, Pithecellobium leptophyllum, Condalia hookeri, Juniperus durangensis* and *J. deppeana* (alligator juniper, known here as *cedro*). *Madroño* (*Arbutus*, a tree) and *manzanita* (*Arctostaphylus*, a shrub) are both recognised by their red trunks; they're often covered with *injerto* (*Phoradendron bolleanum*), a hemiparasite which is the favourite food of white-tail deer. *Muhlenbergia* grasses are found in valleys on Cerro Blanco (with *Pinus arizonica* and *Quercus rugosa*) and in desert grassland, with *Acacia tortuosa* and cacti such as *Opuntia leucotricha* and *O. robusta*.

The last Mexican wolves (*Canis lupus baileyi*) are captives at the Piedra Herrada research station and there's also a deer-breeding programme at the Alemán research station; otherwise mammals are of little interest, with coyotes, foxes, peccary, pumas, bobcats, squirrels and coati here. There are at least 109 bird species here, notably wild turkeys (*cócono, guajolote* or *pavo salvaje/Meleagris gallopavo*), which fly only when alarmed and to their roosts high in trees, and parrots. As regards insects, the *mariposa del madroño* (*Eucheira socialis*) has a semi-social life which fascinates scientists, and termites build nests of soil above ground level, which is very rare in Mexico; there are also lots of dung beetles (especially *Aphodiinae*).

INEGI map F13B33 *San Juan de Michis* covers the most important parts of the reserve; the slightly more up-to-date (1981!) 1:250,000 map F13-2 *El Salto* covers all of La Michilía and the El Salto trackbed hike, but not Durango city. To visit either of the Biosphere Reserves in Durango you should have a permit from the Institute of Ecology, which manages them; contact Juan Antonio Guerra Ramírez, *jefe de unidad administrativo, Instituto de Ecología*, Apdo 632, 34000 Durango (tel: 121 483); their offices are out to the west of town at km5 on the Mazatlán highway, to the left just before the Lomas del Parque junction (Tierra y Libertad buses, westbound on Serdan).

Getting there

A bus runs from Durango's *Central camionera* to San Miguel de la Michilía and San Juan de Michis at 08.30 daily; there's a good road, with a dozen buses a day (and a daily train), as far as Súchil, from where you could probably get a lift. There are hotels in Vicente Guerrero, on the main road, but not in Súchil, 15km on at 1,976m. In Súchil you need to turn right into the centre, then head right across the plaza and leave town on Av del Trabajo and Calle 16 de Septembrie; the asphalt ends after 5km, but a good dirt road continues past San Miguel. Almost an hour's drive from Súchil you'll reach a T-junction: about 2km to the left/southeast is San Juan de Michis, from where a rougher road continues south, parallel to the Sierra de Urica, to Alemán. The more important road goes right past the Rancho de la Peña, over the Mesa El Burro and then south to emerge on the Las Margaritas-

Mezquital road.

Alemán is part of the San Juan *ejido*, a friendly helpful place; the *casa de los scientificos* is just to the northwest of the village, in a loop of the Arroyo el Temascal, where there's plenty of water (and birds) all year. You can camp here, and it makes a good base for exploring the Sierra de Urica (particularly a more humid area known as El Olividado to the southeast of El Alemán). In contrast, the Rancho de la Peña area is private property, but if you stick to the main tracks you should have no problem. Piedra Herrada, the main research station in the reserve, where you should usually be able to find a scientist to talk to (from Monday to Friday), is on the road in this area.

Hiking directions

Here I describe a route from Alemán to Piedra Herrada and then a loop along the edge of the nuclear zone; this will serve as a jumping-off point for explorations in the Cerro Blanco area.

Starting from the scientists' house, head back along the rough dirt road and take a left before the outer gate (by a hut) onto a rougher track. Fork right after ten minutes, and climb steadily; after 20 minutes a better track comes in from the right, and in another 20 minutes you'll reach the plateau, just before the Laguna Mogotes, an artificial water tank. (Coming back, you can turn right about eight minutes after passing the Laguna, to cut down by an obvious route to the oasis-like Arroyo el Temascal for water and relaxation.) Ignore two turnings to the right, and in five minutes you'll pass through a fence and in another 15 minutes reach a gate onto the main dirt road. Hike west, and in 30 minutes you'll pass the entrance to the Rancho de la Peña to the right; it's another 20 minutes to Piedra Herrada, also on the right. To the left is the Rancho Temascal, where the wolves are housed, as well, I gather, as zebra, elk and other oddities (it's not open to the public, but you may get in with a researcher).

To get to the nuclear zone, head through the Piedra Herrada research station and out at the bottom, across the Bordo de la Avena dam and right/ northwest, and then left on a dirt track. You'll pass through a gate from the Potrero La Avena into the Potrero Pericos, and then left into the Potrero de Las Casas, to reach the Rancho de la Peña, 20 minutes from La Piedra. The manager here is Don Manuel, who should point you in the right direction if you say you're heading towards Cerro Blanco. Continue along the track, swing left and after five minutes go through a gate into the Potrero El Taray. Fork right here and again after ten minutes, following a sign *Al Taray*; the road swings right and loops right around the head of the Mesa de San Antonio before dropping down to the west to the Arroyo el Taray after 25 minutes. The track marked on the map goes straight ahead across the streambed (dry in summer) but a newer route follows the valley for ten minutes to a roofed saltlick and a dry water-tank.

From here the track climbs up to the north onto the Mesa del Lobo, meeting the old road in five minutes, then rising to the west; after 30 minutes it takes a right turn and then a left onto the ridge known as the Cordón de las Culebras. In ten minutes it reaches a junction by another roofed saltlick; here one branch heads right and slightly downhill to Pitorreal, from where you can press on towards Cerro Blanco. To the left, the track follows the ridge, only slowly swinging to the left/west, until it finally turns south after 15 minutes around the head of the Taray valley. Another 20 minutes brings you to a gate, and 20 more to the Mesa El Burro, a cattle corral that you can leave to your right. Fork right after 15 minutes (taking the road less travelled by) and in five minutes you'll reach the dirt road at a red gate.

This drops away to the left/southeast, with a broad view ahead, and brings you back to Piedra Herrada, under 5km away. To the right it heads south, eventually meeting a road to Mezquital (on the Tropic of Cancer at 1,468m) and thus back to Durango. This road is served by a daily bus south to Charcas and Canoas, in an area inhabited by the Tepehuan people, who live in thatched houses on stilts and hold powerful animistic ceremonies to bring rain and to bless the corn. North of Mezquital, on the west side of Cerro Blanco, are ancient structures about 2m high which were thought to be the homes of pygmies; in fact they are granaries built by a people of the Oasis America culture, similar to those of the southwestern United States. Downstream, the Mezquital valley is one of the deepest gashes in the flanks of the Sierra Madre; Cerro Gordo (3,354m) is 2,500m above the valley floor 10km away.

Mapimí

There are two routes north from Durango towards the Copper Canyon area: the most direct is as described below, through Parral and Guachochi, but the main route, with a considerable proportion of divided carriageway, is to the east via Gómez Palacio and Ciudad Jiménez and towards the city of Chihuahua. Midway between Gómez Palacio and Ciudad Jiménez the road (and railway) pass through the small town of Ceballos, at the western edge of the Mapimí Biosphere Reserve. This is the Bolsón (Basin) of Mapimí, the lowest and driest part of the state, and not particularly close to the town of the same name.

This is part of the Mexican *altiplano* or plateau, at about 1,150m altitude, and formed of Cretaceous limestone with some Quaternary alluvia and, in the centre, 250,000ha of basalt lavas. The climate is semi-arid, with just 200mm precipitation (80% from June to September), and average temperatures between 11°C and 28°C. It protects the *matorral xerófilo* that covers a quarter of the state, dominated by creosote bush (*gobernadora/ Larrea tridentata* and *L. mexicana*), with agave (*lechuguilla/Agave heterocantha*), mezquite (*Prosopis spp*), candelilla (*Euphorbia antisyphilitica*), ocotillo (*Fouquiera splendens*), *Acacia greggii*, and 13 species of nopal cactus (*Opuntia spp*). You may also see the button-like peyote cactus (*Echinocactus williamsi*), as well as barrel cacti (*Mamillaria spp*) and palms. As with all desert and semi-desert environments, this is in fact highly evolved and differentiated, with subtle changes in slope or soil producing different combinations of plants, and each combination housing specific populations of rodents, lizards and other animals. However, it does help to have specialised knowledge; if you choose to just get off the bus, have a quick look, and get on the next bus, nobody could blame you at all.

Otherwise you should make your way to the *Laboratorio del Desierto*, at the centre of the reserve, where its most famous animal residents can be found in an enclosure. These are the desert turtles (*gran tortuga/Gopherus flavomarginatus*), which used to be widespread but were hunted almost into extinction; now there are virtually none anywhere but here and at the University of Arizona. Their shells measure up to 400mm by 250mm; they hide underground throughout the hot dry months from October to March, spending five months without food or water. Other animals in the reserve include pumas, bobcats, jaguarundis, coyotes, peccary, mule deer, foxes, hares, rabbits, armadillos, ground squirrels and a range of other rodents. Birds include golden eagles, roadrunners, chacalacas, wild turkeys and mockingbirds.

The *Laboratorio del Desierto* is 55km from Ceballos, below Cerro San Ignacio. Take the dirt road east from Ceballos through *ejido* La Flor towards Santa María Mohovano and Carrillo. To the northwest of Ceballos is the "Zone of Silence", supposedly a Mexican Bermuda triangle where radio transmissions vanish and other weird things happen. The truth is out there, somewhere.

CHIHUAHUA

Few backpackers travelling in northern Mexico fail to visit the area of the Copper Canyon (*Barranca del Cobre*), and indeed a remarkable number of them meet at Margarita's hostel in Creel (see below). Most are breaking their journey on the Chihuahua-Pacific railway, from Chihuahua city to Los Mochis, near the port of Topolobampo, from where many take a ferry to La Paz in Baja California Sur. If, however, you're interested in the mountains you may prefer to follow a north-south route, along the lines described here.

Chihuahua state is divided between *altiplano* (which in the north forms the Chihuahuan desert – see p11-12) and the Sierra Madre Occidental, an awesomely rugged series of massifs divided by several deep valleys which effectively block travel across them and don't usually do much to help travel along them either. It can be very tough going, and lack of water in the dry season makes things harder. The flora and fauna are less interesting than in many parts of Mexico, but the amazing scenery more than compensates: for a hiker with no interest in flora and fauna this is the most rewarding part of the country, and even those here for the wildlife would have to be true obsessives to get no pleasure from hiking here. The best season is from January to May, when the weather is dry and cold.

There is also a large indigenous population in this area, with around 50,000 Tarahumara in the Guachochi and Creel region; they call themselves "the runners" or *raramurí*, due to their most famous ability, and form the second largest indigenous group north of Mexico City (after the Navajo in the USA). They still live in their own way, notably adopting only a few superficial features of Catholicism while maintaining their own cosmology based on the sun god and protector of men, Raienari, and the moon god and protector of women, Mecha. Their life is still based on transhumance, spending the winter in the canyons and moving to log cabins in the hills in summer. It's very rewarding wandering around on the backroads meeting people who don't normally see outsiders, but bear in mind that there's also quite a lot of marijuana and worse grown in this area; you'll almost certainly meet police patrols, although they'll probably not be too interested in you. One of the best things about travelling the backroads of this area is that virtually every vehicle will pick you up, and nobody ever has to pay for a ride.

Parral and Guachochi

Leaving Durango by a direct bus to (Hidalgo del) Parral, on what is now a very good road, you'll pass what really are known as *los sets*, where many Western films were made; these can be visited, although by and large they look like regular Mexican villages. At km12 there's Villa del Oeste, and at km14 Chupaderos; these are served by local buses to Canatlán, Flores

Magón and San Juan del Río, as well as the odd train.

Parral, six hours from Durango, is an old mining town (you'll even see mine head-frames in the centre of town) but now it's better known as the scene of Pancho Villa's murder. You'll arrive at the new bus terminal, from where you can walk in twenty minutes, or take a Minero-Pradera bus, down to the centre; cross the river and make your way to Calle Flores Magón, where the budget hotels are found, and, in the Hotel Los Pinos, the office of Transportes Ballezanos, opposite the good Café Los Corrales. Buses for Guachochi leave (in both directions) at 08.00, 12.30 and 16.00; the road has recently been paved throughout to Creel, so it now takes just 3¼ hours to Guachochi, and it's possible to reach Creel the same day.

Guachochi is, like El Salto, a logging town with a rough frontier feel and overpriced hotels – an exception is the Orpimel, in the same building as the bus office, which appears to be closed but is in fact functional enough. There's a laundry and a *torta* shop in town, but otherwise nothing to detain you. However, the first of the big canyons, the Sinforosa, lies just to the west of town; to reach it you should take the main dirt road west from town towards Ciénaga Prieta. Head one block south from the plaza, turn right at the fence to go past the DIF building and a secondary school, and after ten minutes turn left and at once right, and left and right again very soon, at the hospital. After five minutes turn left at a yellow *tortillería* onto a better dirt road, and after ten minutes you'll come to the end of the shanty town and reach a junction at a breezeblock hut and some pine trees. For the Barranca de Sinforosa you should turn left here, and after 6km, just beyond a bridge, turn left again.

Guachochi to Batopilas

Most people will reach Batopilas (see below) either by taking a bus all the way to Creel (departures at 07.30 and 13.00) and then another back, or by changing at Samachique; however, there is a stunning little hike which connects the hinterland of Guachochi with the road to Batopilas. You need to take the right fork at the junction at the breezeblock hut (above) and get *un ride* as far as Yoquivo, 72km from Guachochi; this is a very rough road without much traffic, so don't expect to arrive at any set time – it took me about seven hours to get there. A few junctions are signposted for Yoquivo, but by and large you'll have to rely on the locals for guidance. There is a daily minibus from Morelos to Guachochi, which returns at some point in the afternoon. This is Tarahumara heartland, inhabited by lovely but very shy people who are very much taken aback at the sight of a gringo riding on the back of a pickup.

There's not a lot in Yoquivo; it's a scattered settlement with one restaurant and a couple of unreliable shops. The trail north to La Bufa, on the Batopilas road, starts at the ford, as you arrive from the east, just before a house where *se rentan cuartos* (rooms are rented). Take the track beside the stream, which after ten minutes takes a left and a right to a small shop and becomes undriveable. In 20 minutes more the path enters the woods, where the water is purer than in the village, with tadpoles and tiddlers living in it. The direct route up the valley is closed by a fence, so you should follow a mule-track to the right, which brings you in ten minutes up to a dirt road (branching off the Guachochi road to the east of the village). Heading left or just north of west, you'll soon drop into the valley and cross to the right bank before (after ten minutes) turning right onto an unused road back down to the stream, and continuing on a mule-track on the far side. This reaches a ridge in ten minutes; just beyond this an old forestry road comes in from the right, but you can continue to follow short cuts used by the mules. The route drops to cross a stream and reaches another ridge in ten minutes; just beyond this it reaches a branch of the road, onto which you should turn right/north. This route heads up towards attractive cliffs ahead and after another ten minutes forks right to a pass with the cliffs just to your right.

There's a good viewpoint ahead; to continue, head right along this old forestry track, which runs north along a very chalky ridge and after seven minutes drops down to the left. After ten minutes fork right to continue along the ridge, and at its end (just three minutes further on) turn left. Fork left again after five minutes to take an attractive disused forestry track that runs down and around to the right, with a valley to the left. This crosses a couple of streams that were dry in May, and comes to an end in 20 minutes. A vague path (used mainly by fuelwood gatherers) continues, and it's not hard to drop down into the valley, climbing over a fence. You'll notice a few fields and houses across the valley to the left (a settlement shown on maps as Cordón Colorado), and may meet the Tarahumara residents with their livestock. You need to continue along this valley, crossing the stream and then returning to the right bank; after a couple of minutes you'll come to a fenced watertank where the valley splits. Follow it to the left here, on what soon becomes a good path through a lovely gorge, at about 2,000m.

After 20 minutes the path passes a rock tower (almost a mesa) which is visible from the forestry track; five minutes further on you should fork left to pass some rock shelters by a waterfall (virtually dry in May) and in 15 minutes swing right as a smaller valley comes in from the left. From here you can see all the way to the Batopilas canyon, still a long way below. At this stage the path ahead is rising as much as it's falling, but after 20 minutes it takes a sharp bend to the left and begins to zigzag steeply down the hill. In ten minutes this reaches a great rocky viewpoint, from where there's a very tricky slow, steep, descent with almost no sign of a path: mules take a higher route continuing straight on from the top of the zigzags, and rejoin the path after this steep section. About 20 minutes from the viewpoint you'll reach a small col (marking the end of the most spectacular and difficult section of the hike) where you should turn right and follow more zigzags down, swinging left to reach the first house in ten minutes. This is a scattered settlement of Tarahumara farmers on the eastern flank of a 1,500m hill shown (even on the 1:250,000 map) as sitting in the mouth of this valley. I chose to go to the left around this hill, following obvious paths downwards, reaching the road in 50 minutes right by the La Bufa village limits sign, with a bridge over a side-stream immediately to the left/west. However, looking back from the far side of the canyon, it was obvious that there's a far bigger and better-used path to the right around the north side of the hill, reaching the road just before its bridge over the Río Batopilas.

The Batopilas canyon is narrow by the standards of this area, but deep and impressive enough, and if you head down to the village of Batopilas itself (at 500m) you'll find yourself in a semi-tropical zone with a lush vegetation, including palms and cacti – in fact you may have seen your first small barrel cacti further up the side gorge, and columnar species here at La Bufa.

Batopilas

Batopilas was for many years one of the most productive silver-mining centres in Mexico; now, after years of decrepitude, it's finding new prosperity as a tourist centre. There are quite a few budget places to stay, including the Monsé Guest House and Carmen's Youth Hostel. Being in a canyon, there are basically two directions in which you can hike – downstream or up. Downstream, the so-called *Camino Real* (Royal Road) leads to Satevo, 7km south, where stands an abandoned mission church. It is a truth universally acknowledged that this hike should not be done in the midday or afternoon heat; most travellers spend the afternoon in the church or in the river, returning only when the day cools off.

Upstream, you can return about 4km back up the road towards La Bufa, to Las Juntas, and then turn left up the Munérachi valley to Cerro Colorado, about 6km further. If you want to carry food and water for a couple of days, you could find your way on northwards to Sorichique and then to Cieneguita de la Barranca, from where a dirt road leads right/east to Samachique, the main junction on the Guachochi-Creel road. A rougher track leads west to Urique, in the depths of the Copper Canyon itself, from where a dirt road leads to Divisadero and Creel. There's a more direct route from Batopilas to Urique, heading westwards to Cuesta Colorada and then north up the Urique valley.

Batopilas to Creel

In the other direction from La Bufa, the road climbs 1,000m in a couple of kilometres, in a series of hairpin bends that are so tight that trucks can't get around some in one take. It took 45 minutes for my truck to get to the top, while eagles soared below me and ever more impressive views opened up. No matter how much the Guachochi-Creel road is improved, this will always remain a narrow, difficult road which will not carry much traffic. Once on

Cusárare Mission

the plateau, it passes through Quirare (or Kirare – villages hereabouts have names spelt in both "Mexican" and Tarahumara styles) and Basigochic, to pass the Samachique turning about 2km before reaching the asphalt road from Gauchochi, 75km from Creel. At km150 (km60 by the old markers) the road crosses the Río Urique at the Umira (or Humira) bridge, long before it develops into anything as impressive as the Copper Canyon. At km112.2 and km108 you'll see signs to the Cusárare waterfall, to the west, and at km112 the road turning east to Cusárare village, where there's an old mission church. There's a hotel by the falls, but most visitors come on daytrips from Creel.

Creel

Creel (2,330m) is somewhat more civilised than some of the logging towns nearby, but although you will see groups of middle-aged Americans here the town has not yet been ruined by tourism. It's an obvious place to stop, feed up, do your laundry and exchange tales with other travellers. The usual place for this is the Casa Margarita, on the corner of the plaza between the two churches; you can get a dormitory bed and two meals here for the cost of a bed alone elsewhere, but it has to be said that the staff can be peculiarly grumpy. Tours operating from here to the Copper Canyon, Cusárare, La Bufa and elsewhere are considerably more expensive than those available elsewhere in town, although you can beat them down. Next to Margarita's is *Expediciones Umárike*, where you can rent mountain bikes; at López Mateos 53 (on the main street) *Nuevo Horizonte Internacional* offers helicopter rides and quadbike hire, and all the hotels offer minibus and horseback trips and so on.

Also on the plaza is the *Misión Tarahumara*, which sells crafts, books and maps, and acts as a sort of tourist information centre. There are quite a few glossy US-published guides to the Copper Canyon area and to the Tarahumara, including Richard Fisher's *Mexico's Copper Canyon* (Sunracer) and John Fayhee's *Mexico's Copper Canyon Country: a hiking & backpacking guide* (Cordillera), usually available here. Across the rail tracks from here is the *Estrella Blanca* office, from where buses leave every two hours or so to Chihuahua, as well as a daily bus to Ciudad Juárez (on the border). The rail station is evident, a bit further to the right/north; its ticket office opens just an hour before the arrival of the first-class "tourist" train, which may easily be an hour after the scheduled time (currently 12.30 to Los Mochis and 15.15 to Chihuahua). Tickets for the second-class train (14.10 to Los Mochis and 17.05 to Chihuahua) are sold on the train. There's no point taking the train to Chihuahua, as it's slower and more expensive than the bus, and the scenery is no different. Buses to Batopilas (07.15 on alternate mornings) run from the Restaurante El Herradero/Hotel Los Pinos at López Mateos 37, those to Guachochi (07.30 and 13.00 daily) run from López Mateos 64, and there are buses to Divisadero (16.30 daily) and Norogachi (Tuesday and Saturday at 11.00) from the *Abarrotes Jessy* shop on Francisco Villa, across the tracks.

The Tarahumara people around Creel are now well organised to use tourism as a way of preserving their traditional lifestyle; you'll have to pay to visit most of the local sights but shouldn't begrudge this, especially as some of the money is going to clear up, at long last, problems such as litter and graffiti. Their *Complejo Turístico Arareko* has an information office on López Mateos (tel: 60126 – the same number serves for the cabanas to the south of town – see below). The government is also keen to boost tourism in the area, for instance by road-building; however, the Tarahumara are opposed to this, as easy access for minibuses would reduce the need for guides and local accommodation.

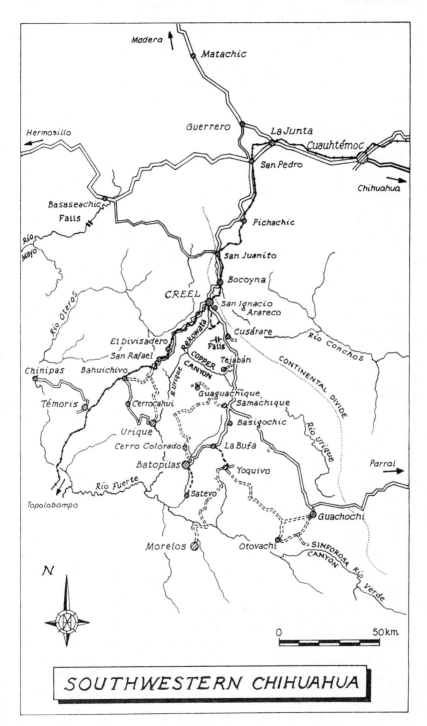

SOUTHWESTERN CHIHUAHUA

Around Creel

Most visitors take relatively easy daywalks to the south of town, notably to the village of San Ignacio Arareko and Laguna Arareko. It takes about 15 minutes to walk south from the plaza along López Mateos to where the railway swings away to the right/southwest under the bypass; a dirt road swings left to San Ignacio, passing the annexe of the Pension Creel (with its name painted on the roof), the cemetery and some troglodytic Tarahumara dwellings. However, it may be more interesting to continue to the right and return by the direct route. The main road (cobbled) swings right and reaches the bypass in two minutes, from where it's three minutes south to km92 (2km from the centre of Creel) and the start of the new road (asphalted for 5km) to Divisadero, San Rafael and Urique. On the far side of this junction there's a typical Tarahumara troglodyte home, with a welcoming family in residence – they now derive a reasonable income from tourists, but that doesn't mean that a *gratificación* is any less appropriate.

An alternative is to take the road to the Pension Creel annexe and then fork right onto the old "road" (you'll understand why the new one has made such a difference) on the far side of the stream, joining the new Guachochi road at a bridge at km93½. This is an open grassy valley, with pineclad hills and rocky outcrops on either side. At km95, at least half an hour south of the troglodyte house (there's little traffic, so it's not an unpleasant walk) a side road heads left/north to San Ignacio, 2km away. You have to pay to visit the village, but you can also visit the mission and the Valle de Hongos ("Valley of Mushrooms", so called after its rock formations) and buy baskets woven from the foot-long pine needles of the area. It's also possible to continue along a dirt track east from San Ignacio to the mission of Sisoguichi; you can camp in this area and find your own way across country (with the help of local farmers and children) to go directly back to Creel.

At about km97½ you'll reach the entrance to the Laguna Arareko, with a campsite and boats for hire, and a longer walking route to San Ignacio. Continuing south, you can also reach the lakeshore at km98, from a layby (with craft stalls) opposite the highways department depot. It's an attractive U-shaped lake with rocky shores and the odd beach, and a dam at its northern end, but the water is not fit for swimming or drinking. Further south, at km98½ and km99, you'll find the cabanas Segorachi and Batosarachi, both operated by the Tarahumara people; friendly rustic places with good log fires (welcome for much of the year!).

Finally, at km100.1 you'll come to the turning (right/west) to the **Rekowata hot springs**, one of the most popular trips from Creel; the road, steadily being improved, runs through pine forest for 20km to the edge of the San Ignacio canyon, where you pay your fee and hike down to the stream. There's a purpose-built thermal bath, about 2m long and 0.5m deep; alternatively, continue downstream for 100-plus metres to a natural waterslide, plunging into a deep cold-water pool. There's more water in the rainy season, but then it's cooler and murky, too. The climb back to the car park can take up to an hour if you're not acclimatised to the altitude, but it's no problem if you are.

It is possible to continue down the San Ignacio (or Tarerecua) canyon to the Copper Canyon itself, and then after a kilometre or so climb west to Divisadero; if you get an early start from Creel with a group visiting the hot springs you might just manage this in a day, but it's more sensible to camp by the river. It's also probably wiser to start from Divisadero, as it can be hard to locate the start of the path from the canyon up to Divisadero. The hike described next is an easy day trip to the upper part of the San Ignacio canyon, ending on the Rekowata road, and can easily be linked with a visit to the lagoon.

The San Ignacio canyon

This is a short hike to a big waterfall with spectacular canyon views, that for some reason attracts almost no vistors. It starts at the road bridge at km93½ on the Creel-Guachochi road, 3½km south of Creel; take the track to the right here and straight down the valley past a few huts (no troglodytism here). In the dry season the best route is down the stream bed, while in the wet there's a track alongside; at this season you should also watch out for flash floods. After 25 minutes you'll pass through a gate, as the valley narrows, although it's hardly a canyon yet. After 15 minutes the valley turns 90° left and 90° right, as it gets more and more attractive. About seven minutes further on, the track heads up to the left; rock-hopping down the valley, progress now gets rather slower, although it's easy enough in the dry season. After another 20 minutes the valley again turns 90° right and left below a jagged cliff, and after five minutes more you'll reach a 2m-high waterfall; it's easy to climb down to the right, or to go about 100m further to the left and then down. Another five minutes on, what's now a small canyon again turns 90° left at a second 2m waterfall, where it's very easy to climb down to the left. It's just two minutes further to the brink of what has been described as "one of those waterfalls you see in movies set in the Andes". The cliffs continue at the same height, while the floor is at least 50m below – from here on it's a full-sized and immensely impressive canyon. However, the falls are totally non-existent by the end of the dry season.

It's easy to climb up to the left/north, barely needing to use your hands, and to follow the clifftop onwards to see the waterfall from the other side; you could climb down from here into the canyon, but it would be wise to use a rope, and there's not a lot of point anyway as the bottom of the canyon is littered with large boulders. If you continue along the cliffs for a couple of hundred metres you'll reach a bluff with great views. Another 15 minutes along to the left (making your way easily through pine, juniper and *manzanita* bushes, although there's no obvious path here), you'll cross a dry (in May) streambed which leads to a two-stage waterfall into the canyon. There's another streambed three minutes further on; you can head left up either of these to join the track that climbed out of the valley upstream of the waterfalls. This heads southeast across the plateau (at about 2,300m) and in ten minutes brings you to a field and another dry streambed; turning left here and following the valley as it curves to the right, it takes 15 minutes to a fence where the path turns right to cross a stream and join a rough road.

To the right this leads to the Rekowata hot springs; to the left it at once crosses the stream again, and after five minutes turns sharp left at a switchback bend, with a farm to the right, and enters denser pine forest. After five minutes more, at the foot of a hill, the old road turns left, while a newer road goes straight up the right bank of a dry stream; they are reunited at the top (about ten minutes on) and continue northwards across the plateau. In ten minutes more you'll pass through a four-way junction and then go through an area of boulders and interesting rock formations; you'll reach the road in under 20 minutes, at km100.1. It's 10km back to Creel, but you'll probably get a ride before too long. It's also possible to hike to Rekowata from Cusárare falls – ask at the hotel.

Copper Canyon

Few people actually visit Copper Canyon (the *Barranca del Cobre* or canyon of the Río Urique), as opposed to getting off the train at Divisadero and gawping from the viewpoint for ten minutes. However, there are settlements on terraces in the canyon where apples and peaches, as well as maize, are grown; these do depend on irrigation, and you must not expect to find water in the streams in the dry season. It's worth hiring a mule to be sure of plentiful water supplies, and you can combine this with taking its owner as a guide. We've heard of various hikers trying to find their way alone and having to give up, faced with a maze of minor field paths, before even reaching the canyon edge.

It's possible to drop down into the canyon from Divisadero (and I don't mean by parachute) and either return the same way or carry on to Rekowata (as above); the other main route in is via **El Tejabán**, reached by a long dirt road from south of Cusárare. There's a small hotel here, which even boasts satellite TV, but it's probably simplest to arrange a trip (transport and a guide, in particular) through Margarita's in Creel. From Tejabán it's about an hour's walk to the canyon rim, and another two to three hours down on a well-marked trail: this leads to the village of Huacaybo, tucked into a terrace high on the far side of the canyon, and it's normal to meet heavily-laden villagers hiking to the highway in half the time it takes us. Locals also still look for gold in the canyon, and it's not unusual to hear the steady beat of a rock-hammer. From here it's possible to return to El Tejabán in the afternoon, or to take a couple of days more to hike down the canyon to Divisadero.

The Chihuahua-Pacific Railway

Construction of the Chihuahua-Pacific railway began soon after the Durango-Mazatlán line, at the turn of the century, but faced with the same problems its builders, the *Ferrocarril Kansas City, Mexico y Oriente*, also had to give up, and the line was only completed after nationalisation, in 1961. The line crosses the Continental Divide three times, but in essence it passes through it by the tunnel immediately northeast of Creel; the highest point on the line is at km583, 19km west of Creel on the north side of Cerro Los Ojitos. (Kilometre posts, starting at Ojinaga, on the US border, are visible on the north side of the line.) At km585 the train inches around El Lazo ("The Lace"), a 360° loop, and there's a similar 180° loop and tunnel at Témoris (km707.5). Divisadero is at km622, and there's another halt at km624 for the hotels there. At km638, west of San Rafael, the train runs along the edge of the La Laja canyon, and then across it; Bahuichivo (for Urique) is at km669.7. Passenger trains terminate at Los Mochis (km921), although freights go on to Topolobampo (km940.5).

Topolobampo (originally known as Port Stilwell, after the Kansas railroad tycoon who first spotted its potential), lies on one of the world's deepest natural harbours; 1.6 million game birds come here each winter from the USA and Canada, pursued by "hunters" from the same countries. There's also good fishing here, with red snapper, yellowtail, snook, bonito, giant grouper, roosterfish, marlin and sailfish, as well as butter clams, oysters, scallops, crabs and shrimps.

Central Chihuahua

Many visitors to Creel also take an excursion to the **Cascada de Basaseachic** (as in many place names in this area, the terminal "c" is optional), to the northwest of Creel on the new Chihuahua-Hermosillo highway. Opinions vary about just how high they are, but 266m seems a safe estimate, making them the ninth highest in the world and the highest single-stage falls in North America. They are surrounded by a largeish national park of about 6,000ha, protecting pine and oak forests and endemic shrubs, as well as pumas, bobcats, jaguarundi, black bears, coyotes, white-tail deer, porcupines, collared peccary, flying squirrels, otters, beavers, golden eagles, peregrine falcon, ocellated quail, parrots, woodpeckers and tree-frogs.

The residents of Chihuahua city are frequent visitors to the **Cumbres de Majalca** national park, but very few tourists get there, although there is a campsite; it's 30km west of the Chihuahua-Juárez highway 35km north of the city. Again it's largely pine, oak, and pine-oak forest, with scrubby *matorral* and strangely eroded rock formations. Animals include puma, coyote, white-tail deer, raccoon, badgers, woodpeckers, falcons and roadrunners.

To the north of the Cumbres de Majalca, the **Sierra del Nido** is where the last Mexican wolves and grizzly bears were seen; it's not a national park, presumably because it's too late, but can still be worth visiting. Head north from Chihuahua for 60km, then 74km west to Santa Catarina, and then north up the Santa Clara valley (populated by Mennonites); from the Rancho El Mesteño you can hike up the Cañón de las Ánimas on a track which ends at the ruins of a sawmill. From here you can hike up a side stream to reach the sierra's highest point, Cerro El Salto (2,820m). Above the *matorral* of oak and *manzanita* there's a forest of yellow pine (*Pinus ponderosa arizonica*), sheltering white-tail deer, wild turkey, quail, woodpeckers, parrots, red-tailed hawks and trogons. There's little water, only 200mm a year, and some of that falls as winter snow.

Madera

In the northwest of Chihuahua state is another area of mountain ranges abruptly broken by deep river valleys; ancient Spanish trails cross the Sierra, but there are still next to no roads, other than dead-end logging tracks. This is the homeland of the 10,000-strong Yaqui people, although the Yaqui museum is near the mouth of the Río Yaqui in Ciudad Obregón (known until 1928 as Cajeme, after "He who never stops to drink", leader of a revolt against Porfirio Díaz's attempts to seize Yaqui land). Castaneda's Don Juan was a Yaqui *nagual* or shaman. In the area of Madera and Casas Grandes you can see the remains of much older cultures, which have nothing to do with the Mesoamerican cultures of the Maya and Aztecs.

Madera is (as its name implies) a logging town, reached by hourly buses from Chihuahua; there's a supermarket (the *Comercial Claudia*), but not a lot else for tourists. The expensive Motel Real del Bosque, on the road south to Chihuahua, is the best place to ask about tours and guides; there's a choice of cheaper places to stay in the centre, although guidebooks don't give much guidance here. A couple of kilometres back down the Chihuahua road, a (signposted) road turns south towards Tres Ojitos, a mission that is still active. Turning left/west in the centre of town onto Independencia (asphalt for one block only), you can follow signs to the Huapoca archaeological site, which includes the famous Anasazi cave dwellings. Heading north, the road parallels the railway, first to its east, then to the west (not as shown on maps), and after about 44km reaches the Cuarenta Casas ("Forty Houses"), another well-known Oasis Culture site, notably the Cueva de las Ventanas ("Cave of the Windows").

SONORA

The road north from Madera (Chihuahua state) continues to the logging settlements of La Mesa del Huracán (75km from Madera) and El Largo, a few kilometres to the west. There are two hotels in El Largo, the Central on the main road, and the El Huerto down the road opposite it. The road is being paved on to La Norteña, from where a dirt track, used by just a few pickups a day, continues over the state border and through the mountains to Tres Ríos, where a dirt road from Casas Grandes to Nacori Chico crosses the Río Bavispe. The northern part of this route, through Pacheco, was originally a forestry railway, built in 1910 by the American Pearson Company; it ought to make a great mountain-biking route, and with patience you'll also be able to get through by hitching rides on pickups, although traffic is hardly heavy.

From Nacori Chico it's a full day's bus ride down to horribly hot Hermosillo, notable only for the excellent *Centro Ecológico de Sonora*, about 5km south down the main highway. Alternatively you can stay in the Sierra and head north to Bavispe, just east of the Sierra del Leone where Geronimo surrendered to the US Cavalry in 1885. In the 1850s Sonora was still paying a bounty for the scalps of Apaches, all presumed to be habitual bandits, and in 1850 the state governor himself killed Geronimo's family, starting a 25-year campaign of revenge that left 500 dead. Geronimo settled on a reservation in the USA but soon broke out, and was cornered here only after a campaign that cost US$25m; he settled as a farmer in Oklahoma and died in 1909.

Directly west of Hermosillo is the **Isla Tiburón Special Biosphere Reserve**, Mexico's largest island (120,800ha) and the traditional home of the Seri people, who were given title to the island by presidential decree in 1978. This did not prevent them from being displaced to Punta Chueca and Desemboque on the mainland when the reserve was set up; however, they are allowed to return to hunt and collect the ironwood (*palo fierro/Olneya tesota*) that they carve and sell. There's a typical arid zone vegetation, largely *gobernadora* and *mezquite*, with ospreys, desert turtles, bighorn sheep, aplomado and prairie falcons, blue-footed and brown boobies and an endemic iguana.

The Sierra del Pinacate and the Desierto del Altar

There is a direct road from Chihuahua to Hermosillo but it's a rough route and not popular; buses to Hermosillo take a long route around by Agua Prieta on the Arizona border. This is also the way to Nogales, Mexicali and Tijuana, via Caborca (where the oldest rocks in Mexico, 1,700-1,800m years old, and the country's oldest fossils, algal stromatolites, are found) and the **Sierra del Pinacate y Gran Desierto del Altar Biosphere Reserve**, west of Sonoyta. The eastern half, El Pinacate, is a bare volcanic landscape centred on the Volcán El Elegante (462m), a crater about a kilometre across produced by a massive steam explosion 1.2m years ago and seemingly virtually unchanged since then. Cerro del Pinacate (1,390m) is the highest of 600 volcanic cones in the reserve, giving fantastic views of the cinder plains in which NASA practised the first moon landing. This section can be visited by a dirt road that links km58 on highway 2 (Sonoyta-Mexicali) with highway 8 (Sonoyta-Puerto Peñasco).

To the west, the Gran Desierto del Altar is the largest sand desert in North America, with dunes similar to those of the African deserts. Other than the highway along the US border, and the railway along the coast, there's next to no access to the desert; but I personally would be more than happy to simply stop at the Cerro Pinto microwave tower at km127 (ie 72km before San Luís Río Colorado) and briefly gaze out over the desert. The climate is fierce, with temperatures over 50°C and only 250mm of precipitation, spread between winter and summer. In the driest places virtually nothing but white bursage *(Franseria dumosa)* can survive, with *gobernadora* (creosote) where there's a drop of moisture. However, despite appearances, there is animal life here, including two small herds of Sonoran pronghorns, mule deer, bighorn sheep, desert turtles, puma, hares (jackrabbits), bats, snakes, lizards, quail, roadrunners, and Gila woodpeckers and Harris' hawks, both nesting in the huge saguaro cactus that's found only here. On the coast, Bahía Adair is visited by wintering birds, and is also of archaeological interest.

In Sonora as a whole, in a total of just 2,634 plant species, there are 200 species of cacti and succulents. The state has been overgrazed for centuries, and buffel grass (introduced from Africa, with triple the yield of native species) is now escaping into El Pinacate. Ironwood and mezquite, the "keystone species of the Sonoran desert", are being plundered for charcoal for barbecues across the border; likewise saguaro cacti, worth up to US$800 each, are being rustled.

The Biosphere Reserve covers 714,556ha; in all over 2 million hectares of Sonoran desert are protected, including Organ Pipe Cactus National Monument and Cabeza Prieta National Wildlife Reserve across the border. The best information source is the International Sonoran Desert Alliance, 6842 East Tanque Verde Rd, Tucson AZ 85175 (tel: 602 290 0828). The aboriginal people of the Sonoran desert are the Tohono O'odham or Hokoham (formerly called Papago, "desert people"); 6,000 live in a million-hectare reserve in Arizona, and just 200 in Sonora.

The Río Colorado Delta

Adjoining the Altar Desert is a newly established reserve of almost 1m hectares at the northern end of the Gulf of California, the **Alto Golfo de California y Delta del Río Colorado Biosphere Reserve**. The Colorado River, 2,330km long, is almost entirely within the USA, as is its tributary the Gila, so the ecological health of its delta is at the mercy of dams north of the border. It took from 1963 to 1980 to fill Lake Powell, during which period flow into Mexico was just a quarter of the average from 1935 to 1963. Since then there have been major floods, in 1979-80 and 1983-85, and the area is also threatened by gas finds. The chief importance of the area is as a wintering spot for many birds, such as the tundra swan and greater white-fronted, snow, Ross's, Canada and Brant geese. There are also 21 endemic species of fish, notably the *totoaba* (*Cynosciom macdonaldi*, now endangered by over-fishing), as well as the *vaquita de mar*, an endemic type of dolphin (*Phocoena sinus*).

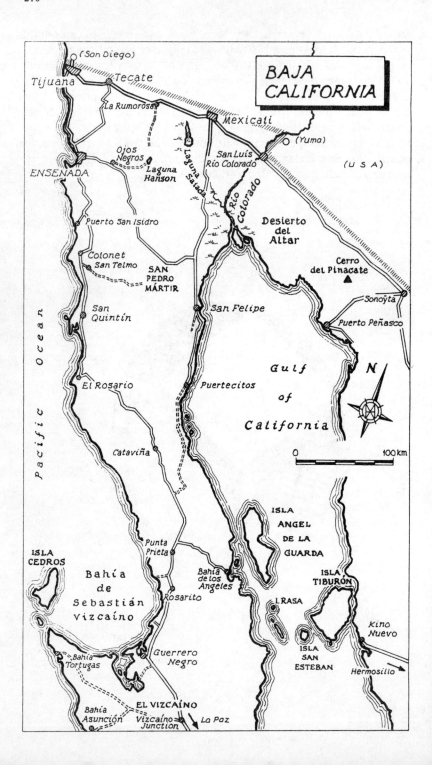

Chapter Twelve

Baja California

Baja is very much a place unto itself, for many years almost empty and unexploited, but now the most rapidly developing part of Mexico and the most visited from the USA. Biologically it's distinct from other parts of Mexico and shows amazing contrasts, with awe-inspiring aridity in many places, yet with cloudforest in a few mountain areas. There's an amazing degree of endemicity, in particular among the plants (especially cacti – 80 of the 110 species in Baja) and reptiles.

Geological and biological orientation
The action of the San Andreas fault (the same one that brings San Francisco its earthquakes) caused what is now the Baja California peninsula to tear away from the mainland about 5mya (million years ago), opening up the Gulf of California, now 3km deep at its mouth. In tectonic terms, the Pacific Plate is being forced under the North American Plate in the Cedros Trench, to the west of Baja, while Baja itself is an errant part of the North American Plate that is being torn off and forced northwards at about 5cm per year. The southern part is moving more slowly than the north, so that Baja is slowly being stretched, but in any case in a matter of a few million years time it will be somewhere off the western coast of the USA. The oldest volcanic rocks date from about 150mya; these were displaced 65-100mya by vast batholiths, upswellings of liquid granite from deep below that melted and transformed the older rocks. These mountains have now been heavily eroded, the resulting sediments forming metamorphic rocks on either side of the spinal range.

The peninsula is almost 1,300km long and as a rule less than 130km wide; however the two coasts are very different in climate and in general character. The Pacific coast enjoys a steady supply of wind (and surf) from the west, while the Gulf of California is quieter and hotter; summer temperatures on the Gulf side are generally 8° to 11°C higher than those at the same latitude on the Pacific coast. Mornings on the Pacific coast can be distinctly cool and misty, and its tip, in Los Cabos, catches an extra supply of precipitation as *chubascos* or storms from the southwest, producing a lush vegetation that comes as a shock after the huge expanse of desert to the north. Baja's northeastern corner, on the border with Sonora, is its hottest, driest and most desolate zone; elsewhere there are wet-season creeks running down from Baja's mountainous spine. As one moves uphill one comes to palm-filled canyons which may have all-year water, and at the highest altitudes (up to 3,096m) there are "islands" of pine forest with lakes and winter snow.

Biologically, almost all of Baja (with the exception of the coast north of El Rosario and the area of La Paz bay and Los Cabos) forms part of the Sonoran Desert, although this includes four distinct habitats. *Gobernadora* (creosote bush) and white bursage, as in the Gran Desierto del Altar (see above), continue along the Gulf coast to the Bahía de los Angeles; the Vizcaíno Desert extends along the Pacific slope from El Rosario to south of San Ignacio, with the Magdalena Plain continuing south to the level of La Paz, and the Central Gulf Coast desert fills the gap between Bahía de los Angeles and the La Paz area (including most of the Gulf islands). The Vizcaíno desert (which may have no rain for four years at a stretch) is characterised by agaves, especially *Yucca valida* (*datilillo*), a 6m-high tree with leaves all along its trunk.

The Magdalena Plain receives slightly more rain, so features real trees, notably *Lysiloma candida* (*palo blanco*), with lots of cacti; by the coast there's also a bizarre "fog desert", with lichen and ballmoss (*Tillandsia recurvata*) growing on cacti, shrubs and indeed phone lines. The Central Gulf Coast boasts some of the weirdest trees in Baja, although they are not endemic to the peninsula, being also found just across the Gulf in Sonora. The *torote* (*Bursera microphylla*) stands up to 10m tall but is disproportionately squat, like a baobab tree, and the *cirio* (*Idria columnaris*) has a bare, ugly trunk, up to 20m tall, and only produces a few scrawny leaves after rain. *Ocotillo* (*Fouquieria splendens*) is related, but it has no trunk at all, but rather 3-4m whip-like branches. You'll also see plenty of *cardones* (*Pachycereus pringlei*), columnar cacti even taller than saguaro (up to 15m) and with even more parallel branches.

The area north of El Rosario is a *chaparral* or scrub typical of southern California, with *chamise* (*Adenostoma fasciculatum*, which flourishes after fire), manzanita (*Arctostaphyllus spp*), laurel sumac (*Rhus laurina*), white sage (*Salvia apiana*), scrub oak (*Quercus dumosa*), and basin sagebrush (*Artemisia tridentata*). Mezquite, of course, is found in all these regions, as are species of *Cercidium* specific to each region (variously known as *palo verde, palo brea* or *palo estribo*), all with green branches, usually leafless and with yellow flowers from March to June. See below for more details of the biology of Los Cabos and the mountains.

North of El Rosario, the bulk of the fauna is similar to that of southern California, with Merriam chipmunks (*Eutamias merriami*), whitetail antelope squirrels (*Ammospermophilus leucurus*), raccoons, ringtails, badgers, coyotes, foxes, and a couple of salamanders; below 1,500m you may see a subspecies of mule deer (*Odoceilus hemionus peninsulae*), with white-tail deer above, and perhaps bighorn sheep too in the rockiest, remotest areas. The ranges of some Californian birds such as the bald eagle, Anna's hummingbird, Hutton's vireo, American and Lawrence's goldfinches extend into this area. South of El Rosario, it's largely desert, with reptiles dominant, such as iguanas, lizards, skinks and snakes.

Historical orientation

Cortés saw Baja California in 1525, and Ordoño Jiménez landed in La Paz in 1533, followed by Cortés again in 1535. Francisco de Ulloa reached the head of the Gulf of California in 1539, and Juan Rodríguez Cabrillo's ship sailed north as far as Oregon in 1542/43, but maps showed California as an island until 1683. Attempts, every ten years or so, to settle California consistently failed, due to lack of water and the hostility of the indigenous population. Nevertheless the "Manila galleon", the annual convoy from the Philippines to Acapulco, took to taking on water at Cabo San Lucas, where English, and later Dutch, pirates lay in wait for them. The Jesuits established their first mission in 1697, in Loreto; they and their guards brought diseases with them which led to the deaths of 90% of the indigenous population by 1800. The Jesuits were expelled in 1767, and were replaced by the Franciscans and Dominicans; the remains of their missions, many in out-of-the-way oases, are now some of the most evocative tourist destinations in Baja. In addition, gold and silver mines flourished from 1748. The first scientific expedition (to observe the transit of Venus) was in 1769.

After independence, California became a Federal Territory; in 1848 Alta California, to the north, was ceded to the USA, and the filibuster William Walker tried to seize Baja California as well in 1853. Development followed slowly; northern Baja California became a fully fledged state in 1952, and Baja California Sur followed in 1974, a year after the opening of the Trans-Peninsular Highway to Cabo San Lucas. This has transformed the peninsular, above all allowing gringo tourists to swarm all over it. A road had existed since 1850, but it linked the missions rather than the present towns on the coast, and was fit for little more than mules. The north has also boomed, with the growth of the *maquiladora* industry, of irrigated agriculture providing winter vegetables for the US and Canada, and of Pacific Rim trade in general.

Practicalities

Many US citizens, Californians in particular, see Baja California as almost an extension of the USA, and many go there at weekends or even for nights out, so there's almost a glut of English-language books on all aspects of

Baja. In addition to the Moon and Lonely Planet guides, and Steinbeck's *The Log of the Sea of Cortez*, listed in Appendix Two, you might wish to look out for the *Adventure Guide to Baja* (Wilbur H Morrison; Hunter/ MPC, 1990), *Camping & Climbing in Baja* (John W Robinson; La Siesta Press, 5/e 1983), *The Baja Adventure Book* (Walt Peterson, Wilderness Press), *Symposium: the Biogeography of Baja California* (edited by Wyatt Durham & Edwin Allison; in *Systematic Zoology* 9(2) 1960), *Field Guide to the Common and Interesting Plants of Baja California* (Jeanette Coyle & Norman Roberts; Natural History Publishing, La Jolla CA, 1976), *Flora of Baja California* (Ira Wiggins; Stanford UP, 1980), *Vegetation and Flora of the Sonoran Desert* (Forest Shreve & Ira Wiggins; Stanford UP, 1946), *Reef Fish of the Sea of Cortez* (Donald Thomson; Wiley, 1979) or the *National Geographic* of December 1989.

International Travel Map Productions (PO Box 2290, Vancouver BC, V6B 3W5, Canada; distributed by Bradt in the UK) produce a superb map of Baja at 1:1,000,000 (3/e 1996), and there's a great hiking map of the Sierra de San Pedro Mártir National Park by Jerry Schad, best found in San Diego, at REI, John Cole's or map shops on University Avenue. Graham Mackintosh walked right around the coastline of Baja, and wrote *Into a Desert Place* (Unwin Hyman, 1988) describing this feat; we're indebted to him for some original material in this chapter.

The capital of Baja California Norte is not Tijuana but Mexicali; the INEGI offices (for maps) is on the third floor of the *Palacio Federal* (CP21000 Mexicali; tel: 65 573 914, fax: 560 995). So there's no need for you to go to Tijuana, the Calcutta of North America – not that it's not worth visiting, but it's not a place to go to on business. There is in any case an INEGI outlet in Tijuana, on the second floor of the *Antiguo Palacio Municipal* at Calle 2 and Constitución (CP 22000 Tijuana; tel: 66 856 786); the capital of Baja California Sur is La Paz, described below – INEGI is at Altamirano 2790, between 5 de Febrero and Navarro (CP23000 La Paz; tel: 112 33150, fax: 24146).

COASTAL HIKES

It's possible to hike Baja's entire coast, from Ensenada to San Felipe, hardly ever encountering a man-made barrier. Proposals by hotel developers to close off sections of beach aroused such violent opposition that beaches nationwide are now state-owned to 100m above the high tidemark, guaranteeing free access to the coastline. Graham Mackintosh walked the whole way, but most sane people will hike just for a day or two; never forget that you will need a large amount of water – oranges are an ideal back-up.

The Pacific coast

Ensenada is the main port in Baja and, by Baja standards, a relatively untouristy place, although it doesn't seem that way to anyone who's spent time in the interior of Mexico. It's the starting point for the Sierra de Juárez hike detailed below. The main ABC bus terminal is at Calle 11 and Av Riveroll; *Aragon* are at Riveroll and Calle 8. The cheapest hotels (not much used by gringos) are near the sea on Av Gastellum and the adjacent streets.

Across the bay, at the head of Punta Banda, a collection of tourist homes and trailers, restaurants, food stalls and curio shops (reached by local buses) clusters around **La Bufadora**, reputed to be the biggest blow-hole in the world – waves rush into a submerged cave, compress the air inside and produce a spout up to 15m in height from a vent in its roof. There are coastal walks here through coastal scrub, with plenty of prickly-pear cacti and agave. Beware the vicious cactus spines, and also the surf: several people have been swept off the rocks and drowned. Sunsets can be magnificent, and between December and March it's a great place to watch the annual migration of the grey whales to calve in the lagoons to the south. Robert Louis Stevenson came here in the early 1880s, and used the Islas Todos Santos, to the northwest of Punta Banda, in his *Treasure Island*.

Heading south along Highway 1, roads run west to a number of spots on the coast, such as Punto Santo Tomás, Punto San Isidro (paved), and San Antonio del Mar. From the south end of Colonet a rough track makes a loop to Bahía Colonet, returning to the highway at the Puente San Telmo, entry-point to the Sierra de San Pedro Mártir (see below). The road runs parallel to the coast as far as El Rosario, where it swings 90° left and heads into truly characteristic Baja desert scenery. In 86km you reach the **Desierto Central de Baja California Natural Area**; this starts with the Cataviña boulder field, an area of weathered granite rocks, some the size of a house. You'll also see plenty of cardón, cirio and yucca here; rare blue fanpalms line the arroyos, which sometimes flow with water. From Santa Inés (one of the few places along this road where you can find dormitory accommodation, 2km south of the settlement of Cataviña) a rough track leads 23km east to the ruins of the old Jesuit mission of Santa María de los Angeles, which makes a worthwhile hike.

South of El Rosario hundreds of miles of magnificently empty coastline – all the way to Guerrero Negro – provide splendid solitude interrupted only by a few fish camps and adventurous offroading gringos. A little-used road broadly follows the southern stretch of this coastline, with occasional links to the highway; don't attempt to walk inland in summer – it's better to wait for a ride at a fish camp. A half-decent road leads (from 26km south of Punta Prieta) 16km to the small fishing village of Santa Rosalillita, and another (from Villa Jesús María, paved for about 6km) to the headland of Morro Santo Domingo. Here you are entering the vast hook of Bahía Sebastián Vizcaíno (or Vizcaíno Bay, named after an explorer who reached

DESERT SURVIVAL
by Graham Mackintosh

Between April 1983 and March 1985 I hiked around the entire coastline of Baja, south from San Felipe on the Gulf side, and then south from Ensenada on the Pacific side. My goal was to survive off the sea and the desert. My diet consisted largely of fish, shellfish, crabs, seaweed, cactus and its fruits, rattlesnakes, and whatever I could obtain from ranches and fish camps. I rarely went hungry. Obtaining drinking water was always my prime concern.

Temperatures in Baja from May to September are hot everywhere except in the immediate vicinity of the Pacific coast and the very highest elevations. Midday temperatures often hover around 38ºC (100ºF); when it's that hot the Baja backpacker should always be aware that *your life expectancy without water is about 24 hours* (assuming complete rest). You need to drink almost continuously and must budget a minimum of four litres (one gallon) of water a day. Don't venture anywhere in Baja without adequate supplies of water, or knowing exactly where you're going to obtain it.

On my journey I would regularly go four or five days without seeing anyone or finding a water source, so I had to make my drinking water from the sea, with one of three different stills. The first was made by Airborne Industries of Leigh-on-Sea, Essex, UK, and described thus in a survival products catalogue: "SOLAR STILL. Specialised inflatable unit designed to supply the occupants of a liferaft with 0.5 to 1.5 litres (½qt to 1½qt) of fresh water a day through solar evaporation of seawater. Can also be used on land. Weighs 0.9kg (2lb)."

My most important still cost less than US$10 and consisted of a kettle, a cork and length of aluminium tubing. I would boil seawater in the kettle and condense the steam by passing it through the tubing. By tending this still through the evenings and long midday breaks I could make several gallons of drinking water a day. There was normally plenty of driftwood or dried cactus for a fire.

The third type was the classic desert still comprising a polythene sheet spread over a freshly dug hole in the ground. The sun draws moisture from the soil, water droplets form on the underside of the plastic sheet and run down to drip steadily into a collecting vessel placed underneath. A good day's yield would be less than a litre.

Even with these stills I came close to dying of thirst on at least three occasions when forced inland by impassable cliffs. Without access to seawater my stills were practically useless. Don't imagine you are going to get enough water from cacti – you have to find water or make your way back to the sea!

San Francisco in 1602 – his first voyage in 1591 was abandoned when the crew mutinied against his sodomy), which offers some of the world's finest beachcombing, with all sorts of intriguing rubbish brought from the north by the California Current.

The highway crosses the 28th parallel into Baja California Sur and there's a short spur west to Guerrero Negro (named after a whaling ship, the *Black Warrior*), the base for the huge El Vizcaíno Biosphere Reserve and some of the world's best whale-watching.

Isla Cedros

Isla Cedros is the large island (about 32km long) north of the Vizcaíno Peninsula; it has a population of about 10,000, mostly dependent on fishing rather than tourism. Nevertheless, the island does have restaurants, guest-houses and taxis, and can be reached by flying from Ensenada. Among its attractions are fine beaches, huge colonies of elephant seals and sea lions, and on Cerro Cedros (1,250m) forests of pine and juniper (known as *cedro*). All along the coast from here to Ensenada are dense "forests" of a kelp called *zargaza* (ie sargasso, *Macrocystis pyrifera*), which grows 40-60cm a day, and houses a complete ecosystem of fish, invertebrates and other creatures. The islands from here northwards are the breeding colonies of Xantus' murrelet (*Synthliboramphus hypoleucus*); Craveri's murrelet (*S. craveri*) breeds here and on the Gulf islands.

El Vizcaíno Biosphere Reserve

At just over 2.5m ha (6.3m acres), this covers an immense area, largely of small-leaved drought-resistant scrub – not really pretty. This is a mixture of mezquite and cacti such as *cardón, garambullo, cholla* and *yuca*, and some pine. However, for most visitors the focus of interest is the coast; here there are some mangroves, pines and on coastal dunes eel grass, *datilillo* (*Yucca valida*), *copalquín* (*Pachycormus discolor*), *cardón, cardón barbón* (*Pachycereus pecten-aboriginum*), and *palo adán* (*Fouquieria columnaris, F. peninsularis*). Wildlife includes the peninsular subspecies of the pronghorn, the bighorn sheep, puma, bobcat, fox, coyote, golden eagle, osprey, peregrine and black falcons, white and frigate pelicans, and migrant water-birds such as northern pintail, blue-winged teal, American widgeon and lesser scaup. There are many endemic reptiles and leatherback, loggerhead and green turtles.

But the main reason for visiting is to watch the **grey whales** (*Eschrichtius glaucus*), from January to March. These amazing creatures migrate almost 10,000km in eight weeks from the Bering and Chukchi Seas to the lagoons of Baja California Sur, where some mate and then others give birth (their gestation period is 13 months). Laguna Ojo de Liebre is also known as Scammon's Lagoon, after Charles Melville Scammon, the first whaler to find the whales here, in 1857. Such a massacre ensued that by 1890 there were few left to hunt; the Atlantic grey whale is extinct, and there are fewer than 100 of the Western Pacific grey whale. The world's first whale refuge was created in Bahía Magdalena in 1972, since when the Californian race has recovered to 22,000, close to its original levels; about 4,000 come to the lagoons each year. These gentle giants measure up to 18m long and weigh up to 40t, with a tongue of 1.5t, feeding only on tiny crustaceans; they are already 3-4m long at birth, weighing up to 800kg. Jim Conrad describes his first encounter with them: "several whales had glided beneath our small fishing boat before one approached and gently nudged it. The

MARINE BIOLOGY

In the Gulf of California as a whole there are at least 800 species of fish, second only to the Red Sea, with 2,200-odd marine invertebrates; 90% are close to shore, making them easily accessible to divers. Reef fish number about 250 species; endemics among them often have a similar "pair" species in the Caribbean, indicating the relatively recent lifting of the Central American land bridge. "Cleaning stations" such as Shepherd's Rock, where fish come to allow smaller fish, that you might expect them to gobble up, to feed on their parasites, are well known hot spots for divers. Diving at night, when many fish can be seen to change colour, is also very rewarding, an ethereally beautiful experience.

The larger gamefish attract huge numbers of American and Canadian "sportsmen", with around 40,000 marlin a year being taken off Los Cabos – thankfully, an increasing number are now being released, alive if traumatised. Billfish (*pecudo*) include black, blue and striped marlin (the blue weighing in at up to 300kg), sailfish, and dorado (or *mahi-mahi*, their Hawaiian name). Marlin are most common in the spring, dorado from May, and sailfish in the summer and autumn; the dorado is reckoned to be the world's third fastest animal, moving at twenty bodylengths/second. Less exciting to catch, but excellent eating, it seems, are bass (larger types are known as *garropas*, ie groupers, and smaller ones as *cabrillas*), jacks (such as yellowtail, which weigh up to 180kg, jack crevalle, Pacific amberjack and roosterfish), tuna (bluefin, albacore and yellowfin), snook, wahoo, rako and many others. Most of these can be found in season in the Gulf, as well as in the Pacific, although Ensenada calls itself the "yellowtail capital of the world" and swordfish are also mostly found in the Pacific.

The Gulf also accounts for 70% of Mexico's commercial fish catch (1.5m tonnes in 1990); even in 1940 Steinbeck was fretting about the depredations of the Japanese shrimp boats (*that* at least was solved by Pearl Harbour), and now the World Bank is helping to wipe out the shrimp population. Sardines are also overfished, harming all the larger fish that feed on them, such as jacks, scad and sawfish which are now commercially useless. Pearl fishing was a major industry for 7,000 years, but was wiped out by disease in 1936-40.

As regards mammals, the common dolphin (*Delphinus delphis*) is seen in pods of thousands, and there are also Pacific white-sided, bottlenosed, spotted, Risso's, spinner and striped dolphins, as well as the *vaquita* ("little cow", *Phocoena sinus*), of which only a few hundred survive in the Río Colorado Delta. See below for

barnacle-covered creature then raised its head vertically from the water to look us over; satisfied with what it saw, it approached the boat over and over again, allowing us to reach out and touch its surprisingly soft flesh. That was the pattern for three days – curious mothers and babies, and "friendlies" galore. These gentle creatures couldn't get enough of us, nor we of them."

Whale-watching is big business now, with 4m people a year involved in North America alone; this of course points the way for the success of ecotourism more generally. In Mexico it's now tightly regulated, so that you can't just ask a local fishermen to take you out in his boat; there are agencies in Guerrero Negro who put on four-hour trips for about US$30, details of the grey whale; twelve other species of whale appear in the Gulf, of which six breed here, including the huge blue whale, which is relatively easy to find between January and April. The Northern elephant seal (*Mirounga angustirostris*), once common, is now mainly found on the Isla Guadalupe and Isla Cedros. There are two types of sea lion (*lobo marino*), like seals with ears: the Steller's sea lion (*Eumetopias jubata*) only along the Pacific coast, and the smaller Californian sea lion (*Zalophus californianus*), of which more than half are found in the Gulf. The latter is a natural acrobat, the classic circus "performing seal".

It was estimated that in 1989 84,000 spinner dolphins died in fishing nets (not only in the Gulf of California), and therefore the USA banned tuna imports from Mexico in 1990; although the death toll has now been reduced to near zero (and considerably less than the US rate) the ban has not been lifted, leading to accusations of economic imperialism and protectionism. Personally, I fail to see much distinction between killing dolphin and killing tuna.

Sharks are generally of more interest to divers than to fishermen. Of the 60 species found here the most interesting are the smooth and scalloped hammerhead sharks (up to 4m long, feeding on stingrays buried in sand), and the whale shark (*tiburón ballena*), the world's largest fish at up to 18m in length and 3.6t in weight; this feeds only on plankton, often at the meeting of two currents, relatively easy to find by looking for plastic flotsam also held by the currents.

There's any number of marine invertebrates, from thatch barnacles, oysters, clams and cowries through crabs, starfish, sea urchins and sea anemones to coral and algae. Most squid are under 30cm in length, but the Humboldt squid can reach 4m and 150kg. Turtles are mostly hawksbills and loggerheads, with leatherbacks, greens and ridleys (with the pond slider *Chrysemys scripta* in fresh water).

Being gringo territory, with lots of resident expats, there are quite a few non-profit groups helping the Mexicans to tackle their environmental problems. In La Paz *Pronatura* is active (with Tim Means, founder of Baja Expeditions, playing a leading role) in campaigning against destructive drift nets and planning artificial reefs (off Loreto and Isla Ballena), and ISLA works for the preservation of the islands' ecosystems. In Los Cabos there's the *Grupo Ecológico de Cabo San Lucas*, Sea Watch, and ASUPMATOMA (the Association for the Protection of the Environment and Marine Turtles in Southern Baja California).

and many of the ecotourism companies listed on p.33-35 come here. The rules are clear and are described in an excellent leaflet; most are obvious, but above all remember not to swim or dive near whales. There are two old wharves just north and west of Guerrero Negro from which you can watch the whales. The official whale-watching area, with a viewing tower, is to the south on Laguna Ojo de Liebre; take the La Paz road for 10km, then head right/west for 24km, and expect to pay about US$3. This road continues to the world's largest salt works, producing 4.7m t/year, most of which is taken by barge to Isla Cedros from where it's shipped to Japan. A new Mitsubishi project (ESSA) is being opposed as environmentally damaging.

You could continue on this track to reach the Vizcaíno Peninsula, but it's better to continue down the La Paz highway for 61km to Vizcaíno Junction (Fundolegal), from where a fairly decent road (paved for 10km) heads west to reach the villages of Bahía Ascunción and Bahía Tortugas. It's 56km to the Bahía Ascención junction, and after 37km more a track heads north for 42km to Playa Malarrimo, which offers the world's best beach-combing. From Bahía Tortugas tracks continue to the Malarrimo fish camp and to the end of the peninsula at Punta Eugenia (known for its lobster and abalone fishing). From Bahía Ascunción a track runs south along the coast for almost 100km to Punta Abreojos (Open Eyes Point) on Bahía de Ballenas (Whale Bay), and then 67km (past the basaltic Sierra Santa Clara, 935m) back to the highway 44km south of Vizcaíno Junction. It's a rough road, and there's no water, so cycling is not recommended, but this is one of Baja's classic 4WD circuits.

San Ignacio

It's another 24km southeast on the highway to San Ignacio, an oasis where the Jesuits established a mission (one of the best-preserved) and introduced the date palm – there are now about 100,000 here. From here a road runs southwest to the south side of Laguna San Ignacio, the other hot spot for watching grey whales, where some US tour companies have luxury camps. A track continues near the Pacific coast to San Juanico, La Purísima and Ciudad Insurgentes. To the north of the highway about 30km east of San Ignacio rises the triple-peaked Volcán Las Tres Vírgenes (1,920m), still classified as active, and one of the more dramatic sights along a highway not known for exciting driving.

San Ignacio is also the base for visiting the amazing **cave paintings** of central Baja; little is known about these, although the oldest seem to be about 10,000 years old. Access to the *Zona Arqueológica* is now strictly regulated along the best ecotouristic lines, with a museum and INAH office in San Ignacio, and employment as guides distributed by rota to the families who live in these bleak hills. You have to use a guide, who can also supply mules; remember you'll have to carry water (but alcoholic drinks are forbidden).

Most of the paintings are in the mysterious Sierra de San Francisco to the north; a relatively decent track runs 37km east from the highway, 45km north of San Ignacio at km118, to San Francisco de la Sierra, where camping is allowed. From here the descent to the canyon bottom is spectacular, and the paintings are more so. After a hard day of exploring caves you can immerse yourself in a warm stream or rock pool and wonder what the artists ever saw in these palm-shaded canyons. A far worse track runs north from about 10km east of San Ignacio to Santa Marta (close to San Francisco, but on the other side of the 2,105m Pico Santa Mónica), 5km from the Cuesta del Palmerito, one of the most visited caves.

Bahía Magdalena

Leaving the Vizcaíno Biosphere Reserve at last, the highway follows the Gulf coast through Santa Rosalía, Mulegé, Bahía Concepción and Loreto, and then swings southwest again to Ciudad Insurgentes. Buses from La Paz run via Insurgentes north to La Purísima and west to Puerto Adolfo Lóez Mateos, on the coast opposite the sand bar of Isla Magdalena.

Ciudad Constitución, 26km south along the highway from Insurgentes, is, with 50,000 inhabitants, the largest settlement between Ensenada and La Paz, although it's of little interest; however, a paved road runs 32km west to Puerto San Carlos (also reached by buses from La Paz), the main town on **Bahía Magdalena**, another major centre for whale-watching and a stopover for yachtsmen from the States.

To the north the barrier islands protect narrow mangrove-lined creeks full of water birds; there's an endemic rattle-less rattlesnake on Isla Magdalena.

The Gulf coast

At the head of the Gulf of California (also known as the Sea of Cortés, and previously called the Vermilion Sea, due to algal red tides) is the delta of the Colorado river, protected by a Biosphere Reserve (see p.208). To its south is the town of San Felipe, reached by good roads from Mexicali and Ensenada. This area is horribly hot in summer and in winter is clogged with camper vans – totally missable in either case.

The road south as far as Puertocitos is well developed, with camper sites and fish camps all along it. The next 137km to the Trans-Peninsular Highway south of Cataviña is a very rough road, although plenty of off-roaders do come this way. The coast here is very rough and rugged, so hikers may have to detour inland to pick up the road for a while. While the desert here is comparatively barren and uninteresting, there are some fine beaches for camping, and the many nearby islands are particularly photogenic.

This is one of the best places in the world for sea kayaking, with calm waters and beautiful empty scenery; be sure to protect yourself from the sun, and to carry stills and water supplies.

Remember that tides in the northern Gulf are enormous – up to 9m (30ft)! Keep this in mind when you pitch your tent.

Bahía de los Angeles

Virtually everyone will follow Highway 1 for a while from here; your next chance to reach the Gulf coast is about 110km south of Cataviña, where a paved road runs 77km southeast to Bahía de los Angeles, a small bay with a growing resort. There's little traffic on this road, but the view as you arrive is one of the most memorable in Baja. The cacti forests around town are some of the tallest and most spectacular in the world. From Las Flores, about 20km south, you can hike inland to the former mine of San Juan

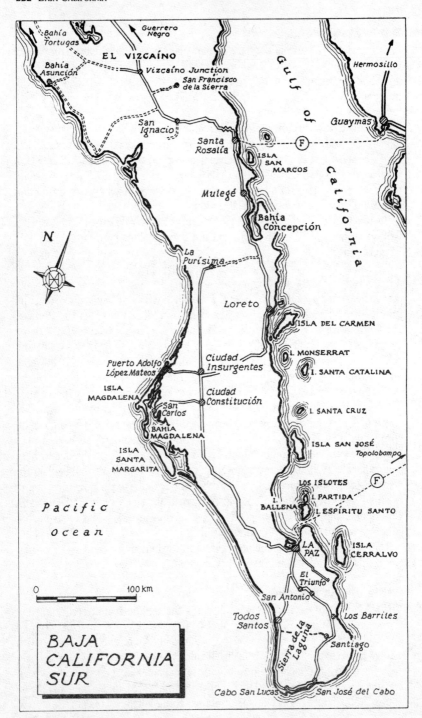

Bahía Tortugas
Guerrero Negro
EL VIZCAÍNO
Bahía Asunción
Vizcaíno Junction
San Francisco de la Sierra
Hermosillo
Gulf of
San Ignacio
Santa Rosalía
Guaymas
ISLA SAN MARCOS
Mulegé
Bahía Concepción
California
N
La Purísima
Loreto
ISLA DEL CARMEN
Puerto Adolfo López Mateos
Ciudad Insurgentes
I. MONSERRAT
I. SANTA CATALINA
ISLA MAGDALENA
San Carlos
Ciudad Constitución
I. SANTA CRUZ
BAHÍA MAGDALENA
ISLA SAN JOSÉ
Topolobampo
ISLA SANTA MARGARITA
LOS ISLOTES
I. PARTIDA
I. BALLENA
I. ESPÍRITU SANTO
Pacific
Ocean
LA PAZ
ISLA CERRALVO
El Triunfo
San Antonio
Todos Santos
Los Barriles
Sierra de la Laguna
Santiago
100 km
Cabo San Lucas
San José del Cabo

BAJA CALIFORNIA SUR

(visit the town's free museum first to learn about the area's mining history).

There's a fish camp 11km north, beyond which the coast is desolate and dangerous – you may see nobody for 130km or more. Summer temperatures, even near the water, can be 43°C (110°F).

To the south the coast is equally rugged, but there is a dirt road inland which only reaches the coast at Playa San Rafael, although there are also side roads to Bahía de las Ánimas and San Francisquito. This eventually emerges at El Arco, 42km from the highway south of Guerrero Negro.

Bahía Concepción
The stretch of Highway 1 from Santa Rosalía through Mulegé to Loreto is fairly touristy, but still offers spectacular backpacking. Bahía Concepción, south of Mulegé, is popular with kayakers and windsurfers, and offers many beautiful camping beaches. Here too there are plenty of cave paintings in the hills inland; trips are organised by most of the hotels and agencies in Mulegé. For kayak, canoe or snorkel hire, contact Roy and Becky of *Baja Tropicales* at Palapa #17, Playa Santispac, or Apdo 60, Mulegé, BCS. South of here the bay becomes more primitive and there may be no water where you camp; a track continues to the eastern side of the bay, where things are even rougher.

South of Loreto the road swings west to Ciudad Insurgentes, crossing the Sierra de la Giganta; this is composed of pyroclastic volcanic rocks, with a gentle slope to the west but a steep scarp to the east, ending in cliffs along the coast. Don't hike here unless you're absolutely sure of your water supplies. There's a scrubby vegetation with columnar cacti such as *cardón*.

The Mission Trail
A relatively well-used jeep track crosses the northern part of the Sierra de la Giganta, from just south of Bahía Concepción to La Purísima; from San Isidro, 55km from Highway 1 (and 8km short of La Purísima) a track leads north for about 10km to the ruined mission of La Purísima Concepción de María Cadegomo (1719).

Another rough road leads 34km southwest from Loreto to San Javier, site of the mission of San Francisco Javier de Vigge-Biaundo (1699), perhaps the finest in Baja, preserved by aridity and isolation. The road follows a little stream along a canyon, shaded by palm trees. About halfway from Loreto to San Javier, another rocky track heads north for 79km to San Isidro, via the ruins of San José de Comondú (1737), another mission set deep in a watered valley between dry barren mesas of volcanic rock.

It's possible to trace the old Mission Trail through much of Baja, but this is the easiest section to follow. Although there is a surprising amount of water at these higher elevations, you might want to hire a local guide, or maybe hire or even buy some pack animals, to be sure of adequate supplies.

The islands

There are two main groups of islands in the Gulf of California, most the remains of ancient volcanoes and most now protected by a Special Biosphere Reserve; biologically, they are of interest because of the high proportion of endemic species. The cold waters around Isla Tiburón also produce large quantities of phytoplankton, which feed zooplankton, which in turn feed sardines which feed birds and larger fish – a huge quantity and variety of them. Some of the islands receive as little as 25mm (one inch) of rain a year, and all have a drought-resistant vegetation of mezquite and acacia scrub, low thorny deciduous forest and endemic cacti, with many types of iguanas and lizards (including the metre-long chuckwalla), while the sea's riches support many sea mammals and sea birds, including ospreys, cormorants, boobies, pelicans and magnificent frigatebirds.

Isla Tiburón is described on p.207; **Isla San Esteban**, just to its west in the middle of the Gulf, is also traditional Seri territory. The tiny **Isla Raza**, to its north, is one of the more important islands for marine birds and mammals; virtually the entire world population of elegant terns (*Sterna elegans*) and Heermann's gulls (*Larus heermanni*), 50,000 birds in all, nest in an area of just 6.9ha, producing large quantities of guano. Rats and mice, accidentally introduced a century ago, were finally eliminated from the island in 1995. **Isla San Marcos**, just south of Santa Rosalía, has a huge gypsum quarry at its southern end, and a seal colony at its north, while Isla Carmen, off Loreto, has salt works produceing 60,000-80,000t per year, mostly for domestic consumption. Further south, **Isla Santa Catalina** is home to an endemic rattle-less rattlesnake and giant barrel cacti.

Just north of La Paz, and much visited by boat trips, **Isla Espíritu Santo**, and the much smaller **Isla Ballena**, **Isla Partida** and **Los Islotes**, are important breeding grounds for seals, sea lions and birds; the black jackrabbit (*Lepus insularis*) and a subspecies of the ringtail (*Bassariscus astutus palmarius*) are both endemic to Isla Espíritu Santo and **Isla San José**, to the north. Espíritu Santo is also of archaeological interest. Isla Ballena boasts the densest known breeding colony of ospreys, as well as herons, brown pelicans, double-crested cormorants (*Phalacrocorax auritus*) and Caspian terns (*Sterna caspia*). Los Islotes are home to sea lions which, unusually, are friendly to visitors, actually seeming to welcome swimmers. You shouldn't go ashore unless absolutely necessary, and be careful during the breeding season (May to August), when males (up to 2m in length and 300kg) may drive you away. You'll see blue-footed and brown boobies, brown pelicans, cormorants, magnificent frigatebirds and gulls here too.

Out in the Pacific are far more isolated islands with even higher degrees of endemicity. **Isla Guadalupe**, 260km offshore on the 29th parallel (level with Bahía de los Angeles), rises 4,000m from the oceanbed, and is now a Special Biosphere Reserve; however, it's too late to save much of what was a place of extraordinary biological richness. Woodland (mostly thorny shrubs, with salt-resistant cacti) originally covered 10,000ha of the island's total 24,400ha, but is now reduced to a mere 393ha, and of 168 native plant species, 26 have not been seen since 1900. The last Guadalupe juniper died in 1983, and there are just 40 Guadalupe oaks left, all old. The damage has been done almost entirely by goats, introduced in the 18th century as a food reserve for the whalers. In addition, feral cats kill birds, of which at least five species are no longer found there, including the Guadalupe caracara and the Guadalupe storm petrel. Elephant seals, which come from California to breed, were killed by whalers and believed extinct by 1869, but reappeared; the Guadalupe fur seal *Arctocephalus townsendi* was also almost wiped out. There is still an army base on the island, as well as visiting abalone and lobster fishermen.

The **Revillagigedo Islands** (or Islas de Santo Tomas), part of Colima state, lie 400km southwest of Los Cabos, on the same parallel as Mexico City. This is the meeting point of the American, Pacific and Cocos plates, and there are two active volcanoes, as well as underwater fumaroles; Cerro Evermann (1,130m) erupted in 1993. They also form a Biosphere Reserve, with no fishing allowed within 20km of the islands. The terrestrial portion of the reserve is covered by typical arid zone salt-resistant scrub. There's a naval base on **Isla Socorro**, the nearest island to the mainland. The Socorro dove survives only in captivity; the Socorro mocking bird was thought to be extinct, but has reappeared.

Companies such as Baja Expeditions offer diving cruises here from Los Cabos. The big attraction is swimming with giant manta rays (with a 7m "wing" span and weights of almost 2t), which tow scuba divers along on their backs; there are also plenty of big sharks, tuna and wahoo, and smaller fish such as bass, angelfish, triggerfish and trumpetfish.

LOS CABOS

The Cape region is distinct from the rest of Baja California, an area that is already distinct from the rest of Mexico. It's the fastest developing tourist area in the country, with flights from most cities in the western USA to the airport of San José del Cabo. This is a bizarre all-American enclave, with a runway long enough for 747s but virtually no internal flights from elsewhere in Mexico; these use La Paz airport, as do flights from Los Angeles and Tucson. The Cape receives more precipitation than the rest of the peninsula (300mm a year in San José), and its flora is related to the thorn forest of the mainland's Pacific coast rather than to the Sonoran desert immediately to the north. For a naturalist's view of Los Cabos, see Ann Zwinger's *A Desert Country near the Sea* (Harper-Row 1983).

Of Baja's 2,958 plant species about 880 are found in the Cape, of which 272 are endemic to the Cape; at 31%, this is a relatively low proportion, probably due to the area's relatively recent separation from the mainland.

Nevertheless, 22 of 35 cacti species are endemic, as are 40 of 103 *Fabaceae* (peas/legumes), 19 of 50 *Euphorbiaceae* (spurges), 48 of 97 *Asteraceae* (daisies), four of six *Agavaceae*, four of seven *Polygonaceaea* (buckwheats), two out of four oaks, sumacs, passionflowers and willows, and one orchid, one campanula, one fig, one mistletoe and one ocotillo. All three persimmons (*Ebenaceae*) are endemics, and the *Amaryllidaceae, Begoniaceae, Geraniaceae, Ericaceae, Loganiae* and *Crassulaceae* are all represented by a single endemic species. On the other hand just one of 47 grasses is endemic.

The bird population is much the same as that to the north, with no natural barriers in between; apart from a few subspecies, the only endemic is the black-fronted hummingbird (formerly Xantus' hummingbird; *chuparossa de Xantus/Hylocharis xantusii*). Baird's junco was thought to be a distinct species, but is now classified as a subspecies of the yellow-eyed junco (*ojilumber mexicano/Junco phaenotus*), and likewise the San Lucas robin is now seen as a subspecies of the American robin (*primavera real/Turdus migratorius*). There are quite a few endemic rodent subspecies, such as the southern pocket gopher (*Thomomys umbrinus alticolus*, at La Laguna), little desert pocket mouse (*Perognathus arenarius arenarius*, on the Pacific side of the Cape, and *P. arenarius sublucidus*, in the La Paz region), Merriam's kangaroo rat (*Dipodomys merriami melanurus*, in the foothills of the Sierra Victoria), and the piñon mouse (*Peromyscus truei lagunae*, at La Laguna). The most common lizards in the Cape region are the Coast horned lizard (*Phrynosoma coronatum*) and the orange-throated whiptail (*Cnemidophorus hyperythrus*); there's also the endemic Cape skink (*Eumeces lagunensis*).

La Paz

The Cabos resorts are all right if you want to enjoy overpriced drinks in a "fun" but totally unMexican atmosphere; they do offer ample opportunities for all water sports and other activities. In comparison **La Paz** seems a real Mexican town full of real people (160,000 of them); the gringos are mostly in beach hotels a few kilometres away, and the town-centre hotels are used by Mexican visitors. The *Yeneka, Pensión California* and *Hostería del Convento* are all places where travellers should feel comfortable, but the best value for money is the *Villa Juvenil* (youth hostel), on the highway towards the Cape. This is 3km from the centre (by the 8 de Octubre bus or *colectivo*), but convenient for the ABC/Aguila *camionera* – turn right/east on Jalisco, left/north on Olachea Aviles, follow the righthand lanes and turn right at 5 de Febrero and right again to reach the hostel. There's a laundry opposite, and the Drambupo supermarket – but the best supermarket is the CCC (*Centro Comercial California*) at Bravo/Isabel la Catolica (on the 8 de Octubre route), and also at Colima/Madero. There's a small free museum, but not a lot else to see in town.

South from La Paz

Buses in the Cape area are relatively primitive, even compared to those in
northern Baja; at first it can be a welcome change from hermetically sealed
air-conditioning and addictive videos, but then it may all get a bit tiresome,
especially drivers' reluctance to pick you up by the roadside or to put your
rucksack in the locker. Most buses from La Paz serve both San José del
Cabo and Cabo San Lucas; the term *via corta* usually refers to the western
route, to Cabo San Lucas, so to go directly to San José you in fact usually
need a *via longa* bus for Cabo San Lucas. There are three companies, of
which *Enlaces Terrestres Peninsulares* and *Autotransportes La Paz*, both
on Degollado by the market, mainly use the *via corta* to Cabo San Lucas,
while *Aguila*, connecting at the *camionera* with services from the north,
uses both routes.

The roads to Los Cabos split about 31km south of La Paz at km185; on
the *via longa* you'll see the remains of 18th century gold and silver mines
in El Triunfo and at the pass (km159½) before San Antonio. You could
take a short hike here, or along the roads to the microwave stations from
San Antonio (km156) or San Bartolo (km129); a longer road leads from
km147½ to San Antonio de la Sierra, on the northern flanks of the Sierra
de la Laguna. It's also possible to take a bus from La Paz to just beyond
San Juan de los Planes and then follow a dirt road along the Gulf coast
through Boca de Alamo and El Cardonal, to meet the main road at the
wind-surfing centre of Los Barriles (km111).

Another dirt road, rapidly being improved, follows the coast on to San
José del Cabo, via Cabo Pulmo; occasional buses go as far as La Rivera via
the paved road from km93½. The **Parque Marino Nacional Cabo Pulmo**
protects the only coral reefs on the northern Pacific coast; these are relatively
young, between 5,000 and 20,000 years old, and are mostly composed of
Porcillopora elegans, a branched coral which needs very clear water and
steady salinity. Others include the green *Porites california* and the massive
non-branching *Pavova gigantea* and *P. clivosa*. Dinoflagellates live
symbiotically in coral tissue, photosynthesizing for much of the time, but
in their animal phase forming the red tides that led to the Gulf once being
named the *Mar Vermejo*. There is, as you'd expect, a huge range of fish
here, and diving and snorkelling are superb.

The junction to Santiago is at km84; this is a pleasant small oasis town
2km from the highway and the start of one route into the Sierra de la Laguna,
and it also boasts the only zoo in Los Cabos. You'll find a filling station at
the junction west to Miraflores (km71); there's talk of building a road
through the Sierra de la Victoria from Miraflores to Todos Santos, over a
900m pass, but no immediate sign of it happening. San José airport is just
a kilometre to the west from a flyover at km44; if you're coming by bus
from La Paz you should allow three hours to get there. A four-lane highway
from the airport to Cabo San Lucas was completed in 1993, and no matter

what taxi-drivers tell you, there is now a regular minibus shuttle service (tel: 31220).

San José del Cabo

The centre of San José is to the left/east at the traffic lights at km32: the ETP bus office is to the right a few longish blocks along Doblado, and the Aguila terminal is on Valerio González, a few blocks further down Highway 1. Following Doblado to its end, you'll reach Mijares, the touristic centre of the old town; the plaza and tourist information (better than most) are a block to the left/north. Heading south, Mijares runs down to the estuary, where the first mission in Los Cabos was founded in 1730; in 1753 it was moved 8km north to San José Viejo, and then moved back to the site of the present church, on the plaza. The estuary (about 1km by 200m, now closed off by a sand bar) is now a state ecological reserve, being the only place in the state where ruddy ducks and blue-winged teals nest, and there's a museum on its western shore, at the end of Mijares. From here the Paseo San José runs parallel to the coast to Highway 1 (km30), serving all the big hotels. There's nowhere cheap to sleep in town; the so-called youth hostel at the San José Inn (at Obregón and Guerrero, tel: 22464) is poor value. In fact a dormitory bed here, even if they admit one is available, costs more than a single room elsewhere in the country, and almost twice as much as the hostels in La Paz and Cabo San Lucas.

A few hundred metres towards Cabo San Lucas you'll come to the Brisa del Mar RV Park, home to the Baja Bicycle Club and Los Lobos del Mar (tel: 22825), where you can arrange sea kayak and snorkel hire and trips. Here and elsewhere in Los Cabos ATVs (All-Terrain Vehicles) are big business: these are more like go-fast golf carts than proper cross-country quadbikes, but they'd do for larking about on the beach in an offensive polluting manner. Immediately east of Las Brisas is Serrano EcoTours (tel: 88657), who will take you horse-riding or kayaking on the estuary.

Between here and Cabo San Lucas, Highway 1 follows the coast past a chain of ten excellent beaches; the best surfing is at Costa Azul (km29) and Canta Mar (km16), and the best swimming and snorkelling at Punta Chileno (km14) and Santa María (km12). At "Shipwreck Beach" (Playa Barco Varada, km9) a sunken trawler provides interesting diving.

Cabo San Lucas

At km0 (as you'll have guessed) the highway ends at Cabo San Lucas, on the north side of a small bay; the Cape of San Lucas itself is on the south side, with a spectacular rock arch right through it. You can hike out past the Hotel Finisterra to the highest point of the Cape, El Vigía, which was a lookout point for English pirates awaiting the Manila convoy. It's not possible to walk to the beaches below the arch, but there are plenty of boat trips. There's really nothing left of the original fishing village; this is now a brash noisy resort, with a younger crowd than San José and plenty of party venues such as a Hard Rock Cafe and the similar Cabo Wabo, Pancho's, Squid Roe and the Giggling Marlin. There is a youth hostel, to the north at Morales and Juventud (tel: 30148), which is the only budget accommodation in the Cape. There are three RV Parks, where you can camp.

TIO Sports (tel: 32986) rent and sell gear for diving, kayaking, mountain-biking, snorkelling, sailing and most other sports, Underwater Diversions (tel: 34004) is the main diving outfitter, and Lucina's Broken Surfboard restaurant has a noticeboard for yacht skippers seeking crews. There's spectacular diving right offshore, in a 600m-deep canyon.

The *via corta* heads north from Cabo San Lucas, back towards La Paz, along a fairly featureless coast with a few empty beaches: at km 56½ the *Campo Experimental* houses a botanical garden with a good display of cacti and other desert plants. **Todos Santos** (km51½) was founded as a mission in 1734, and remains remarkably pleasant and unspoilt. Buses stop on the plaza, where the Café Santa Fé is probably the best restaurant in the Cape. During the winter this area crawls with gringos, especially around the *Super Mercado Hermanos Castro*, at the south end of town, where they load up their RVs with supplies before looking for free beach camping. Just south of town the Playa Punta Lobos is popular, but not ideal for camping; it's better to head south to the Playa San Pedrito, north of km59, where there is a very attractive RV park and also plenty of scope for camping wild.

MOUNTAIN HIKES

These three hikes show you a totally different face of Baja California, relatively high mountains with real forests of tall trees. In the north, the Peninsular Range, comprising the Sierras de Juárez and de San Pedro Mártir, is similar in many ways to the mountains of California, and it freezes and even snows regularly here. Evenings can be chilly at any season, so be prepared. There has been far more logging, grazing and burning here than in the Californian parks, leading to a less "natural" environment, but they really are just as attractive. The Sierra de la Laguna, far to the south in Los Cabos, is an area of cloudforest, which seems totally out of place in Baja.

The Sierra de Juárez/Laguna Hanson

A continuation of the coastal mountains of California, the Sierra de Juárez has been tilted as the Gulf of California has opened, so that it now has a fairly gentle slope to the west but a high escarpment of huge granite blocks to the east, mixed with metamorphic rocks and overlaid by some sedimentary rocks and volcanic debris. To the east are spectacular gorges, notably the Cañón de Guadalupe, with water all year, including thermal pools (at 45°C);

this is lovely but a bit too visited, with the occasional armed robbery. The highest parts, essentially a 160km² plateau at an average altitude of about 1,700m, have been protected since 1962 by the **Parque Nacional Constitucion de 1857**; nobody ever uses or recognises this name, but if you mention Laguna Hanson everyone will immediately understand – even though this should in theory be called Laguna Juárez. This lake, the focus of the park, is named after a Norwegian named Jacob Hanson, who bred cattle here in the 19th century and was murdered due to tales of a hidden fortune (which was never found). The area has been inhabited for a long time: the Kumaia people (whose last members survive in the villages of San José de la Zorra, San Antonio Necua and La Huerta) left cave paintings; there was a gold rush in 1873; and there was logging until quite recently.

The lake is filled by rain water alone, and in a dry summer can turn into a bog or disappear altogether, although there was still plenty of water when I visited during the drought of 1996. The climate in the higher parts is classified as dry temperate and sub-humid semi-cold, with winter rain, and often snow.

To the west, the lower slopes are covered by a shrubby **chaparral**, mainly of *chamizo* (*Adenostoma fasciculatum*), with *jojoba* (*Simmondsia chinensis*), *manzanita* (*Arctostaphylos spp*), scrub oak (*Quercus dumosa*) and other shrubs up to 4m in height. Above about 1,000m there's a mix of juniper (*guata/Juniperus californica*) and piñón (*Pinus monophylla* and *P. quadrifolia*), and above that pine-oak forest, of ponderosa, jeffrey, sugar and coulter pines (*Pinus ponderosa, P. jeffreyi, P. lambertiana* and *P. coulteri*), canyon (or golden) oak (*Quercus chrysolepis*) and quaking aspen (*Populus tremuloides*). To help you tell the pines apart, the ponderosa (or Western yellow) pine has pinky-yellow bark and needles about 20cm long in groups of three; the jeffrey pine is a beautiful symmetrical tree up to 60m tall with scaly plates of reddish-brown bark, with a vanilla smell on warm days, and needles up to 30cm long also in threes; the sugar pine is up to 75m tall with a similar bark, and needles up to 10cm in fives; and the coulter pine is only 25m tall, with needles up to 30cm long in threes, and is found on dry rocky slopes below 2,000m. The piñón pines are up to 15m in height with edible nuts, and needles about 3cm long either singly (*P. monophylla*) or in fours (*P. quadrifolia*). The much drier eastern slopes, up to 1,400m, have a *matorral* like that of the Sonoran desert, consisting of creosote bush, ocotillo, maguey and jojoba.

The fauna includes mule deer, puma, bighorn sheep, hares, rabbits, skunks, coyote, rattlesnakes, lizards, frogs, toads, woodpeckers, golden and bald eagles, hawks and falcons, vultures, ravens, piñón jays, quails, roadrunners, doves; and in winter ducks and geese.

Map I11D84 (*Arroyo del Saúz*) covers the whole park, but not the way in, which is possibly more important.

Getting there
In theory a road runs all the way through the park from La Rumorosa (on the Mexicali-Tijuana highway) to the Ensenada-San Felipe road; but in reality this is only practicable with a mountain bike or a long hike.

Taking the *via libre* (not the new *via cuota*) west from Mexicali, the turning to the Cañón de Guadalupe is at about km30, there's a spectacular 1,326m pass at km64, and you enter La Rumorosa at km68. The turning to San Francisco and El Topo (76km) is unmarked, at about km72, and there's another route from El Cóndor, just before km83, to Pino Suárez, Margarita and El Topo; neither carries much traffic, and there's no way of deciding which gives you the better chance of a ride to the national park. It's wiser to approach from the south, where there's more traffic and it all uses the same route.

There are only two buses a day, at 08.00 and 18.00, from Ensenada (see p.215) to San Felipe, on a road which climbs steadily over two impressive ridges; get off at the Ojos Negros junction at km39½, just after a filling station. It's little more than a kilometre to the village, but pickups meet the buses and you should get a lift in any case. Turn right at the crossroads by the Oasis restaurant, which offers tourist information and an English-language menu, although there's little sign of many gringos stopping here. There's no accommodation, so the 18.00 bus is a bit on the late side. It's 4km along a broad sandy road to a smaller village, Puerta Trampa, at the end of which you should turn right and then left past a shack selling Tecate beer. The dirt road continues straight on into near-desert (with lots of hares), climbing steadily, and forks right after 4km. The road begins to wind through foothills past a small *rancho* and across a small stream; after 2½km turn left at a T-junction, at a spot probably called La Choya. There's another small stream about 1½km north; the road winds upwards, never quite seeming to reach a ridge, but eventually ends up on the plateau.

From here you'll begin to find National Park signs. By a reedy pool the road turns 90° left (at a turning right to Rancho Laguna Seca) and in about 1km passes a farm at El Rayo. In another 3km you'll reach a turning to the left across a ford, beyond which is the settlement of Aserradero ("Sawmill"), also known as Arroyo del Saúz ("Creek of the Willow"). Follow the main dirt road through the settlement, following signs for "La Laguna"; the road crosses a pleasant plateau strewn with pines, boulders and outcrops, and after 45 minutes walk reaches the National Park gate, 500m before the visitor centre.

Around Laguna Hanson
The visitor centre is potentially lovely, but seems abandoned. In theory there's a charge of US$1.50, but I saw no sign of anyone collecting it. The track splits here to pass on either side of the Laguna Chica ("Little Lake"); to the left it soon reaches the *campamento*, by Laguna Hanson itself, with

some run-down cabins and an empty barn-like building that was once a tourist lodge.

From here the track continues along the lakeside, a truly beautiful area with naturally sculpted rocks among the pines (some of the latter are up to 2m in diameter); there are plenty of lovely spots for camping, and there are outhouses dotted around, although these can be rather smelly. Some areas are marked as "ecological recuperation zones", with no camping allowed, but as cows graze here as much as anywhere else this seems a bit pointless. There's quite a bit of litter in some areas (although chipmunks are happy to use much of it for nest-building), but there are plenty of attractive spots. Obviously, lake water should be purified before drinking.

The eastern/right-hand side of the lake is far quieter; the track to the west continues northwards through the park, passing to the west of its highest peak, the Cerro Torre Blanco (1,800m, little above the plateau). Turning right a couple of kilometres north of the lake, you can follow a track northeast to San Luís (1,500m), at the springs at the head of the Cañón de Guadalupe; however it's not practicable to make your way into the canyon from here. Keeping left on the main track and then turning right after the Arroyo San Pedro, you'll reach the El Topo gate of the park and the road to La Rumorosa. However, for most people it's best to spend a day or two scrambling around the rocks here and then return to Ensenada.

The Sierra de San Pedro Mártir

Further south in the Peninsular Range, the Sierra de San Pedro Mártir (named after the mission of St Peter of Verona, on its southwestern slopes, abandoned in 1806) is similar to the Laguna Hanson area, but considerably higher and wilder. The access road is longer and emptier, but there is some traffic to astronomical observatories, and tourist traffic at weekends. Again it's largely granitic, with a huge drop, and spectacular canyons (with all-year water), to the east. It receives an annual average of 20cm of snow, and in some years over a metre.

In addition to the trees found in the Sierra Juárez, you may also see the endemic mountain cypress (*Cupressus montana*), which can be 20m in height and 5m in diameter, and is found only in isolated parts of the eastern escarpment, as well as lodgepole pine (*Pinus murrayana*), up to 20m in height with paired needles 3-6cm long, found above 1,600m; incense cedar (*Librocedrus decurrens*), 25-35m high, found from 700m to 2,500m, and white fir (*Abies concolor*) with furrowed ash-grey bark, found in dry rocky places from 1,000 to 3,000m. In isolated pockets there's also an oak-piñón combination not found in the Sierra Juárez (although it apparently extended to sea-level before the Pleistocene warming).

Map H11B45 (*San Rafael*) covers the most visited area from Vallecitos to the north, including the Guadalupe canyon, but not the highest area, to the south, which is covered by map H11B55 (*Sierra de Santa Cruz*).

Getting there
The road in is generally in good condition; it starts at the Puente San Telmo (km140), reached by second-class buses from Ensenada to Vicente Guerrero, San Quintín or Lázaro Cárdenas. This runs up a broad fertile valley, passing San Telmo at km9 and the Hacienda Sinaloa at km18, and then heads into emptier foothills, crossing a broad valley at km34. At exactly km49 there's a turning left/north to El Coyote, and about 400m on there's the right turn to the Melling Ranch at San José. This is a tourist resort, but surprisingly affordable, given its isolation, offering guided horse-riding up into the mountains. (From the Ensenada-San Felipe road there's access to a similar place, Mike's Sky Rancho, on the northern edge of the park, but I gather its style is more trail-bikes than horses.) The main road drops to the left, crossing a broad valley and a stream (with some water even in May) at km51½ (just after a road coming in from the Melling Ranch) and then winds up into the hills. At km68 there's a road left to the Ranchos La Joya and Concepción, at km74 (just after entering pine) there's the Los Manzanos campsite (where you can also rent a plot to build your own cabin), and at km78 you'll reach the National Park gate, where you might have to pay US$5, although again it was pretty much abandoned when I was there, even though it was the Memorial Day weekend with plenty of gringo visitors.

The road crosses a ridge at Corona de Arriba (km83½) and drops to a plateau and the clearing of Vallecitos, where there's a little white shelter like a cricket scorer's box. It's a nice spot to camp, with a view of the observatory, but there's no obvious source of water. At the far end of the clearing (km91) there's a junction by a corrugated iron toilet; the track to the right leads to La Tasajera, 10km away, and the main road swings left to wind uphill again. From km95 a track heads north for 2km to a logging camp, and at km98 you reach the gate into the observatory, which is only open to visitors on Saturdays from 11.00 to 13.00. UNAM, the National University, has a 2.13m reflecting telescope set on an east-facing ridge at 2,804m, taking advantage of the crystal-clear air.

The astronomers' accommodation is to the right here; behind the oil tanks you can cut down to an old forestry track which runs eastwards up a small attractive valley, dominated by conifers but with attractive copses of quaking aspen. You can also reach this by taking a short-cut up the hillside from a hairpin bend at km96½ (km102 before the bottom part of the road was straightened out). In about 15 minutes this reaches a camping place (with two tables) where two streams meet at about 2,580m, although there's barely enough water. About five minutes further on the track ends at a couple of fallen trees, but it's easy to follow the valley gently uphill for ten minutes more, to suddenly emerge on the edge of the escarpment at about 2,640m. There's a great view to the Gulf, and to your right you'll see Cerro de la Encantada (also known as Picacho del Diablo), the highest peak in the park at 3,096m. Much nearer to your left you'll see the peak marked on the 1:50,000 map as Picacho El Diablo; this is definitely not the highest point.

You could scramble up the granite slope to the right/south, but you probably wouldn't get much further. To climb Cerro de la Encantada you need to take the track to La Tasajera and then drop into the Cañón del Diablo, camping there before climbing up. It's definitely more than a simple scramble, and should only be tackled by a group led by someone who knows the way; you need to carry enough water for three or four days. According to CEMAC (the Mexican Exploring Club), it was not climbed until 1968. From La Tasajera it's also possible to reach the Cañón del Chorro (or Arroyo de las Garzas), which drops 724m in under 1½km, with a spectacular series of waterfalls; this is inaccessible without plenty of climbing equipment and experience.

The Sierra de la Laguna

This hike takes you across 20km of hot desert and steeply up through various vegetation zones to a wonderful clearing in forest that's cool (or even cold) and moist (or soggy) and thus quite unlike anything you'd expect to find in Baja. As you climb, the view towards the Pacific becomes more and more spectacular, and you'll hear surf breaking on the beach 25km away!

The Sierra de la Laguna is a name often applied to the whole chain of granite mountains south of La Paz, but strictly speaking it only applies to the northern half, including this hike. The southern half is the Sierra de la Victoria, whose dominant peak, the Picacho San Lazaro (1,558m) overlooks the airport of San José del Cabo. Unlike the Peninsular Range to the north, these mountains are steep to the west and gentle to the east; of the seven canyons cutting the range, only two are on the Pacific side. The highest parts of the Sierra de la Laguna have a temperate sub-humid climate, with 600-800mm of precipitation a year, up to 200mm of it in August, and an average temperature of 14°C; it can freeze in January and February. An area of 112,437ha was declared a Biosphere Reserve in 1994, but it is not yet fully established, with cattle still grazing in the clearing of La Laguna.

What looks to a lay person like a desert, below about 400m, is in fact a drought-resistant *matorral* of thorny shrubs, with columnar cacti, barrel cacti, spiney and spineless cholla, and agaves. From about 400m to 800m this is mixed with deciduous tropical thorn forest, with trees such as *torote* (*Bursera microphylla*), *lomboy* (*Bursera microphylla*) and *datilillo* (*Yucca valida*). You'll see desert birds such as the endemic black-fronted hummingbird, Scott's orioles, caracaras, white-winged doves, ladder-backed woodpeckers, San Lucas cactus wrens and ash-throated flycatchers; in the forest you'll also find blue-gray gnatcatchers, California quail and doves. Then from about 750m to 1,200m you'll pass through oak forest (the most vulnerable to erosion) with *Quercus deviata* and *Q. tuberculata*, and then oak-piñón forest, with *Pinus cembroides* as well, and arbutus, laurel sumac, willows, poplars and *palmita* (*Nolina beldingii*); there are isolated populations of Hutton's vireo and the plain titmouse here, as well as scrub jays. When you reach La Laguna you may see black phoebes (and in winter Say's phoebes), acorn woodpeckers, kestrels, yellow-eyed juncos, bandtailed pigeons, Xantus's screech-owls, white-breasted nuthatches, rufous-sided and brown towhees, rufous-crowned sparrows, and (in summer) warbling vireos. Mammals include the endemic piñón mouse (*Peromyscus truei lagunae*), mule deer, pumas, coyotes, bats, foxes and raccoons. The Pacific treefrog (*Hyla regilla*) is lurking up there in the trees, and snakes, notably rattlers and the endemic bullsnake are seen at all levels, though most often in the desert.

Map F12B24 (*Las Cuevas*) shows the La Laguna clearing and everything to the east as far as Las Barriles; F12B33 covers Todos Santos, and the path also cuts through the corner of F12B23.

Getting there

The standard route is from the highway south of Todos Santos, and involves crossing about 20km of hot arid desert, on a track which only carries a pick-up truck every two or three hours or so. You might wish to avoid this, either by renting a vehicle in Todos Santos, by hiking at night (a potentially exquisite experience if the moon is full, but watch out for rattlesnakes!) or by taking another route in. Studying the map, you might well think that it would be easy enough to hike in from the east, but it's not so simple. Jim Conrad has scouted the upper end of this route, and I've tackled the lower end, and we have each concluded that it is not advisable except for experienced hikers with good maps and plenty of water. Trails habitually begin by seeming well-used, but gradually peter out or end at a cliff-edge or in a thicket of excoriating *uña de gato* or cat-claw acacia.

If you do wish to hike in from the east, this is a brief outline of the route: from km84 on the old route from La Paz to San José del Cabo, walk the 2km down the road to Santiago, cross the riverbed and take the first right, before the plaza. This sandy road runs through the oasis for 400m and then climbs a low escarpment, forking right at the top where a track turns left to San Jorge. It's 20km to the end of the road at San Dionisio, across the bare Mesa Los Chorritos and up the San Dionisio valley. The mesa is just as hot and arid as the desert near Todos Santos, and there are far fewer vehicles on this road, so you're little better off here; however, you will occasionally find water in the riverbed. At San Dionisio you can either go through the yard or around to the right, but you'll soon come to the end of the track and continue up the riverbed. There's a clear path, well used by livestock, but it's probably mobile, needing to be re-established after each rainy season. After a while it settles down in the trees on the left/north bank; it takes about an hour and a half to reach a point where two valleys meet, just below the 700m contour, where you'll find lovely pools shaded by

Washingtonia fan palms. This is a lovely camping spot, except in the wet season when you should beware flash floods.

From here it's possible to scramble up by waterfalls on the northern branch, the Portezuelo Hondo, and I'm told that it's possible to continue all the way up this creek and then loop south to La Laguna. It's not possible to climb up the southern branch, although there are some beautiful pools here; the direct route to La Laguna is a small path up the hill to the south which starts just three minutes before the junction of the valleys, at a large Indian fig tree (*Ficus indica*), with an impressive root system draped over rocks. You have to follow animal droppings to find the correct path broadly westwards to La Laguna.

The main route into the reserve starts just north of km55, between Todos Santos and the botanic garden; you'll see a good dirt road heading east over a cattle-grid. After about 5km swing right past a forestry service hut and then left where the road splits, to keep heading east towards the mountains rising ahead. You'll pass a path left to El Salado, and continue to La Burrera, about 20km from the highway. There's a gate (and maybe some loafing soldiers) by an army base; if you hear a vehicle on these roads, you'd be wise to vault out of its way, as these lads drive those big trucks the way you'd expect young guys with big engines to drive. There's also a sign advising visitors to check in at park headquarters, but there's no hint as to where this is – unfortunate, as water should be available there.

From La Burrera, beyond the gate on the San Juan del Aserradero stream, you'll be following a mule track, often sunken and narrow. This climbs steadily for 11km, taking between five and seven hours. About halfway (c1,200m) you reach a fine place for camping, and there's usually water in the stream here. Due to livestock further uphill you should definitely purify the water. About twenty minutes before reaching La Laguna, there are great views back to the Pacific.

Finally you drop down into the meadow with its frog-filled water-seepages draining into small streams. Unfortunately, wherever there's accessible water there are also mushy piles of cattle poop. The air is delightfully cool and moist, if not cold and wet; remember that the peaks can be wrapped in cloud and drizzle for long periods, especially in winter, so always bring warm waterproof clothing, no matter how silly it seems in the desert. Push on for another ½km or so to the rangers' hut and main camping area, set in a luscious valley about 1km by 500m, at c1,750m altitude. This is a magnet for naturalists, and, even for those with no great knowledge of biology, a restful contrast to the rest of Baja. As its name implies, there was a lake here until c1870 when a natural dam broke and the water flowed out down the San Dionisio valley; some locals seem to believe it's still here. The rich soil is ideal for growing potatoes, as well as for grazing cattle; however, rangers are now resident here for two-week spells, exercising at least some control.

At the far end of the clearing you should find the path east to the San Dionisio valley; to the southeast, not far from this route, another path leads to a waterfall and bathing pools. From the northwestern edge of the clearing a path branches north from the path on which you arrived from La Burrera, leading to the summit, El Picacho (2,163m), from which you can see both seas – not to be confused with the peak of 1,980m, with radio towers atop, which rises immediately northwest of the clearing. There's also the 2,083m peak of Cerro Las Casitas, just southeast of La Laguna.

APPENDIX ONE: HIKERS' SPANISH

There are plenty of places where you can stop for as long as you want to study Spanish with more or less professional teachers. But however competent you become with the language there are certain words and phrases that are essential for hikers or 'ecotourists' but are unlikely to form part of your language course.

Pronunciation is fairly straightforward, and more so than in Castilian (European) Spanish:

'd' is like English 'th' except when it's the first letter in the word, when it's 'd';

'g' is as in English except before 'e' or 'i' when it's 'h'

'h' is always silent

'j' is a guttural 'h'

'll' is like 'y'

'ñ' is like 'ny'

'v' is like 'b' (and words can often be spelt either way)

'x' is like 'sh' in Mayan words, or else a guttural 'h'

'r' is rolled, and throughout the region football commentators can be heard on the radio competing in rolling 'r's more absurdly than their colleagues, and yelling 'Goooooooooooal!!' for longer without drawing breath.

Two useful phrasebooks have recently been published: the *Rough Guide to Mexican Spanish*, and *Maya for Travelers and Students* by Gary Bevington (University of Texas Press); rather more abstruse is the *Outline Dictionary of Maya Glyphs* (Dover), while the *Diccionario de Mejicanismos* (Editorial Porrua, México City, 1959) is large and dated.

PHRASES

You can't get lost	*No puede perdirse*
What's this place called?	*Como se llama este lugar?*
What village is this?	*Que aldea es esta?*
Where does this trail go?	*A donde va este camino?*
Where are you coming from?	*De donde viene?*
Where are you from (your country)?	*De donde es?*
How far is it to ... ?	*A que distancia ... ?*
How much is it?	*Cuánto vale?*
May I ... ? Is it possible ... ?	*Se puede ... ?*
I would like (to eat)	*Quisiera (comer)*
Without meat	*Sin carne*
Bon voyage	*Vaya bien, Buen viaje*

WORDS

Left/right	*izquierdo/derecho*
North/south	*norte/sur*
East	*este* or *oriente*
West	*oeste, occidente* or *poniente*
Northeast/northwest	*noreste/noroeste* (easily confused)
Straight ahead	*todo recto*
Backpack	*mochila*
Boat or motorized canoe	*lancha, panga*
Bridge	*puente*
Campsite	*camping, campamento*
Cave	*cueva*
Cloud	*nube*
Crossroad	*cruce*
Environment	*medio ambiente*
Farm or ranch	*finca, hacienda, rancho*
Farmer or peasant	*campesino*
Field	*campo, milpa*
Forest	*montaña, bosque*
Frontier	*frontera*
Gorge	*desfiladero, cañón*
High	*alto*
Hill	*cuesta, cerro*
Junction	*cruce, desvio*
Jungle	*selva*
Lake	*lago, laguna*
Landscape	*paisaje*
Lookout, viewpoint	*mirador*
Marsh	*pantano, marisma*
Meadow	*llano, llanura*
Mountain	*cerro, pico, montaña*
Mountain range	*cordillera, sierra, fila*
On vacation	*paseando*
Pass	*puerto, paso*
Pasture	*pasto, pradera*
Path	*camino, sendero*
Peak	*picacho, pico*
Rain	*lluvia*
Restaurant	*restaurante, comedor*
Ridge	*cumbre, cadena*
River	*río*
Rock	*roca*

Saddle	*puerto, paso*
Shop	*tienda, pulpería, kiosco*
Slope	*cuesta, vertiente, ladera, falda*
Spring	*fuente, manantial*
Steep	*abrupto, escarpado*
Stream	*arroyo, chorro*
Summit	*cima*
Tableland	*mesa*
Tent	*carpa, tienda de campaña*
Tired	*cansado* (not *casado* – married)
Valley	*valle*
Village	*aldea, pueblo, poblado, ejido*
Wandering	*errante*
Wood (material)	*madera*

APPENDIX TWO: SELECTED READING

Health

The best books we've seen are:

Healthy Travel: Bugs, Bites and Bowels by Jane Wilson Howarth (Cadogan 1995).

Wilderness Medicine by William W. Forgey (ICS Books, USA, 4/e 1994).

The Tropical Traveller by John Hatt (Penguin 1993).

More general are:

Health Guide for International Travellers by Thomas Sakmar *et al* (Passport, 1994).

International Travel Health Guide by Stuart Rose (Travel Medicine Inc, Massachusetts, 6/e 1995).

In Britain you can also contact **MASTA** (Medical Advisory Service for Travellers Abroad), at the London School of Hygiene and Tropical Medicine, Keppel St, London WC1E 7HT (tel: 0171 631 4408), or any of the travel clinics run by British Airways, Thomas Cook, Trailfinders and others.

In North America try **IAMAT** (the International Association for Medical Assistance to Travellers) at 417 Center St, Lewiston, NY 14092 (tel: 716 754 4883) or 40 Regal Rd, Guelph, Ontario N1K 1B5 (tel: 519 836 0102), or the **Center for Disease Control** in Atlanta, GA 30333, USA (or by their automated hotline on 404 332 4559, fax: 404 332 4565); their annual bulletin *Health Information for International Travel* is also available from the US Government Printing Office, Washington, DC 20422, and they're on the Internet (http://www.cdc.gov/travel/travel.html).

Natural History

The books listed here are all published in the USA. UK readers may like to contact the Natural History Book Service (tel: 01803 865 913) for their catalogue.

I've not found any decent overall guide to the wildlife of Mexico, but there are plenty of bird guides.

Wildlife of Mexico by AS Leopold (California UP, 1959). Game birds and mammals only.

Biological Diversity of Mexico by TP Ramamoorthy et al (Oxford UP, 1993). An excellent but very academic text.

On the Road to Tetlama by Jim Conrad (Walker, New York, 1991).

Mexican Wilderness and Wildlife by Ben Tinker (Texas UP, 1978). Northwestern Mexico – dated, but of historical interest.

Guide to the Birds of Mexico & Northern Central America by Steve NG Howell & Sophie Webb (Oxford UP, 1995). My favourite, above all because it gives Spanish names, as well as scientific and English names, making it possible to discuss birds with the locals.

Peterson Field Guide to Mexican Birds by Roger Peterson & Edward Chalif (Houghton & Mifflin/Cassell, 1990). Includes Guatemala, Belize and El Salvador.

Field Guide to the Birds of Mexico & Central America by L Irby Davis (Texas UP, 1972). Now very dated, but covers a wide area.

A Birdwatcher's Guide to Mexico by Margaret Wheeler (Minutiae Mexicana). Slim, but available in Mexico.

Checklist of the Birds of Palenque by Steve Howell (Sierra Madre).

Survey of the Birds of Oaxaca by L Binford (American Ornithologists' Union monograph 43, Washington DC, 1989).

Audubon Guide to the Butterflies of North America & Northern Mexico by Robert Pyle (Knopf, 1981).

A Plague of Sheep – environmental consequences of the conquest of Mexico by Elinor Melville (Cambridge UP, 1994).

Defending the Land of the Jaguar – a history of conservation in Mexico by Lane Simonian (Texas UP, 1995).

US-Mexican Border Environment Directory (Texas UP, 2/e 1996).

Guidebooks
You'll need a general guide to Mexico, and there's a seemingly limitless choice, especially in Canadian and US bookshops.

Mexico: Travel Survival Kit (Lonely Planet, 4/e 1993). Most European and Antipodean backpackers will carry this, and it's pretty much in tune with their needs, covering the basics well.

Lonely Planet also have *La Ruta Maya: Yucatán, Guatemala, Belize: Travel Survival Kit* (by Tom Brosnahan, 1991) & *Baja California* (by Wayne Bernhardson & Scott Wayne, 1994).

Mexico: the Rough Guide by John Fisher (Rough Guides, 1995). As usual, a cut above the Lonely Planet guides in style and attention to detail, and also in their target market, although it doesn't cover as many places.

Mexico & Central America Handbook (Footprint Publications, annually in September). This is the one to take if you're planning to get well off the beaten track, but it has few town plans and relies overmuch on readers' letters – this means that whereas new hotels and so on get added quickly, dead information is not weeded out. It pays plenty of attention to the needs of business travellers and those travelling by car. More experienced travellers, who can cope with the risk of information overload, may prefer this to the backpackers' guides.

Peoples' Guide to Mexico (10/e by Carl Franz, Lorena Havens & Steve Rogers, John Muir Press, 1995; also newsletter from World Wide Books & Maps, 1911 N45th St, Seattle WA 98103; tel: 206 634 3453). Many North American backpackers see this as the bible, and it's a shame it's not more widely available in Europe. It's been published since 1972 and carries the weight of years of experience – almost nothing on hiking, however.

Moon Guide to Mexico (Moon Publications, 1996). This is a conflation of eight separate guides, to Baja California, Los Cabos, Cancún, Central Mexico, Northern Mexico, Pacific Mexico, Puerto Vallarta, and the Yucatán Peninsula; they're particularly good on fauna and flora.

The Berkeley Guide: Mexico on the Loose (Fodor, 1996). The first edition, part of a hip, readable and informative series.

Everyman Guide to the Route of the Mayas (David Campbell Publications, UK, 1995). From southern Mexico to El Salvador, with good illustrations.

The Cadogan Guide to Mexico by Katharine & Charlotte Thompson (Cadogan Guides/Globe Pequot, 1991). A more cultural view of the country.

Bicycling Mexico by Erika Weisbroth and Eric Ellman (Hunter, 1990).

Latin America by Bike by Walter Sienko (The Mountaineers, Seattle WA, 1993). This covers 17 countries, so is rather sketchy.

Mexico by Rail by Gary Poole (Hunter). This is above all a guide to places along the main rail routes, so it may be of use even if you don't travel by train.

Mexico's Volcanoes: a climbing guide by RH Secor (Mountaineers, 1981, o/p). Old and thin.

Traveller's Tales
There are two compilations of writings on Mexico: *Mexico: Some Travels and Some Travelers There* by Alice Adams (Simon & Schuster, 1992), and *Traveler's Tales Mexico* by James O'Reilly & Larry Habegger (Chronicle/Traveler's Tales, San Francisco, 1994), which includes contemporary American writers only, so no DH Lawrence or Aldous Huxley.

Two 19th-century travellers left good accounts of Mexico: Frances Calderón de la Barca's *Life in Mexico* (first published in 1843, by the Scottish wife of the first Spanish ambassador to free Mexico; Century 1987) and John Lloyd Stephens' *Incidents of Travel in Central America, Chiapas and Yucatán* (Dover: the classic 1841 account of the discovery of the great Mayan ruins and much more; *Incidents of Travel in Yucatán* is the 1843 follow-up).

More recent accounts include *Mornings in Mexico* by DH Lawrence (1927; Penguin), *Beyond the Mexique Bay* by Aldous Huxley (1934; Flamingo), *The Lawless Roads* by Graham Greene (1939; Penguin), *The Log from the Sea of Cortez* by John Steinbeck (Mandarin), *The Old Patagonian Express* by Paul Theroux (Penguin/Pocket Books, 1980), *So Far from God* by Patrick Marnham (Penguin, 1985), *Time Among the Maya* by Ronald Wright (Bodley Head, 1989), and *A Trip to the Light Fantastic* by Katie Hickman (Flamingo, 1993).

Historical books include *Ancient Kingdoms of Mexico* by Nigel Davies (Penguin, 1982), *The Maya* (Thames & Hudson, 5/e 1993) and *Breaking the Maya Code* (Penguin, 1994) by Michael Coe, three books all entitled *The Aztecs*, by Serge Gruzinski (Thames & Hudson, 1992), Inga Clendinnen (CUP, 1991), and Richard Townsend (Thames & Hudson, 1992), the definitive *The Conquest of Mexico* by Hugh Thomas (Pimlico/Simon & Schuster, 1994), and *The Conquest of New Spain* by Bernal Díaz (Pelican/ Linnet). The best general history is *Fire and Blood – a History of Mexico* by TR Fehrenbach (Da Capo 1995), and a good guide to contemporary politics is *Politics in Mexico* by Roderic Camp (Oxford UP, 1993).

Broader guides to the economic, social and political background are *Mexico: a Country Guide* (ed. Tom Barry, Inter-Hemispheric Education Resource Center, New Mexico, USA) and *Mexico in Focus* by J Ross (Latin American Bureau, UK, 1996).

The best Mexican **novelists** are Carlos Fuentes, Octavio Paz and Carlos Cuauhtémoc Sánchez, all now translated into English. Foreigners, mostly North Americans, who have set novels in Mexico include many of the above, and Malcolm Lowry, Jack Kerouac, B Traven and Richard Brautigan.

246

INDEX